SPACE AND SOCIETY IN THE ROMAN WORLD

We cannot properly understand history without a full appreciation of the spaces through which its actors moved, whether in the home or in the public sphere, and the ways in which they thought about and represented the spaces of their worlds. In this book Michael Scott employs the full range of literary, epigraphic and archaeological evidence in order to demonstrate the many different ways in which spatial analysis can illuminate our understanding of Greek and Roman society, and the ways in which these societies thought of, and interacted with, the spaces they occupied and created. Through a series of innovative case-studies of texts, physical spaces and cultural constructs, ranging geographically across North Africa, Greece and Roman Italy, as well as an up-to-date introduction on spatial scholarship, this book provides an ideal starting point for students and non-specialists.

MICHAEL SCOTT is an assistant professor in Classics and Ancient History at the University of Warwick, and formerly the Moses and Mary Finley Research Fellow at Darwin College, Cambridge. He is the author of *Delphi and Olympia: the spatial politics of Panhellenism in the Archaic and Classical Periods* (Cambridge, 2010), and has also written and edited books for interdisciplinary academic audiences and the wider public (*From Democrats to Kings* in 2009 and *Risk* (co-edited with Layla Skinns and Tony Cox) in 2011). He is active in making the study of the ancient world accessible to as wide an audience as possible by talking to schools across the country, writing for international magazines and newspapers, taking part in outreach initiatives with the Mayor of London and Olympics 2012, and writing and presenting TV documentaries for the BBC, History Channel and National Geographic.

KEY THEMES IN ANCIENT HISTORY

EDITORS

P. A. Cartledge
Clare College, Cambridge

P. D. A. Garnsey
Jesus College, Cambridge

Key Themes in Ancient History aims to provide readable, informed and original studies of various basic topics, designed in the first instance for students and teachers of Classics and Ancient History, but also for those engaged in related disciplines. Each volume is devoted to a general theme in Greek, Roman or, where appropriate, Graeco-Roman history, or to some salient aspect or aspects of it. Besides indicating the state of current research in the relevant area, authors seek to show how the theme is significant for our own as well as ancient culture and society. By providing books for courses that are oriented around themes it is hoped to encourage and stimulate promising new developments in teaching and research in ancient history.

Other books in the series

Death-ritual and Social Structure in Classical Antiquity, by Ian Morris
978 0 521 37465 1 (hardback) 978 0 521 37611 2 (paperback)

Literacy and Orality in Ancient Greece, by Rosalind Thomas
978 0 521 37346 3 (hardback) 978 0 521 37742 3 (paperback)

Slavery and Society at Rome, by Keith Bradley
978 0 521 37287 9 (hardback) 978 0 521 37887 1 (paperback)

Law, Violence, and Community in Classical Athens, by David Cohen
978 0 521 38167 3 (hardback) 978 0 521 38837 5 (paperback)

Public Order in Ancient Rome, by Wilfried Nippel
978 0 521 38327 1 (hardback) 978 0 521 38749 1 (paperback)

Friendship in the Classical World, by David Konstan
978 0 521 45402 5 (hardback) 978 0 521 45998 3 (paperback)

Sport and Society in Ancient Greece, by Mark Golden
978 0 521 49698 8 (hardback) 978 0 521 49790 9 (paperback)

Food and Society in Classical Antiquity, by Peter Garnsey
978 0 521 64182 1 (hardback) 978 0 521 64588 1 (paperback)

Banking and Business in the Roman World, by Jean Andreau
978 0 521 38031 7 (hardback) 978 0 521 38932 7 (paperback)

Roman Law in Context, by David Johnston
978 0 521 63046 7 (hardback) 978 0 521 63961 3 (paperback)

Religions of the Ancient Greeks, by Simon Price
978 0 521 38201 4 (hardback) 978 0 521 38867 2 (paperback)

Christianity and Roman Society, by Gillian Clark
978 0 521 63310 9 (hardback) 978 0 521 63386 4 (paperback)

Trade in Classical Antiquity, by Neville Morley
978 0 521 63279 9 (hardback) 978 0 521 63416 8 (paperback)

Technology and Culture in Greek and Roman Antiquity, by Serafina Cuomo
978 0 521 81073 9 (hardback) 978 0 521 00903 4 (paperback)

Law and Crime in the Roman World, by Jill Harries
978 0 521 82820 8 (hardback) 978 0 521 53532 8 (paperback)

The Social History of Roman Art, by Peter Stewart
978 0 521 81632 8 (hardback) 978 0 52101659 9 (paperback)

Ancient Greek Political Thought in Practice, by Paul Cartledge
978 0 521 45455 1 (hardback) 978 0 521 45595 4 (paperback)

Asceticism in the Graeco-Roman World, by Richard Finn O P
978 0 521 86281 3 (hardback) 978 0 521 68154 4 (paperback)

Domestic Space in Classical Antiquity, by Lisa C. Nevett
978 0 521 78336 1 (hardback) 978 0 521 78945 5 (paperback)

Money in Classical Antiquity, by Sitta von Reden
978 0 521 45337 0 (hardback) 978 0 521 45952 5 (paperback)

Geography in Classical Antiquity, by Daniela Dueck
978 0 521 19788 5 (hardback) 978 0 521 12025 8 (paperback)

Space and Society in the Greek and Roman Worlds, by Michael Scott
978 1 107 00915 8 (hardback) 978 1 107 40150 1 (paperback)

SPACE AND SOCIETY IN THE GREEK AND ROMAN WORLDS

MICHAEL SCOTT

CAMBRIDGE UNIVERSITY PRESS

CAMBRIDGE UNIVERSITY PRESS
Cambridge, New York, Melbourne, Madrid, Cape Town,
Singapore, São Paulo, Delhi, Mexico City

Cambridge University Press
The Edinburgh Building, Cambridge CB2 8RU, UK

Published in the United States of America by Cambridge University Press, New York

www.cambridge.org
Information on this title: www.cambridge.org/9781107009158

© Michael Scott 2013

This publication is in copyright. Subject to statutory exception
and to the provisions of relevant collective licensing agreements,
no reproduction of any part may take place without the written
permission of Cambridge University Press.

First published 2013

A catalogue record for this publication is available from the British Library

Library of Congress Cataloguing in Publication data
Scott, Michael, 1981–
Space and society in the Greek and Roman worlds / Michael Scott.
pages   cm. – (Key themes in ancient history)
Includes bibliographical references.
ISBN 978-1-107-00915-8 (hardback) – ISBN 978-1-107-40150-1 (paperback)
1. Space and time – Social aspects – Greece.   2. Space and time – Social aspects – Rome.   3. Cultural geography – Greece.   4. Cultural geography – Rome.   5. Greece – Civilization – To 146 B.C.   6. Rome – Civilization.   I. Title.
DF78.S36   2012
304.2 30937–dc23
2012017899

ISBN 978-1-107-00915-8 Hardback
ISBN 978-1-107-40150-1 Paperback

Cambridge University Press has no responsibility for the persistence or
accuracy of URLs for external or third-party internet websites referred to
in this publication, and does not guarantee that any content on such
websites is, or will remain, accurate or appropriate.

For James, Maria and especially my niece Sophia, whose journey in life only just began as this book was being completed.

Contents

List of illustrations		*page* x
Acknowledgements		xiv
Abbreviations		xvi
	Introduction	1
1	Inheriting and articulating a community: the agora at Cyrene	14
2	Networks of polytheism: spaces for the gods at Delos	45
3	Spaces of alienation: street-lining Roman cemeteries	77
4	A spatial approach to relationships between colony and metropolis: Syracuse and Corinth	110
5	The place of Greece in the *oikoumene* of Strabo's *Geography*	137
	Conclusion: space and society in the Greek and Roman worlds	159
Bibliographic essay		170
Bibliography		177
Index		198

Illustrations

1.1	The region of Cyrenaica and the city of Cyrene (© Figures 1.10 and 1.38 in Luni, M. ed. (2006) *Cirene 'Atene d'Africa'*. L'Erma di Bretschneider, Rome)	page 16
1.2	The agora of Cyrene 650–400 BC (adapted from © p. 63 Bonacasa, N. and Ensoli, S. eds. (2000) *Cirene*. Electa)	18
1.3	The tomb of Battus in the agora of Cyrene *c.*550 BC (© Figure 51 in Stucchi, S. (1965) *L'Agorà di Cirene I: Il lati nord ed est della platea inferiore (MAL 7)*. L'Erma di Bretschneider, Rome)	21
1.4	The agora of Cyrene 400–96 BC (adapted from © p. 64 Bonacasa, N. and Ensoli, S. eds. (2000) *Cirene*. Electa)	27
1.5	The 'Nike and Ship' statue from the agora of Cyrene *c.*250 BC (© p. 88 Bonacasa, N. and Ensoli, S. eds. (2000) *Cirene*. Electa)	31
1.6	(a) The agora of Cyrene by the third century AD and (b) in late Antiquity (adapted from © p. 77 Bonacasa, N. and Ensoli, S. eds. (2000) *Cirene*. Electa)	35
1.7	The Augusteum (former wellhouse) in the agora of Cyrene in the first century AD (© Figure 180 in Stucchi, S. (1965) *L'Agorà di Cirene I: Il lati nord ed est della platea inferiore (MAL 7)*. L'Erma di Bretschneider, Rome)	36
1.8	The temenos of Aristaeus (Anax) covered over by paving in the second century AD (© p. 83 Bonacasa, N. and Ensoli, S. eds. (2000) *Cirene*. Electa)	38
1.9	The ruins of the agora of Cyrene as they stand today	42

List of illustrations

	(© p. 133 in Luni, M. ed. (2006) *Cirene 'Atene d'Africa'*. L'Erma di Bretschneider, Rome)	
2.1	The island of Delos and its main excavated regions (Figure 1 in Bruneau, Ph. and Ducat, J. (2005) *Guide de Délos* and Figure 104 in Papageorgiou-Venetas, A. (1981) *Recherches urbaines sur une ville antique: Délos*. © EfA)	46
2.2	Reconstruction of the sanctuary of Apollo and Artemis on Delos (© Figure 39 in Bruneau, Ph. and Ducat, J. (2005) *Guide de Délos*. EfA)	47
2.3	The sanctuaries on Delos by the end of the Archaic Period (Plan E in Gallet de Santerre, H. (1958) *Délos primitive et archaïque*. Paris)	49
2.4	View from the Apollo and Artemis sanctuary to Mt Cynthus, Delos (© Michael Scott 2011)	49
2.5	View from Mt Cynthus over Delos (© Michael Scott 2011)	50
2.6	Model of the main sanctuaries on Delos 500–314 BC (© Michael Scott 2011)	55
2.7	Model of the main sanctuaries on Delos 314–166 BC. (© Michael Scott 2011)	58
2.8	Map of the Terrace of Foreign Divinities (© Dépliant 5 in Bruneau, Ph. and Ducat, J. (2005) *Guide de Délos*. EfA)	63
2.9	Model of the main sanctuaries on Delos 166–69 BC (© Michael Scott 2011)	67
2.10	Watercolour reconstruction of the area of the Apollo and Artemis sanctuary, Delos in the first century BC (© Aquarelle de Délos in Bruneau, Ph., Brunet, M., Farnoux, A. and Moretti, J-C. (1996) *Délos: Ile sacrée et ville cosmopolite*. EfA)	69
3.1	Map of the city and surroundings of Ostia with main burial areas marked (adapted from Figure 1 p. 15 in Heinzelmann, M. (2000) *Die Nekropolen von Ostia: Untersuchungen zu den Gräberstrassen vor der Porta Romana und an der Via Laurentina*. © Verlag Dr Friedrich Pfeil)	79
3.2	Burials at Ostia in the Porta Laurentina area	82

xii *List of illustrations*

	(adapted from Figures. 21–4 p. 44–5 in Heinzelmann, M. (2000) *Die Nekropolen von Ostia: Unterschungen zu den Gräberstrassen vor der Porta Romana und an der Via Laurentina.* © Verlag Dr Friedrich Pfeil)	
3.3	Burials at Ostia in the Porta Romana area (adapted from Figures. 15–19 p. 36–7 in Heinzelmann, M. (2000) *Die Nekropolen von Ostia: Unterschungen zu den Gräberstrassen vor der Porta Romana und an der Via Laurentina.* © Verlag Dr Friedrich Pfeil)	84
3.4	The city of Pompeii (adapted from map p. xxiv in Richardson, L. (1988) *Pompeii: an architectural history* © Johns Hopkins University Press)	87
3.5	Burials at the Nucerian gate, Pompeii (adapted from map 1 in De Caro, S. (1983) *Un impegno per Pompeii: Fotopiano e documentazione della necropoli di Porta Nocera* © upon authorisation of the Ministry for Cultural Heritage and Environment, Soprintendenza di Pompeii)	90
3.6	Burials at the Herculaneum gate, Pompeii (Plan V in Mau, A. and Kelsey F. (1899) *Pompeii: its life and art.* London)	92
3.7	Tombs of Eumachia and Navoleia Tyche, Pompeii (© upon authorisation of the Ministry for Cultural Heritage and Environment, Soprintendenza di Pompeii)	93
3.8	Map of Rome (adapted from Map 9 in Grundy, G. B. (1917) *Murray's Small Classical Atlas.* London)	97
3.9	Tombs of Caecilia Metella, Cestius and Eurysaces on the roads outside Rome (A: adapted from Figure 35 in Castagnoli, F. (1956) *Appia Antica* © British School of Rome; B: Figure 26 in Castagnoli, F. (1956) *Appia Antica.* Milan; C: Figure 12 in Castagnoli, F. (1956) *Appia Antica.* Milan; D: © upon authorisation of the Ministry for Cultural Heritage and Environment, Roma Capitale; E: Figure 112 in Roullet, A. (1972) *The Egyptian and Egyptianising monuments of Imperial Rome.* Leiden)	100
3.10	View of 'alienating' streets of tombs at Nucerian and Herculaneum gates, Pompeii (© upon authorisation of the Ministry for Cultural Heritage and Environment, Soprintendenza di Pompeii)	108

4.1	Syracuse and the surrounding region (p. 221 and 228 in Coarelli, F. and Torelli, M. (1984) *Guide archaeologiche Laterza (Sicilia)* @ Laterza)	112
4.2	Corinth and the Corinthia (Plan V in Williams, C. and Bookidis, N. eds. (2003) *Corinth: the centenary 1896–1996* © courtesy of the American School of Classical Studies, Corinth Excavations)	114
5.1	The world according to Strabo (Figure facing p. 238 in Bunbury, E. (1879) *History of Ancient Geography vol. 2*. London)	138

Acknowledgements

My thanks go to Michael Sharp at Cambridge University Press as well as Paul Cartledge and Peter Garnsey, editors of Key Themes in Ancient History, for their initial invitation to write a volume in this series, and for their constant encouragement and insight through the different stages of its planning and execution. Part of this book was written while working at the Fondation Hardt, Geneva, Switzerland, and I offer my thanks both to the Fondation for providing such an extraordinarily productive working environment and to the other scholars in residence there at the time who offered good comradeship, guidance and diversion when needed.

My thanks go also to EfA, the French Archaeological School in Athens, for allowing me to stay in their dig house on Delos. Not only did this allow me the necessary time to understand the site, but also the privilege of staying on the island. The sight of Delos' Apollo sanctuary lit by the moon will not be forgotten for a long time. My time there was also much enhanced by the excellent company and insight of several scholars working on different aspects of the Delian material, for which I offer my thanks. I had envisaged a similar trip to the archaeological site of Cyrene in Libya, but sadly this was not possible due to the turbulence in the region.

The majority of this book was written at Darwin College and the Faculty of Classics, Cambridge, during my time as Moses and Mary Finley Fellow in Ancient History at Darwin College. My thanks to the Faculty and to Darwin College for providing such a supportive and enjoyable working environment, made all the more so by my colleagues at both College and Faculty. It has been both a pleasure and an honour to work alongside you and discuss many of the issues in this book. My thanks go also to the organisers and attendees of several conferences concerned with issues of spatial analysis across a wide variety of sources, in which I had the good fortune to participate. Each provided thought-provoking analysis and discussion.

Acknowledgements

Finally, my thanks go to Dr Marion Boos from the University of Darmstadt, Germany for help with images of several tombs at Pompeii; to Maria Pia Malvezzi at the British School of Rome for help with image permissions, and to Prof. Robin Osborne for his comments on earlier drafts. In addition, I offer my sincerest thanks to Thomas O'Reilly at Cambridge University Press and his editorial team for their efficient, expert and congenial shepherding of this book through to publication. All remaining mistakes are, of course, my own.

Abbreviations

ABSA	*Annual of the British School at Athens*
Aesch.	Aeschylus
AIA	Archaeological Institute of America
APA	American Philological Association
App.	Appian
B. Civ.	*Bella civilia*
Ath. Mitt.	*Mitteilungen des Deutschen Archäologischen Instituts. Athenische Abteilung*
AWE	*Ancient West and East*
BABesch	*Bulletin Antieke Beschaving*
BCH	*Bulletin de Correspondance Hellénique*
BEFAR	*Bibliothèque des écoles françaises d'Athènes et de Rome*
Cic.	Cicero
Leg.	*De Legibus*
Phil.	*Philippics*
Sull.	*Pro Sulla*
Tusc.	*Tusculan Disputations*
Verr.	*In Verrem*
CIL	*Corpus Inscriptionum Latinarum*
Diod. Sic.	Diodorus Siculus
Dion. Hal.	Dionysius of Halicarnasus
EAD	*Exploration archéologique de Délos*
G&R	*Greece and Rome*
Hdt.	Herodotus
Hor.	Horace
Sat.	Satires
ID	*Inscriptions de Délos*
IG	*Inscriptiones Graecae*
JDAI	*Jahrbuch des Deutschen Archäologischen Instituts*
JHS	*Journal of Hellenic Studies*

JRA	*Journal of Roman Archaeology*
JRGZ	*Jahrbuch des Römisch-Germanischen Zentralmuseums*
JRS	*Journal of Roman Studies*
Juv.	Juvenal (*Satires*)
Ling.	*De Lingua Latina* (Varro)
MAL	*Monografie di Archeologia Libica*
Mart.	Martial (*Epigrams*)
Ov.	Ovid
Fast.	*Fasti*
Paus.	Pausanias
Petron.	Petronius
Sat.	*Satyricon*
PBSR	*Papers of the British School of Rome*
Pind.	Pindar
Ol.	*Olympian Odes*
Pyth.	*Pythian Odes*
Pl.	Plato
Resp.	*Republic*
Plin.	Pliny (the elder)
HN	*Historia Naturalis*
Plin.	Pliny (the younger)
Ep.	*Epistulae*
Plut.	Plutarch
Vit. Dion.	*Life of Dionis*
Vit. Sull.	*Life of Sulla*
Vit. Tim.	*Life of Timoleon*
Polyb.	Polybius
QuadALibia	*Quaderni di Archeologia della Libia*
RStPomp	*Rivista di Studi Pompeiani*
SEG	*Supplementum Epigraphicum Graecum*
Sen.	Seneca (the younger)
Ep.	*Epistulae*
Stat.	Statius
Silv.	*Silvae*
Tac.	Tacitus
Ann.	*Annales*
Thuc.	Thucydides
TRAC	*Theoretical Roman Archaeology Conference*
ZSS	*Zeitschrift der Savigny-Stiftung für Rechts-Geschichte*

Introduction

INTRODUCTION: SPACE AND SOCIETY

On 28 October 1943, Winston Churchill commented, apropos of how to rebuild the House of Commons following its destruction in a wartime air raid, 'We shape our buildings and afterwards our buildings shape us.' Over the last thirty years, in the fields of anthropology, sociology, geography and archaeology, in what has often been labelled the 'spatial turn', Churchill's observations have been endorsed, investigated and expanded at an ever-increasing rate. Today, we think about spaces – from the individual room to the widest landscape – in an exciting variety of ways. Spaces can no longer stand solely or primarily as static geographical entities, but instead as fluid social constructs. They reflect and articulate practices of social behaviour. They exist in physical and perceptual forms, constructed through material, literary and epigraphical sources. Their meanings are dynamic and multiple thanks to the vibrant, subtle, complex and often unpredictable ways in which they interact with their (many and varied) users over time.[1]

This book asks what use such a reconfigured understanding of space can be to the study of ancient history. That different resolutions of space are firmly fixed on the historian's radar is undeniable: recent commissions for this Key Themes in Ancient History series, for example, include L. Nevett *Domestic Space in Classical Antiquity*; A. Zuiderhoek *The Ancient City* and D. Dueck and K. Brodersen *Geography in Classical Antiquity*. In addition, recent large-scale research projects across Europe, such as HESTIA, PELAGIOS and TOPOI, have sought to examine spatial issues within both literary and physical contexts.[2] What this book sets out to achieve,

---
[1] For a discussion of the relevant theoretical works on space, see the bibliographic essay.
[2] HESTIA: Herodotus Encoded Space-Text-Imaging Archive (Open University, UK); PELAGIOS: Enable Linked Ancient Geodata in Open Systems (Open University, UK), as well as related project GAP (Google Ancient Places); TOPOI: Formation and Transformation of space and knowledge in Ancient civilisations (Berlin, Germany).

in contrast, is not so much to understand one particular level or type of space, but rather to set out an argument for (and the potential of) a much broader engagement between history and space across the study of the Greek and Roman worlds.

In the first section of this introduction, I investigate the particular kinds of (literary and physical) spaces in which current Greek and Roman scholarship has been interested. Such an analysis in turn will provide some insights into how Greek scholarship and Roman scholarship have each approached the study of space as well as into how those kinds of spaces framed, and functioned within, the ancient world. In the second section, I ask how such spatial investigations can be useful for the study of broader historical themes, and make the case not only for casting a wider net in terms of the different kinds of spaces suitable for analysis, but also for the advantages such a broader spatial approach can offer when 'doing' history. In the final section, I outline five case-studies, to be discussed over the course of the book, which seek to demonstrate the potential of spatial analysis in ancient history. In the subsequent chapters, each case-study – the majority of which cross the time span of the Greek and Roman worlds – focuses on a different kind of space. These spaces range: in size (from agora to the lived *oikoumene*); in nature (from physical to perceptual); in tenor (from political to religious to funerary), and in the evidence through which they are represented and constructed (from archaeological material to epigraphic to literary and to a combination of all three) as well as in their geographical location in the Mediterranean world (from Cyrene to Delos to Rome to Syracuse).

At the end of this book, I sum up how these case-studies have helped us improve our understanding of the ancient world, and finish by examining how these approaches to different kinds of spaces across the Greek and Roman worlds help us also to think about how these two worlds thought differently about space, and negotiated space as part of the broader interaction between them. In so doing, I hope to demonstrate not only that a spatial approach is a feasible and useful tool in the historian's arsenal, but that a spatial approach is, actually, indispensable to constructing a well-rounded, textured and credible understanding of the complexity of the ancient world.

SPACE: THE STORY SO FAR

Some of the earliest discussions of space as reflecting and articulating social behaviour, perception and outlook within Greek and Roman studies took place not in relation to physical space, but rather in relation to spaces created within literary works. Vidal-Naquet, in his seminal work *The Black Hunter* (Vidal-Naquet 1986), for example, underlined the Kantian belief that space and time functioned as the basis of all intuitions, and examined how the changing conceptualisation of space, particularly liminal spaces, within different literary works, both reflected and constructed changing spatial structures in both the social and the physical Greek world over time. The study of the way in which different ancient authors constructed and thought about space has also developed with an eye to the philosophers in the work of Sorabji (1988), Algra (1995) and Stevens (forthcoming), to the tragedians particularly in the work of Rehm (2002), Lamari (2010), Seaford (2012), to Hellenic poetry both ancient and modern in Leontis (1995), Fitter (1995) and Calame (2009), and to the ancient novel (Paschalis and Frangoulidis 2002). The focus continues through major research projects such as HESTIA and the Amsterdam-based Space in Literature project (Jong 2012), with digital projects such as HESTIA responding to the interactive possibilities created by the now vast numbers of ancient texts online (e.g. via Perseus).

Space in Roman-period literature has equally been a subject for study (e.g. Leach 1988; Spencer 2006; Jones 2011), particularly focusing either on the period of the early Empire or on travel writers such as Pausanias who presented the Greek world to a Roman audience. Scholars, for example, now speak of Pausanias' *Periegesis* as a 'cognitive map' that interweaves spaces, monuments, myths and legends to express 'a particular ideology of Hellenism' (Hutton 2005: 314), and in which his landscape of Greece is a 'rhetorical discourse' (Elsner 2001: 18). The key points to emerge so far from the study of space in literature have been: the presence of multiple 'views' of, and ways of understanding, the same physical landscape at one time and over time (e.g. the meanings of mountainous spaces: Buxton 1992); the occasional disjuncture and contradiction in the portrayal of spaces between the literary and the physical world (e.g. the changing importance of the boundary between city and countryside: Jones 2004; Rosen and Sluiter 2006), and the wider, culturally contrasting ways of using and talking about space demonstrated in the Greek as opposed to the Latin sources (e.g. the preference for simultaneous double-action spaces in the Greek novel in contrast to preference for single-action space in Latin ones: Konstan 2002).

Such literary interest has of course been fuelled by the increasing deployment of different kinds of spatial analysis on different physical resolutions and kinds of space across a range of civilisations (cf. Étienne 1996;

Osterhammel 1998; Schroer 2006; Schlögel 2007). For example, a major focus has been the study of the individual building, particularly domestic, both within and outside the classical world (e.g. Rapoport 1969; Rapoport 1982; Kent 1990). In scholarship focused on the Greek world, as Nevett's recent Key Themes in Ancient History volume, alongside her earlier work, points out (Nevett 1999; 2010), housing – from architectural layout, to furnishings, to room use – is shaped by culturally specific expectations and systems. The analysis of Greek domestic space has thus brought important insights to bear on particular cultural activities undertaken within that space (such as symposia) and on the gendered division of particular spaces, but also on strategies of definition and engagement within wider communities (cf. Cahill 2002) as well as across regions and in different periods (cf. Souvatzi 2008).

In Roman scholarship on domestic space, thanks to plentiful surviving evidence at key sites such as Ostia and Pompeii, studies have focused even more closely on how domestic space reflects and articulates sequences of movement and interaction, helps us understand the continued interaction between the 'function' and the 'character' of particular spaces (e.g. of individual rooms within a house), as well as how such spaces play an important part in wider issues of identity, power display, community structure and hierarchy (cf. Wallace-Hadrill 1988; Wallace-Hadrill 1994; Laurence and Wallace-Hadrill 1997; Grahame 2000; Hales 2003; Allison 2004). Because of the important part gardens played in the space of the Roman house, as well as the focus on them within Latin literature, these have also been a strong focus for Roman spatial scholarship (e.g. Jashemski 1979; von Stackelberg 2009; Jones 2011). What such studies of Greek and Roman domestic space continue to emphasise, in conjunction with studies of the home as a literary topos, is a series of fundamental differences between the Greek and Roman house, particularly in terms of their metaphorical meaning and spatial articulation (e.g. the Roman house as an important extension of the self: Bergmann 2007: 224).

Another increasing focus of spatial scholarship has been at the level of the city, again reflected in Zuiderhoek's forthcoming Key Themes in Ancient History volume on the ancient city, and in recent cross-cultural treatments of ancient world city development (cf. Smith 2003; Gates 2011). Yet in comparison to the study of the city in other periods, particularly the modern and the Renaissance city, the study of the ancient city as a series of connected and overlapping spaces, formulated and understood through dynamic and multiplicitous cultural expectations, individual experiences and human needs, rather than simply as a collection of different, changing forms of architecture, is really only just taking off (cf. Blake 2004: 239).[3] Early work on the ancient Greek *polis* and Roman *urbs* consisted of studies of their architectural organisation (e.g. Ward-Perkins 1974), or development over time (e.g. Murray and Price 1990). Yet more recently in scholarship on the Greek world, the focus has shifted to the relationship between town and countryside (e.g. Osborne 1987; Rosen and Sluiter 2006), and, thanks in part to the work of the Copenhagen Polis Centre (e.g. Hansen and Nielsen 2004), the development of the polis not simply in terms of architecture, but as a space of interaction, negotiation, memory and identity display (e.g. Vlassopoulos 2007; Ma 2009; Owen and Preston 2009).

In contrast to the study of the Greek polis, because of the high degree of material survival of 'cities' in Italy such as Rome, Ostia and Pompeii as well as throughout the Empire, Roman scholarship on space and the city has been in many ways much more diverse and intricate. There have been studies of user-movement through, and interaction with, civic space in Pompeii (Bon and Jones 1997) and Rome (Bjur and Santillo-Frizell 2009; Laurence and Newsome 2011), studies of the varying ways of experiencing the different sites of Rome (Larmour and Spencer 2007; O'Sullivan 2011) and cities around the Roman Empire (e.g. Spieser 2001; March 2009; Laurence et al. 2011), as well as the spatial construction and perception of different kinds of urban space (e.g. Flohr 2007). Underlining such studies is the critical importance of the centrality of Rome as a model for urban space within the Roman world, and the constant referencing back to Rome in cities that were spread through the Empire in a way that never happened in the Classical Greek world and only to a more limited extent in the Hellenistic Period (Kaiser 2000; Purcell 2007).

In comparison to urban space, sacred space has received a great deal more attention. In Greek scholarship, this has focused on three aspects: first, the roles of sacred space within the wider landscape (Alcock and Osborne 1994; de Polignac 1995; Cole 2004); second, the spatial dynamics and development of sacred space itself (e.g. Scully 1969; Doxiadis 1972; Scott 2010) and third, most recently, an interest in the user-experience of, as well as changing perception of and interaction with, sacred space, particularly during the Hellenistic and Roman Periods (e.g. 'Rethinking the Gods: Post-Classical Approaches to Sacred Space', Oxford Conference 2010; Burrell 2009). In Roman scholarship, while much work has been

---

[3] Modern city: e.g. Benevolo 1980, Certeau 1984, Brand 1994, Smagacz 2008. Renaissance city: e.g. Trexler 1980, Muir and Weissman 1989, Zimmerman and Weissman 1989.

done on Roman religious practice, the focus on the dynamics of sacred space has interestingly most often been in areas outside Rome (e.g. Smith 2001; Steinsapir 2005; Veronese 2006), or on the changes to the sacred landscape as a result of the supremacy of Roman over Etruscan culture, particularly in the way boundaries and networks of sacred spaces were conceived of and understood in the landscape (Grey 2005; Edlund-Berry 2006), or indeed through wider cross-cultural comparisons with Roman attitudes to sacred space (Woodard 2006).

Such integrated analyses of sacred space in both Greek and Roman scholarship, have, however, often been hindered by the publication style of many sanctuary excavation reports, which tend to split off architecture, sculpture and epigraphy from one another, or else study individual structures in isolation from their contexts, thus making the forming of a contextualised spatial view (and a conception of spatial development over time) a difficult enterprise. Yet what spatial study in both Greek and Roman scholarship is increasingly making clear is the crucial role sacred space plays as a resource for the articulation and transmission of culture and practice within the Greek and Roman worlds as well as between them.

Linked into the study of the place of sacred space within the wider landscape has been the study of the landscape itself. How communities constructed both physical and perceptual patterns in their native landscapes has been the subject of much study at both theoretical and practical levels across different cultures, especially those of Greece and Rome (e.g. Tilley 1994; Ashmore and Knapp 1999; Thomas 2001; Tilley and Bennett 2004). The data used for such analyses have migrated from prominent monuments and features in the landscape (e.g. Bender 1993) to data collected and interpreted through Geographical information systems (GIS) and surface-survey techniques (e.g. Broodbank 1999; van Haverbeke et al. 2008), although concerns have been raised recently over the interpretations associated with such techniques (e.g. Fitzjohn 2007). At the same time, the development of network theory has encouraged scholars to create integrated analyses of the networked landscape of the Mediterranean (e.g. Horden and Purcell 2000) as well as case-study-based analysis of different types of networked space within the Greek and Roman landscapes (e.g. Constantakopoulou 2007; Dürrwächter 2009; Malkin et al. 2009; Carruseco 2010).

Here too, however, an important practical distinction is to be drawn between the conduct of archaeology in Greece and Italy. In Greece, surface-survey still counts as one of the maximum five projects allowed to each foreign country per year, and all of those applications have to be submitted *via* that country's archaeological school based in Athens. In Italy, by contrast, surface-surveys are not subject to a maximum, nor does any project have to be 'queued' through a foreign school but can be carried out in direct agreement with the local Soprintendenza. This allows for the possibility (other factors such as finance taken into consideration) for more extensive landscape work to be carried out there than is possible in Greece. As a result, in Italy-based landscape studies, there has been, particularly in the last fifteen years, the freedom for a tremendous effort to counteract the overwhelming focus on Rome by developing a detailed understanding of regional history, rural demography and particularly the villa landscape (e.g. Barker 1996; Dyson 2003; Terrenato 2007; Witcher 2009; Launaro 2011).

Landscapes and networks on their grandest scale connect with studies of how the ancients understood and conceptualised the whole extent of their world (cf. Romm 1992; Dueck and Brodersen 2012), its continuing interconnectedness and 'globalisation' (cf. La Bianca and Scham 2006). Much work has been done on the changing Greek spatial and geographical constructs of the world (e.g. Cole 2010; Romm 2010), from Achilles' shield description in the *Iliad*, to the early development of world maps by Anaximander of Miletus, through Herodotus' three-continent division of the world, to Plato's 'frogs around a pond' and the Aristotelian tendency to place Greece at the centre of the earth and link geographic placement to political and military value.

In contrast, it has traditionally been acknowledged that, while the Romans obviously imposed themselves strongly on the landscape with definitive lasting impact, the attitudes and techniques with which they made sense of the world are more difficult to grasp in any precise detail (cf. Foxhall et al. 2007: 108; Talbert 2010). Such attitudes are even harder to fathom thanks to the loss of maps such as Marcus Agrippa's *orbis terrarum* and the scanty survival of the Justinian marble plan. But there has been strong debate, for example, about the degree to which Romans understood the world from a 'hodological', 'itinerary-led perspective' (discussions about which are often focused on the surviving thirteenth century Peutinger map, the only surviving copy of the Roman *cursus publicus*: Brodersen 1995; Salway 2007; Talbert 2004). As a result, the different ways in which the Greeks and Romans conceptualised their worlds is becoming slowly clearer, e.g. in their attitudes to crossing open water (Salway 2004).

SPACE AS PART OF THE STUDY OF HISTORY

Many of the themes brought out in this short review of the different genres of space and spatial study will have immediate and obvious use for the historian (cf. Sauer 2004). Perhaps above all else, space has been involved in two recent major (interrelated) historical and archaeological fields of enquiry in the Greek and Roman worlds: memory and identity. The way in which spaces reflect and articulate social behaviour, meaning and belief, thus making them charged and valuable arenas in which to act and interject, ensures that they are fundamental to the physical construction of memory within a community and the presentation and experience of that community's identity (cf. Jones 1997; Malkin 2001; Lomas 2004; Meskell and Preucel 2004). Such presentation and experience are often likely to be complicated by the fact that different spaces may offer overlapping or conflicting interpretations, and are certainly likely to be experienced and understood in multiple, unpredictable ways by different users (cf. Alcock 2002). Equally, over time, such physical spaces will also reflect a multitude of changing attitudes towards, as well as projections of, the collective memory and identity of that community (cf. van Dyke and Alcock 2003). To this mix needs to be added the ways in which the different literary sources construct their own views not only of issues of memory and identity (cf. Hall 1997), but also of the nature, interpretation and experiences of particular spaces, which often can contrast starkly with the picture inferable from the material evidence. As Bintliff (2006) points out with reference to the relationship between city and countryside in the Greek world, if the physical evidence is often taken to highlight a complete blurring of the boundaries between the two, why does the literature seem to work so hard to create such a strong distinction between them (for further debate on this issue: Osborne 1987; Jones 2004)?

Yet my belief is that spatial study has the ability to be of much broader use to the historian in a wider variety of fields of enquiry than simply memory and identity, because it taps into, focuses on and makes possible a number of routes of enquiry currently much sought after in the study of ancient history. A focus on space demands an interest in linkages and relationships between spaces, architecture, objects and users. It foregrounds the importance of human movement and visual perspective in creating multiple experiences and understanding of the world and society (cf. Burrell 2009; O'Sullivan 2011). It links different levels of space (house, city, landscape, wider world) and offers different resolutions of activity through its privileging of contextuality. All of these elements help to draw us away from the tendency to consider objects, buildings and sites in isolation from the networks in which they exist and which they help to constitute.

Equally, such studies, particularly using techniques of GIS and field survey, are increasingly providing data which can transport us outside the major settlements that have been such a long-term focus for study (Rome, Athens, etc.), and which are now increasingly recognised as atypical examples rather than normative ones. At the same time, spatial study opens up for analysis arenas of social interaction at lower levels of ancient society (e.g. smaller settlements, housing for all levels of society, patterns of use of everyday as well as prestige objects), which rarely are the focus of the often elite-orientated literary sources, thus allowing for an increasingly sophisticated appreciation of how social change is conducted, as well as motivated, from the bottom up as part of a gradual process as well as imposed from the top.

Spatial study also focuses our attention on the decision processes and active choices involved in the design and creation of different spaces and what fills those spaces (cf. Tanner 2006; Scott 2007; 2010). Yet it also forces us to think about these 'intended' meanings as but one of the ways in which such spaces can be conceived, 'used', experienced and understood, by underlining the mutability of meaning and number of participants active in creating that meaning (for the continuing debate around concepts of agency: cf. Gell 1998; Dobres and Robb 2000; Gardner 2004a; Osborne and Tanner 2007). Spatial study thus opens up an opportunity to shake loose some of the positivisms still remaining in ancient world scholarship and think about a much more textured, complex ancient world. Moreover, in an effort to understand that texture, spatial study requires an appreciation of both the material and literary sources, prodding us towards a much more integrated approach to the ancient world and helping to pull down the disciplinary boundaries that we have historically imposed on ourselves.

In addition, because of the ubiquity of spatial structures across cultures, spatial study offers an invaluable opportunity for feasible and worthwhile cross-cultural study. For our purposes, that allows us to think particularly about the ways in which the Greeks and Romans conceived of, constructed and reacted to particular kinds of space at different levels of society, and in turn how the two cultures interacted over, and within, different spaces. We have already seen some of the distinctions in attitudes to space between the Greek and Roman worlds outlined in current scholarship (for example, the spatial articulation of different social needs and desires in the Greek and Roman house seen through both material and literary evidence, the importance of the centre-and-periphery model for the spatial mimicking of Rome in cities throughout the Roman world, in contrast to the much more local differentiation in the less unified Greek world, the Roman 'hodological' ('itinerary-led') understanding of the wider world in contrast to Greek bird's-eye, all-encompassing interest in geography). Yet there is still much to discover, particularly in relation to how these two approaches to space interacted, conflicted and reshaped one another within the several spatial arenas and periods in which these two cultures interacted.

Through spatial study, therefore, I argue that we can gain greater texture and depth for our historical understanding of particular places and events, a better appreciation of the experience and perception of cultural phenomena, and a clearer picture of the detailed interaction between different groups of peoples and entire cultures. This is an extremely useful reminder of the overlaps and contradictions between literary and material evidence as well as the plurality of ways in which the ancient world could be, and still can be, seen and understood.

MOVING FORWARD

What follows is a series of five case-studies. Each case-study looks at a different type of space in a different geographical part of the Greek and Roman worlds, constructed through combinations of literary, epigraphic and archaeological sources. In each, I first seek briefly to situate my analysis within the major scholarly debates surrounding the case-study, in order to think about how a spatial approach can most usefully contribute to furthering our understanding in that particular area.

In Chapter 1, I examine the spatial development of the agora at Cyrene from the city's inception to the fourth century AD. Within Greek and Roman studies, recent spatial analysis of private space has been much more prevalent than that of public space – an imbalance perhaps itself motivated by the traditional historical focus towards public architecture and civic space within both the study of ancient literature and site excavation. In Greek scholarship, for example, the examination of the agora as public space has been dominated by that of Athens (e.g. Thompson and Wycherley 1972; Millett 1998; Vlassopoulos 2007); the last major cross-polis comparison conducted before the advent of modern spatial studies was done in the 1950s (Martin 1951). What has become clear from these and similar studies is the importance of the agora within Greek culture and the flexibility of its purpose: as meeting place, market, place of politics and law, whose boundaries were marked and to which entry was controlled, thus creating communities of permitted users. Yet more recent investigations of 'agora-type' spaces in other cultures (e.g. Low 2000) have also underlined their ability to reveal complex interactions, overlaps and conflicts between the physical, 'produced' space and the 'perceptual', 'imagined', 'lived', 'constructed' space, both at one time and over time, as meaning is continually etched into the social and physical structure of the public space by a variety of users. In short, the agora still has much to tell us about the complexities of ancient Greek society. This chapter seeks to focus in on the complex spatial evolution of the particular structures within the agora at Cyrene, a city rarely given sufficient attention in the historical or archaeological scholarship, in order to understand how the agora both reflected and actively formulated the changing political, social, economic and religious realities, attitudes and beliefs of the city, particularly as a result of the turbulent political upheavals through Cyrene's history as part of the Greek world and its significant reorganisation under Roman power.

In Chapter 2, I move from polis space to sacred space and to a wider spatial resolution. I also move from examining each individual structure within a defined space, as I did in Chapter 1, to focus on the relationships created between spaces, in this case the relationships between different divinities worshipped on the island of Delos from its earliest religious use through to the devastation and slow decline of the island after the first century BC. The unique nature of Delos as home to so many deities from a host of different traditions, religious beliefs, periods and origins over a long period encompassing both the Greek and Roman worlds makes it the perfect example for an in-depth study of spatial relationships. This chapter seeks to investigate how those operating on the island sought to construct and manage relationships between different divinities through the spatial locations of their shrines, and, in turn, how those spatial relationships expressed and influenced later worship and contributed to the complex political, social and economic position of Delos within the ancient world.

In Chapter 3, I move from sacred space to the study of funerary space, again at a wider spatial resolution, but this time more exclusively in the Roman world. Much has been made of the tombs that lined the streets entering the cities of Rome, Ostia and Pompeii, not least because of the huge amount of evidence available to us at these sites (despite its occasional poor state of publication particularly as regards Rome). Recent investigation has underlined how these tombs provide evidence for a whole range of Roman attitudes towards death, burial and status within Roman society. Yet what interests me in this chapter is the extent to which these 'streets of tombs' projected different kinds of identities over time between different streets serving a particular city and between different cities within Italy. In turn, I am interested in the degree to which these different tombs and streets of tombs contributed to an experience of community or alienation for the city visitor, and thus contributed to a sense of a united Roman world, especially given the traditional scholarly model of Roman practice which often underlines the centrality of Rome and the keenness of many Roman towns to mimic the practices of the centre.

Chapter 4 takes us to an even wider resolution of spatial analysis (stretching across the Mediterranean), but also represents a sharp shift in the nature of the space under consideration. No longer am I focused on a particular kind of space (political, sacred, funerary), nor simply a particular physical space. Instead, this chapter looks at ways in which an examination of the nature of both physical and perceptual space, as constructed through literary, material and epigraphic evidence, can be used to think about the relationship between two physically distant places. I situate my case-study in the wider ongoing debates about colonisation (and specifically the supposed 'dead end' that is the study of the relationship between metropolis and colony). I take as my primary example the relationship between Corinth and Syracuse from its inception through to the second century AD. What interests me here are the multiple ways in which a sense of the 'space' between these two settlements (their actively constructed – as well as perceived and experienced – proximity and distance, similarity and difference) was enunciated through a range of material, epigraphic and literary evidence originating from both Syracuse and Corinth, as well as from the wider Greek and Roman worlds. In so doing, I hope to revitalise the study of such relationships through a better consideration of the polyvalent and manipulable nature of the spatial relationship between them as constructed through a much wider variety of evidence.

In Chapter 5, I move to the largest resolution of spatial study, that of the whole inhabited world, the *'oikoumene'*. At the same time I move entirely from the realm of space as seen through material culture to space as constructed within literature. My focus is on Strabo's *Geography*, and how he seeks to construct the space of the inhabited world and particularly the 'place' of Greece as a country within that world. Greece as an entity within Strabo's world has languished recently, in comparison to study of other parts of the *oikoumene*, under a scholarly consensus of Greece's past historical importance and present impotence. But by thinking about how

Strabo structures his narrative, as well as how Greece as a space is present in other parts of Strabo's world, as well as his representation of Greece itself, I will argue not only that there are novel ways in which space is shown to gain meaning in Strabo's landscape, but also that Greece has a more important part to play than scholars have conceded.

In the conclusion, I will focus on how the different case-studies have helped us to understand better not just the particular topics on which they were focused but also more generally the ways in which Greeks and Romans understood and responded to space and, in turn, how these two cultures interacted over approaches to space. By so doing, I hope that this book will have made the case for a consideration of space, at a series of different levels, in different forms and through different sources, as an inestimably important and extremely useful part of a well-rounded historical investigation of the ancient world.

CHAPTER I

Inheriting and articulating a community: the agora at Cyrene

INTRODUCTION

In a recent *Companion to Ancient History* (Erskine 2009), little mention is made of Cyrene. Such absence is not unusual: the volume on *Greeks beyond the Aegean* (Karageorghis 2002), for example, contains nothing on Cyrene at all. But where it is mentioned most in Erskine (2009) is instructive: not in the chapter on North Africa, but in the chapter on concepts of citizenship. A quick look through the surviving ancient literature and modern scholarship on Cyrene shows an overwhelming interest in the story of its foundation, the celebration of its ruling kings, the arrangement of its later democratic constitution and the intrigue of its political place and stance within the Hellenistic and Roman worlds. Running through all these approaches is a common thread: that Cyrene is, from the standpoint of the literary sources, most often a creation of other writers, times and places.

There has also been a significant amount of work conducted on the physical remains of Cyrene. Many of the key parts of the city have been excavated, and, equally importantly, so have several of the major settlements in the wider region of Cyrenaica (cf. Figure 1.1). That material has been published in a series of excavation reports. Yet the excavations and publications are still far from complete, and some of the finds have been extremely difficult to date. Moreover, where particular spaces have been well excavated, such as the city's agora (cf. Figure 1.9), the tendency in the resulting publications has been to split up different sides of the agora into individual volumes, the maps of which show only the particular structures under consideration rather than the agora as a whole. This is coupled with a primary focus on the borders of the agora rather than its centre, and with a decision to concentrate on finding architectural parallels for the structures from around the Greek world rather than thinking about how those structures related to others immediately surrounding them.

As a result, there has been a consistent failure to link the political history of Cyrene with the spatial and architectural development of its key public spaces, and this in turn reflects, as outlined in the introduction, a lack of recent engagement with the agora as public space more generally. In this chapter, I will examine the spatial development of the city's agora during Cyrene's changing political fortunes from its foundation in the late seventh century BC to its discontinuation as a public space after AD 365. This is not in order to prove that the spatial development of the agora reflected those fortunes – it would be distinctly odd if it did not. What I am interested in exploring is *how* the agora space was inherited, adapted and employed by, amongst others, the changing political elites, and in turn *how* such a space actively contributed to the articulation, negotiation and perception of the city's politics. In so doing, I hope not only to offer a more interconnected way of exploring the material evidence than has previously been adopted, but also, more importantly, to offer a viewpoint for historical discussions of Cyrene's development which is distinctly Cyrenean.

LOCATION AND INITIAL DEVELOPMENTS (650–550 BC)

The region of Cyrenaica is in the eastern part of today's Libya. This area, abundantly fertile, exists as a sort of island, separated from Crete and Greece by the sea on one side and from the rest of Africa by the desert on the other. Within Cyrenaica lies the city of Cyrene. The settlement is spread over an irregular landscape: a long spur of higher ground, surrounded by a 'moat-like' depression, in turn surrounded at one end of the spur by higher hills and at the other by open plains. On one end of the long spur of land that runs through the site like a dorsal fin can be found the city's acropolis (about 625 m above sea level) and, in the middle of the spur, the city's agora. The height above sea level of the agora itself varies only slightly across its width (from 616 m above sea level at its northern end to 617.5 m at its southern end). To the north-west of the central spur can be found the city's sanctuary of Apollo, to the south the sanctuary of Demeter and Core, and to the north-east the sanctuary of Zeus. On the slopes of the hills surrounding the central spur can also be found the city's large necropolis (Figure 1.1).

It has been argued by Calame (1990: 280; 2003: 41), amongst others, that there is no authoritative narrative of the foundation of Cyrene, but rather a number of legends, bound together by genre. Perhaps the most well-known of these is that Cyrene was founded in 631 BC by colonists from the island of Thera (Santorini) in the Aegean (for the

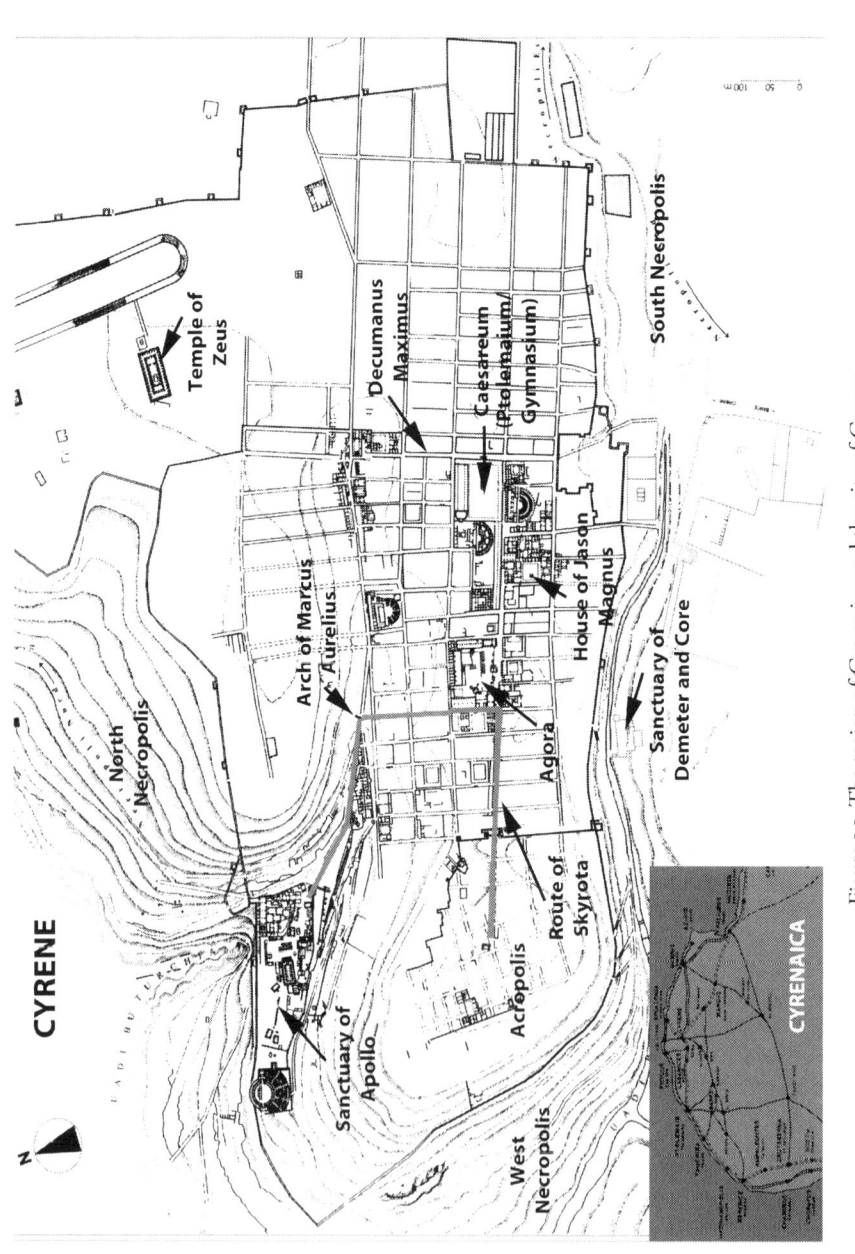

Figure 1.1 The region of Cyrenaica and the city of Cyrene

story cf. Herodotus *Histories* 4.150–8). These colonists, directed by an oracle from Delphi, and aided by a man named Battus, arrived and settled on the coast of Libya some years earlier before being shown the well-watered and defensible inland site of Cyrene by local Libyan tribes. The archaeological evidence suggests that the earliest habitation at the site was on the later acropolis and around the sanctuary of Apollo (Figure 1.1). Over the course of the next one hundred years, the settlement was reinforced by further arrivals from across the Aegean (the pottery found comes from Corinth, Athens, Laconia, Rhodes and Chios as well as from Thera) and spread to occupy the spur of land on which the agora was situated (for discussion see: Applebaum 1979: 14; Osborne 2010: 8–17; Boardman 1999: 154; Bonacasa and Ensoli 2000: 19). Cyrene is said to have been governed in this period by kings, of which Battus, the oikist founder of the colony, was the first. Yet its political system appears to have been rocked both by regular clashes with native Libyans and Egyptians, as well as by feuding amongst the royal family (cf. Hdt. 4.159–66).

It is in this context that we find the earliest structures developed within what would become the agora of the city. In the last quarter of the seventh century BC, an oikos structure was erected in the south-east corner (E1) covering over two small altars, and in the south-west corner, a larger oikos structure was built facing east (Figure 1.2).[1] The south-east oikos is believed to have been dedicated to Orpheles, a local divinity associated with good luck, fortune, health and wealth (Stucchi 1965: 34). The south-west oikos was dedicated to Apollo Archegetes (Purcaro 2001: 25).

Two things are striking about these structures. The first is that these earliest buildings define what will always be the east and west limits of Cyrene's agora throughout its history: the agora space was only ever expanded to the south. Second, their orientation: unlike every other building to come in the agora, these two were orientated in perfect alignment with the road approaching the agora from the west, which split at the corner of the Apollo structure, one branch turning north and the other east, running immediately to the south of both the oikos of Apollo and Orpheles (cf. Figure 1.1). This road has been identified as the processional route (known as the '*skyrota*' in Pind. *Pyth.* 5.93) that linked the acropolis, agora and sanctuary of Apollo at Cyrene (Chamoux 1953: 132). Such a route underlines, however, that the agora, in this period, was not to be found at the centre of its community, but in fact at (and as) one of its boundaries.

---

[1] All reference numbers to structures in the agora are taken from the excavation reports (see bibliographic essay).

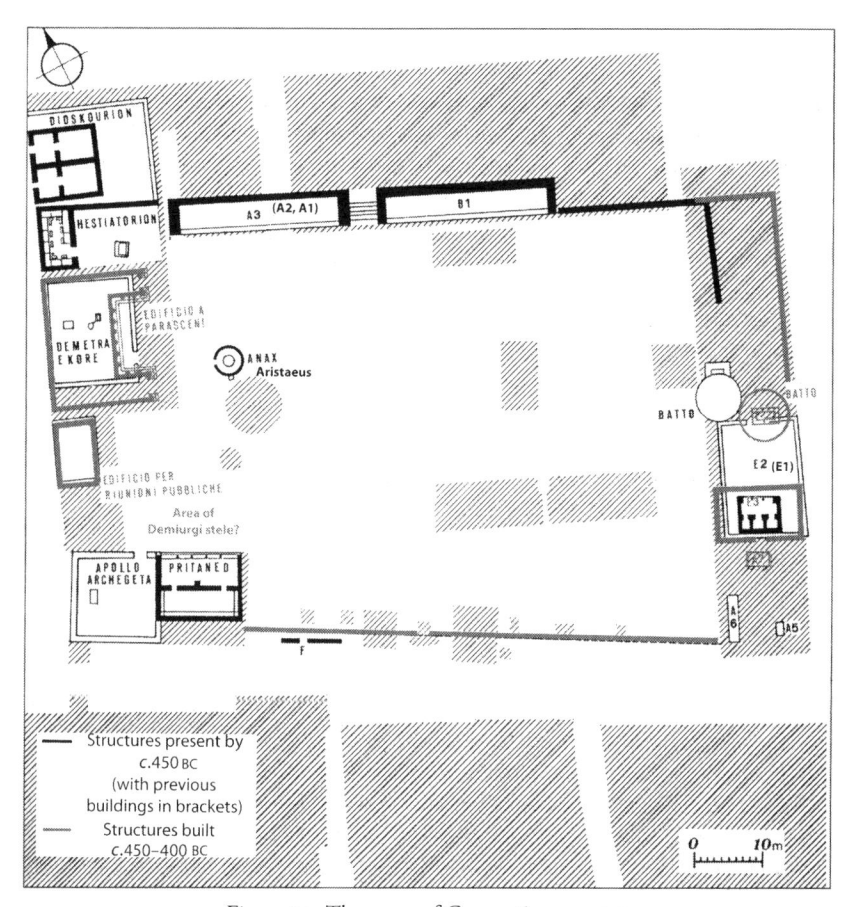

18   *Inheriting and articulating a community: the agora at Cyrene*

Figure 1.2   The agora of Cyrene 650–400 BC

In the first quarter of the sixth century BC, this liminal dimension of the agora, if not its physical location, was dramatically reduced. The south-east oikos (E1) was enveloped by a larger one (E2), flush with which stood a tumulus (Figure 1.2). This tumulus, with a small rectangular appendage to the north, contained the ashes of a human cremation mixed with earth, suggesting to the excavators that the remains had been moved here from their place of initial burial (Stucchi 1965: 58). It has been identified in line with Pindar (*Pyth.* 5.93) – although not without dispute – as the tomb of the colony's founder and first king, Battus, who would be the only king buried in the agora. The intentional movement of such important remains perhaps reflects a desire to reduce the liminality of this area within the wider settlement, as well as to focus ritual attention on the ruling kingship by placing Battus' tomb in such physical proximity (indeed practically linked) with that of Orpheles, the divinity of good luck and good fortune.

DELINEATION, INTEGRATION AND ENLARGEMENT (550–500 BC)

During the second half of the sixth century BC, Cyrene underwent a sustained period of political and military turbulence, first in conflict with local Libyan tribes who felt threatened by the settlement's expansion, then within its own community by a struggle directed against the overly tyrannical rulership of its kings (c.544–530 BC). Eventually, the Cyreneans appealed to Delphi for help. The oracle sent a mediator, Demonax of Mantinea in Arcadia, to oversee reform, which resulted in a new political system in which the power of the kingship was limited to royal property and priesthoods, and the citizen body reorganised into three tribes based loosely on the area from which they had migrated to Cyrene. That system was not accepted without dispute, which was spearheaded by the new king, Arcesilaus III (ruled 530–514 BC), who had the support of Cambyses, king of Persia and conqueror of Egypt, and which may have led to the invasion of Cyrene and damage to the city. An eventual settlement was reached in which Cyrene and the ruling Battiad kings sent regular tribute to Egypt, and, as Egypt was now part of the Persian Empire, Cyrene consequently became a Persian vassal (Applebaum 1979: 18–26; Bonacasa and Ensoli 2000: 61).

It is perhaps no surprise that the period immediately after the middle of the sixth century BC saw a strong attempt to delineate the boundaries of the agora space and transform it into an integrated working civic entity. Such a move was given special emphasis coming as it did in the midst of the constitutional reforms empowering the citizen body by Demonax. The delineation is most obvious on the northern side (Figure 1.2), with the construction of a stoa colonnade structure (A1) and terracing wall, and to the west with the construction of a small temenos (bounded sacred space) thought to be dedicated to Demeter and Core (although not allocated an identification number in the excavation reports). The space of the agora was further synergised through the addition of new paving in this period (Stucchi 1965: 69–77; Bacchielli 1981: 34–7).

There are three key points to note, though, in this articulation. First, that, aside from stoa A1 to the north, the delineation of the agora was still effected primarily through ritual structures (Orpheles and Battus to the east, Apollo and Demeter and Core to the West). The second is that the alignment of the stoa, terracing wall and Demeter and Core temenos is different from that of Orpheles and Apollo, as if there has been a deliberate attempt to regularise the dimensions of the new civic space, thus establishing a visible break with what came before (Polidori et al. 1999: 197). The third is that, as part of this process of delineation, the eastern side of the agora, with the tomb of Battus and oikos of Orpheles, was perceptibly marked as physically different from the rest of the agora space. The new terracing wall to the north stopped before it reached anywhere near the agora's eastern edge, as did the agora's new paving. The agora's delineation and integration seem deliberately to have portrayed the founder's tomb and associated oikos of Orpheles as different, older, less monumentalised, more 'rustic' space. Such differentiation is perhaps suggestive of the desire to stress the primacy and antiquity of their founder's cult, but equally it could be the opposite: a result of the ongoing constitutional tension within the city, which left those improving the agora uncertain as to the degree to which its Battiad kings should be fully included within the city's civic space.

What is more surprising perhaps is that, despite the growing disturbance, possible invasion and absorption of Cyrene as Egyptian/Persian vassal, the last quarter of the sixth century BC witnessed increased growth and articulation of the city's civic space, which included the rebuilding of structures only recently themselves completed. Such enlargement is again most noticeable on the north side of the agora, during which time the recently constructed stoa A1 was rebuilt as A2, and was accompanied a little later by a second stoa (B1) to the east (Figure 1.2). A new staircase entrance was constructed between the stoas to allow easy access from the lower road to the north. The north side terracing wall was continued further east and turned to run along the east side of the agora, although tantalisingly stopping short of the tomb of Battus and oikos of Orpheles (cf. Figure 1.3), to which new altars were added in this period (Stucchi 1965: 81). To the east, the Demeter and Core temenos was significantly enlarged and reorientated with its entrance now openly onto the central agora space (Bacchielli 1981: 38). The oikos of Apollo was substantially added to on its eastern side with a structure securely identified as a *prytaneion* (cf. Figure 1.2), or 'city-hall', a key building within Cyrene's administrative system in which the *prytaneis* (officers of the government) sat (Purcaro 2001: 48). To the south, part of a wall (F) has been found marking the boundary of the agora and the processional road which can be dated to this period (Stucchi and Bacchielli 1983: 23).

During a period of political turbulence, in which Cyrene ceded itself to Egyptian/Persian control, such sustained enlargement and articulation of

Delineation, integration and enlargement (550–500 BC) 21

Figure 1.3 The tomb of Battus in the agora of Cyrene *c.*550 BC

the agora as a working civic space require explanation. Yet it is also important to note that it was not only the agora that received attention: to this period also should be dated the enlargement and marble adornment of the temple of Apollo in the hillside Apollo sanctuary (cf. Figure 1.1), as well as the elaboration of the temples of Zeus and Demeter and Core at the edges of the settlement as a whole (Chamoux 1953: 156). To this period also should be assigned the striking of Cyrene's first coinage (Applebaum 1979: 28). But within this, the agora is distinct in not just its elaboration, but also its development as an increasingly key space within the wider settlement. Its ritual structures devoted to Apollo and Demeter and Core mirrored the settlement's main sanctuaries to these deities at its boundaries, a relationship articulated by ritual processions beginning at the agora and leading to the respective sanctuaries (Chamoux 1953: 340; Laronde 1987: 363–5; Robertson 2010: 293).

The agora, however, did not develop solely as a religious centre, but also as a civic one. The addition of the *prytaneion* structure here is crucial, particularly as the previous structure for the meeting of the *prytaneis* had most likely been the temple of Apollo in the Apollo sanctuary on the hillside (Applebaum 1979: 14). *The* civic structure par excellence not only was given its own independent structure, but was relocated from the heart of a sanctuary heavily associated with the city's aristocracy and monarchy to the city's agora, a space which still left the city founder's royal tomb just outside (or rather not *clearly* inside or outside) its new walled boundaries (Figure 1.3). Such spatial development thus provides an interesting and important undercurrent to the wider political story of Cyrene in this period: in the midst of a general elaboration of the settlement there was a very visible, determined and expensive articulation of the agora as the city's physical, political and religious centre, reinforced by the reallocation of an important civic structure and its corresponding activities.

THE 'TRIUMPH' OF DEMOCRACY (500–401 BC)

After the political turbulence of the last part of the sixth century BC, Cyrene appears to have enjoyed a relatively peaceful and prosperous first half of the fifth century BC, a state of affairs which is often attributed to the energetic King Arcesilaus IV. Arcesilaus is said not only to have ensured closer ties with the local Libyan tribes from the desert, but also to have focused on Cyrene's international relations, maintaining relationships with Delphi, Olympia and Athens (despite Cyrene's ties to Persia). He is also said to have extended Cyrene's power within Cyrenaica through the colonisation and annexation of surrounding settlements and, within Cyrene, to have patronised the arts, issued new coinage and embellished the city (cf. Applebaum 1979: 31; Laronde 1990: 44–8). He was also the king for whom (and *by* whom) Pindar was commissioned to write victory odes following his victories at Delphi in 462 BC (*Pyth.* 4 and 5). It is in *Pythian* 5 that Pindar describes not only the '*skyrota*' processional way, but also the eastern corner of the agora where the tomb of Battus lay. Pindar describes it as '*prumnois*' (*Pyth.* 5.93), 'prow-like', 'frontier-like', 'separate', or as the Loeb translation has it 'and there, at the end of the agora, he has lain apart since his death'.[2] The separation of the royal tomb, which is so noticeable in the spatial elaboration of the agora since the mid-sixth century BC (cf. Figure 1.3), is here echoed by Pindar as still evident in the fifth century BC (cf. Stucchi 1965: 62; Laronde 1987: 172).

The agora without doubt benefited from Cyrene's increasing prosperity (Figure 1.2). On the north side of the agora, stoa A2 was replaced by an even larger stoa A3, and a new monumental stairway entrance was constructed over the previous one (Stucchi 1965: 101). Apart from this, however, all the activity in the first half of the fifth century BC was heavily concentrated on the western side of the agora. In the north-west corner between stoa A3 and the Demeter and Core temenos, following heavy terracing work, a *hestiatorion* (public dining room) structure was built, identified through its rear room containing stone couches and remains of a hearth in the front section. By the middle of the fifth century BC, a structure had been added further to the north, which, though not part of the agora (it was situated on a lower

---

[2] Pindar *Pythian Odes* translated by W. Race, Loeb, Harvard University Press, 1997.

level and faced onto the processional road heading for the sanctuary of Apollo), was structurally linked to it through its use of the *hestiatorion* terracing wall as one of its own boundary walls (Bacchielli 1981: 47). This two-chamber oikos (shrine) has been identified (again, thanks to Pindar) as a shrine to the Dioscuri. Just opposite the sanctuary of Demeter and Core, in the as-yet unoccupied open space of the agora, was constructed a circular shrine with outer walls 2 m high, which has been identified as that of Aristaeus (often known simply as Anax), the son of Apollo and the huntress Cyrene (Santucci 1998: 530–5; Bonacasa and Ensoli 2000: 62).

These new structures, concentrated in the western, indeed north-western corner of the agora (Figure 1.2) suggest a continuing and marked emphasis on the needs and concerns of the citizenry rather than on honouring their energetic king. This is not simply thanks to the construction of another civic building, the *hestiatorion*, to complement the *prytaneion* in the south-west. It is also due to the nature of the gods being worshipped (Demeter and Core, the Dioscuri and Hestia), all of whom can be associated with the cares and concerns of the working agro-pastoral citizenry (Bonacasa and Ensoli 2000: 83), and who, in turn, diverted ritual attention away from the deities traditionally associated with the aristocracy and monarchy (e.g. Apollo and Zeus). This new emphasis was more, however, than just a diversion. The impressive two-metre-high circular shrine to Aristaeus on the western side of the agora, prominent because it occupied the hitherto unoccupied open space of the agora, architecturally mirrored (and surpassed) the circular tumulus of Battus on the eastern side, and offered a divine counterpart to the royal foundation story (Santucci 1998). Equally, through this focus on Aristaeus, the existence of Cyrene was pushed much further back in mythological time. In addition, combined with the new focus on the Dioscuri, it added a definite Spartan flavour to the agora, reflecting the increasing interaction between Sparta and Cyrene on display elsewhere in the city (cf. White 1990: 101–2). The eastern side of the agora, associated with Battus and Cyrene's seventh-century BC foundation, was thus not only ignored in the first half of the fifth century BC, but actively rivalled and surpassed (cf. Figure 1.2).

The history of Cyrene in the second half of the fifth century BC is unclear, except for the fact that it seems to have been a period of continuing tension leading to civil war in 401 BC (cf. Diod. Sic. 14.34.3–6) and the eventual establishment of a new constitution (cf. Applebaum 1979: 35; Robertson 2010: 372). Yet in this period the spatial development of the agora could not make the direction of the transition more clear. On the western side, the sanctuary of Demeter and Core was entirely built over by a new winged stoa (cf. Figure 1.2, the 'edificio a Parasceni'), the architecture of which appears actively to have mirrored that of the stoa of Zeus Eleutherius in the democratic Athenian agora (Bacchielli 1981: 65; 1985: 2; Polidori et al. 1999: 210). A little further to the south, still on the western side, the first building for meetings of Cyrene's civic council (the *bouleuterion*) was constructed (Bonacasa and Ensoli 2000: 65).

It was also at this time that the first inscribed stele was erected in the western corner of the agora near the temple of Apollo by the *Demiurgi*, who were the city's leading financial officers and/or magistrates (cf. Jeffery 1973–4; Applebaum 1979: 39;). These stelae displayed lists of agricultural produce and price, along with civic expenditure from estates managed by the *Demiurgi* for the polis of Cyrene. Land management had been one of the few responsibilities left in the hands of the monarchy following the reforms of Demonax of Mantinea in the sixth century BC, a responsibility which seems now, very publicly, to have been given to a civic committee from which the community demanded transparency (Applebaum 1979: 87), as perhaps was a wider range of fiduciary transactions (cf. Gasperini 1990).

Yet the western side of the agora was not the only place to see demolition and subsequent construction in the second half of the fifth century BC. The eastern edge of the agora was also expanded by approximately 12 m with a new terracing wall and new floor paving, which not only finally integrated this area into the agora space but also completely covered over the (destroyed) tomb of Battus and accompanying oikos of Orpheles (E2). The tomb was subsequently moved (again) and rebuilt further east (again at the very edge of the agora), in an architectural style similar to that of many tombs from the *necropoleis* of Cyrene in this period (cf. Figure 1.2). The destroyed oikos of Orpheles was also entirely rebuilt in a new orientation to the south (E3), along with a new altar that served it. The oikos may have been rededicated at this point to a (relatively new) god who had only recently been officially welcomed from Epidaurus at Athens: Asclepius (Stucchi 1965: 109; Bonacasa and Ensoli 2000: 65).

The development of the agora in this period is instructive for adding texture to our understanding of the pace and nature of political change in Cyrene in the second half of the fifth century BC. That change was expressed first through a willing demolition of places of ritual worship in favour of the emulation of the physical structures, architectural styles (and perhaps deities) of Athenian democracy, second through a visual display of the changing nature of land and fiduciary control, and third through a demonstration of power over the physical remains of the city's royal foundation history. By the end of the fifth century BC the western side of the agora was even more fervently that of the democracy (with *prytaneion*, *Demiurgi* stelae, *bouleuterion*, Athenian-style stoa, sanctuary of Aristaeus and the Dioscuri), while the eastern side was integrated and rebuilt with the royal founder kept at the boundary, his tomb remodelled to resemble contemporary styles of burial at Cyrene and thus denying him a perceptibly historic presence (Figure 1.2).

At the same time as the agora was made to reflect and construct so clearly the changing nature of Cyrenean governance, it was also, at a more macro level, increasingly being fashioned as a space of key importance within the wider settlement. At the southern end of the agora, which was the last side of the agora to remain undelineated, a new boundary wall was built in this period, with a set of steps offering a new official entrance mirroring that to the north (Stucchi and Bacchielli 1983: 28). As a result, just as the agora became more and more a space that actively represented the changing nature of Cyrenean civic life, it was also marked more and more definitively as a monumental space to which attention should be paid.

PROSPERITY AND UNCERTAINTY (401–300 BC)

The first half of the fourth century BC saw a strengthening of the democracy at Cyrene. The 'stele of the founders' (*SEG* 9,1,3), set up in approximately 375 BC (although where it was originally placed is uncertain), reiterated a close bond between Thera and Cyrene, admitted to *isopoliteia* ('equal citizenship') new Therans in residence and arranged them into smaller civic units, indicating that a full democratic system was in place (Meiggs and Lewis 1988: No. 5; Polidori et al. 1999: 184). Yet this period of prosperity was reflected in the agora by only the most modest of changes to the north side of the agora. Stoa B1 was replaced by a longer stoa B2 and stoa A3 was given internal subdivisions to create three separate chambers, perhaps for civic offices (Stucchi 1965: 124).

In the second half of the fourth century BC, Cyrene's history becomes once again extremely fast-paced and complex. By 331 BC Cyrene (along with Egypt) had passed into the hands of Alexander the Great. Following his death in 323 BC, Cyrene suffered further unrest as supporters of oligarchy and democracy wrestled for control of the city, as did, after 305 BC, the new ruler of Egypt Ptolemy I. Between 323 and 301 BC, there occured several invasions of the city, two revolts in 312 BC and 305 BC, and even the brief assumption of full monarchical powers not by Ptolemy, but by one of his representatives. In 301 BC, another of Ptolemy's representatives, this time his son Magas, was installed, and he initiated a much needed period of stability. At some point in this turbulent epoch, a new timocratic constitution at Cyrene was instituted by Ptolemy I, which we know about through the *Diagramma* document, a copy of which was found in Cyrene's sanctuary of Apollo (*SEG* 9,1,1). This prescribed the balance of power (Ptolemy as supreme general, but Cyrene as autonomous in day-to-day matters) and the organs of government in Cyrene (a *gerousia* ['senate'] of 101 members, a *boule* ['council'] of 500 members, five *ephors* ['overseers'], five *nomothetai* ['law-givers'] and five *nomophylakes* ['law-upholders']), a mix which interestingly echoes parts of both the Athenian and the Spartan systems of government.

Such dramatic and fast-moving political changes are difficult to follow in the archaeological evidence, given the difficulty of precise dating for many structures. But what is clear is that the second half of the fourth century BC saw massive changes to the nature of the agora. On the west side, all the buildings (the Athenian-style stoa, *hestiatorion* and sanctuary of the Dioscuri) were demolished and replaced with a single, gigantic, 39-metre-long stoa (O1), which may have been the location for meetings of the *boule* (Figure 1.4). This new structure was built flush with the pre-existing small *bouleuterion* to its south (which may now have housed the *gerousia*), and seems to have been completed before the political unrest which followed the death of Alexander the Great (Bacchielli 1981: 91–100). On the north side, there was also a complete overhaul between 350–300 BC: stoa B2 was replaced with stoa B3, extending the agora's dimensions a little further to the north and then, almost immediately, B3 was itself pulled down and replaced by an even larger stoa B4 (Figure 1.4). At the same time, stoa A3 was abandoned, pulled down and replaced with a monumental entrance staircase and new terracing walls. To the east, the tomb of Battus was (yet again) rebuilt and this time given a large temenos enclosure wall, and a new large altar was created south of the oikos of Orpheles/Asclepius (Stucchi 1965: 129–42). To the west, the *prytaneion* was detached from the temple of Apollo, and the temple was rebuilt on its archaic foundations (with solid walls mimicking its archaic oikos style) and given its own altar on its eastern side (Purcaro 2001: 61–83).

Yet these changes were not the most dramatic. In the last quarter of the fourth century BC, there was a large extension of the agora to the south, across the processional road, which had traditionally demarcated its southern limit. Although excavations in this area are still to be fully published, it seems clear that this new agora zone to the south was filled with a number of

Prosperity and uncertainty (401–300 BC) 27

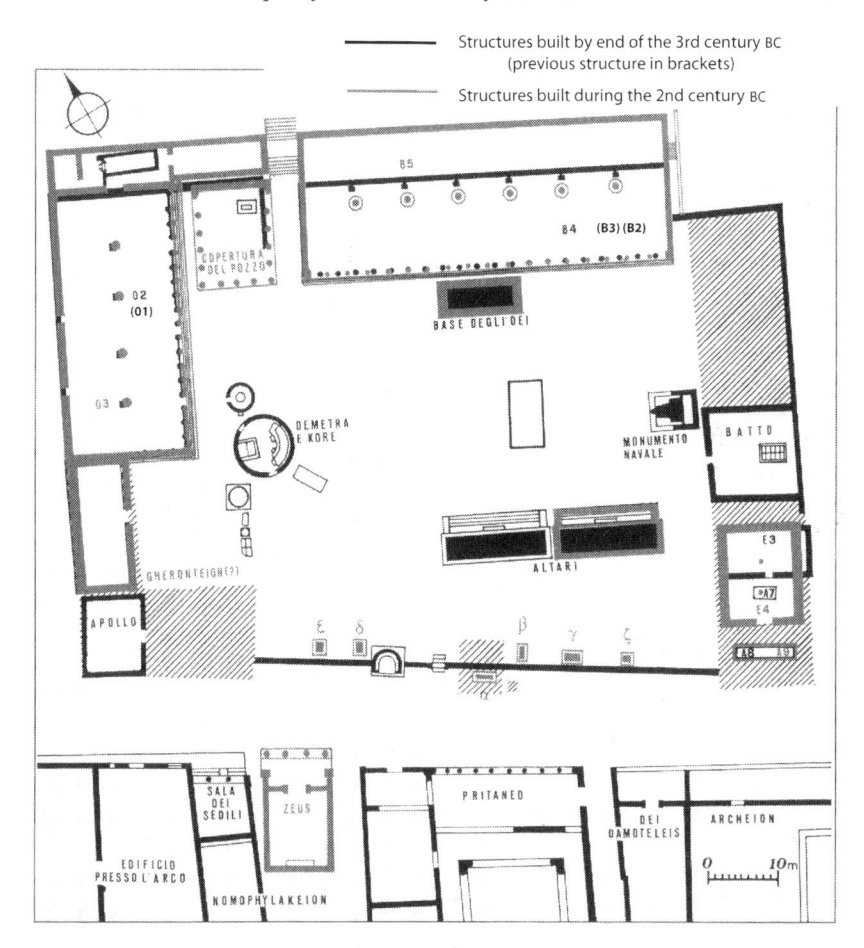

Figure 1.4 The agora of Cyrene 400–96 BC

structures by the end of the fourth century BC: a new *prytaneion*, a *nomophylakeion* ('law archive'), magistrates' building and a temple of the, ostensibly democratic, '*Damoteleis* divinities', who are thought to have performed a protective function (Figure 1.4). Finally, at the very end of the century, on the exact mid-axis of the agora, there was erected a monumental altar in white marble (Bonacasa and Ensoli 2000: 66, 87).

The complex changes to the space of the agora demonstrate the way in which the agora was perceived as a key 'battleground' in this period. The redevelopment of the west side (the construction of stoa O1) underlined the prioritising of civic over religious space, indeed particularly 'open' civic space: the architecture of this building, colonnaded on two sides, was a great deal more physically 'open' than its predecessor (despite that building's stylistic affiliation to the stoa of Zeus Eleutherius in the agora of Athens).

The excavators have also noted some signs of damage to the remains of stoa B3, which may explain why it needed to be replaced so quickly after its construction by stoa B4, damage perhaps sustained during the turbulent times after the death of Alexander the Great. The constant shifting in power between oligarchic and democratic factions in the last quarter of the fourth century may also explain the simultaneous elaboration of structures with both more democratic and more autocratic connotations (stoa O1 was constructed, but the tomb of Battus was also monumentally elaborated and differentiated). At the same time, it is harder to understand the introduction of a well in the north-west corner of the agora at this juncture (Figure 1.4 'copertura del pozzo'), right by the newly constructed stoa O1 (Stucchi 1965: 137). Should it be interpreted as an attempt to draw more people to the agora space on a daily basis, or as an attempt to turn this once intensely democratic area of the agora into a less politically functional zone?

If Bonacasa and Ensoli (2000) are correct in arguing for all the construction in the new southern part of the agora occurring in the last twenty years of the fourth century BC, then it stands as a testimony to the continuing life of the city during those politically and militarily very turbulent years, not to mention the continued pursuit of a greater variety of civic offices as a buttress against oligarchy. It may have been a goal that was greeted with a certain irony as the agora failed to keep pace with the rapidly changing situation. But the final settlement – that of Magas as Ptolemy's ruler-representative in Cyrene – was made very obvious in the agora, for it is to the very end of the century that the addition of the monumental marble altar in the middle of the agora should be dated (cf. Figure 1.4). It is more than timing, however, that ties this altar to Magas: a very similar altar had also recently been donated in the sanctuary of Apollo by a fellow aristocrat (Laronde 1987: 175). Moreover, its sheer cost and high profile position dominating the centre of the agora lend credence to its attribution to Magas as part of a demonstration of control, power and affluence.

But it is also important to note that, once again, the agora was not the only space to receive significant elaboration in Cyrene (cf. Figure 1.1). This period also saw intense construction in the sanctuary of Artemis and Apollo, and some scholars identify the sanctuary of Apollo as the stronghold of the oligarchic faction thanks to the many monumental votives offered there

The Ptolemaic period (301–96 BC)

(Laronde 1987: 178). It was, after all, in the sanctuary of Apollo that Ptolemy's *Diagramma* stele, laying out Cyrene's new timocratic constitution, was found. If so, then Cyrene had not only placed different spaces within its city in political opposition, but also significantly raised the bar for civic adornment, in terms of number, size, luxurious style and quality of their constructions. Though enduring a period of significant turmoil, Cyrene, and particularly its agora, emerged looking more impressive than ever before. This was accompanied by a strengthening of the position of Cyrene in the wider Greek world, witnessed not least by the building of its treasury at Delphi (cf. Scott 2010: 127), and the survival of the record inscribed in the 320s BC of the plentiful amount of grain supplied to Greece and Greek individuals during times of bad harvest (Rhodes and Osborne 2003: No. 96).

THE PTOLEMAIC PERIOD (301–96 BC)

Magas' assumption of power in Cyrene in 301 BC (cf. Paus. 1.6.8) ushered in a period of much greater stability in the region. Between 278–274 BC, Magas was granted the right by his father Ptolemy to rule Cyrene as an independent monarch, which he did until his death in 250 BC. Following his death, through the marriage of Berenice of Cyrene to Ptolemy III of Egypt, Cyrene was once again brought back under Egyptian control, where it would remain until 163 BC. During the second century BC, power at Cyrene increasingly slid back into the hands of the ruling monarch and landed elites: the *Demiurgi* stelae, for example, appear to have been discontinued. In 162 BC, the Cyreneans rebelled against their king, Ptolemy VIII Euergetes II (Ptolemy *Physcon* 'Bladder'), who was re-established on the throne only with help from the Roman senate (Polyb. 18.9; 31.10). Thereafter Ptolemy declared his intention to gift the city to Rome if he died without heirs (*SEG* 9,7). In 96 BC, under Ptolemy *Apion*, the city did finally pass into Roman hands (Tac. *Ann.* 14.18).[3]

During this period, there were both important changes to the agora and important shifts in the focus of the city as a whole (Figure 1.4). By the mid-third century BC, some significant rebuilding had taken place at the borders of the agora: the western stoa O1 had been remodelled as O2 (the main difference being that half-level walling had been introduced in the intercolumniations, reducing the stoa's 'openness'), and the *bouleuterion*/

---

[3] For further discussion of this complex period: Applebaum 1979: 53–63, Laronde 1987: 430–44, Bonacasa and Ensoli 2000: 21.

gerousia structure just to its south had also been remodelled with a new entrance on its eastern side facing towards the agora (Bacchielli 1981: 111; Bonacasa and Ensoli 2000: 84).

Much more important than this, however, were the changes which took place within the agora's open central space. Just to the south of the circular sanctuary of Aristaeus in the western half of the agora, a second, much larger, circular stone structure was built as a temple to Demeter and Core in the mid-third century BC (Figure 1.4). This not only reintroduced the worship of these divinities to the agora, since their previous temple had been built over in the fifth century BC, but also pressed these goddesses into the religious programme of the ruling monarchs; a statue of the king seems to have been incorporated in amongst the statues of Demeter and Core (Bonacasa and Ensoli 2000: 82). Once a symbol, along with the other agro-pastoral divinities in this north-western corner of the agora, of the civic prowess of the people of Cyrene, Demeter and Core now symbolised a stable conjoining of people and ruler within a building that mirrored the style not only of the shrine right by it (which was testimony to the mythical and divine founding of Cyrene), but also to the current style of the human founder's royal tomb to the east (Bonacasa and Ensoli 2000: 82). Indeed, for a long time in the initial excavation of the agora, this new sanctuary of Demeter and Core was mistaken for the tomb of Battus (cf. Stucchi 1965: 62; Laronde 1987: 172–4).

Almost directly opposite this new temple to Demeter and Core, on the eastern side of the agora's main space, there soon followed a unique monument. With its back to the founder's tomb, a tall statue of a female figure was set atop the prow of a ship made out of marble (Figures 1.4 'monumento navale', 1.5). This structure has been dated to the mid-third century BC and linked to the marriage of Berenice and Ptolemy III and their subsequent agreement of peace with the Seleucids in 241 BC. The style of the prow replicates that of a ship in the Ptolemaic navy, its marble 'timbers' covered with images of dolphins, sea divinities and the goddess Isis and Queen Berenice (Figure 1.5). The female figure, standing with feet apart as if moving forward, is reminiscent of the fifth-century BC Nike statue by Paionios at Olympia, and foreshadows the Nike of Samothrace (also perched on top of a ship prow) that would be erected in the second century. Its style and positioning, the excavators argue, had been carefully stage-managed so as to offer a perfect view of the sculpture to those entering the agora in the south-west corner from along the processional road (cf. Figure 1.4).[4]

---

[4] For more detail on the sculpture: Ermeti 1981: 21–9, 54 (design); 79–80, 84–98 (decoration); 129–30 (position in the agora); 131–3 (date of dedication). For an alternative dating: MacKendrick 1980: 123.

The Ptolemaic period (301–96 BC)

Figure 1.5 The 'Nike and Ship' statue from the agora of Cyrene *c*.250 BC

This monument was a game-changer in the story of Cyrene's agora. It was the first monumental dedication to honour so explicitly the achievements of the city's ruling monarchs, set in a location which was intended to link to and overshadow the founder's tomb, while at the same time dominate the central agora space and command the attention of all those in it and entering it.

By the end of the third century BC, there had been several attempts (probably by subsequent rulers) to match it. Statue bases were erected lining the front of the north stoa B4, and, along the low wall dividing the north from the new southern half of the agora, a large exedra monument was set up close to a new archway construction over the steps that allowed access between the two halves of the agora (cf. Figure 1.4).[5] But it was the addition

---

[5] Statues by north stoa: Laronde 1987: 431, Bonacasa and Ensoli 2000: 82. Exedra and arch: Stucchi and Bacchielli 1983: 33–47.

of a second monumental altar probably at the very end of the third century BC, in exactly the same style and size as that offered at the very beginning of the century, that finally succeeded in overshadowing Ptolemy and Berenice's ship monument (Bonacasa and Ensoli 2000: 87). This second altar broke the line of sight from the south-west processional entrance and succeeded in weakening the monument's domination over the central agora space (cf. Ermeti 2002: 129).

The changes to the agora during the second century BC were no less dramatic, being focused on its borders as well as on its newly occupied centre (Figure 1.4). At the beginning of the century, stoa O2 on the western side was again remodelled into stoa O3 with the addition of an L-shaped wing on its northern end, which was divided into distinct chambers (perhaps with one as a dining room). At the same time, the structure was given new entrance doors on its western side, opening up straight onto the processional *skyrota* road outside the agora, increasing the number of potential entrance ways into the agora space (Bacchielli 1981: 142–54). At the same time, on the north side, stoa B4 was transformed into an enormous two-level stoa measuring 53 m x 21 m (now stoa B5). On its lower level, facing out onto the road to the north of the agora, were spaces for shops, and on its upper level, facing onto the agora, was a new open colonnaded civic space (Stucchi 1965: 148–80). To the east, the temenos of Orpheles/Asclepius (E3) was once again rebuilt (although still in archaic oikos form) as temple E4 and given a new altar (A9) to its south (Stucchi 1965: 182–90).

It is more difficult to date precisely when within the second century BC the new construction work in the south of the agora took place. But it was wide-ranging in its scale. The magistrates' building was remodelled and added to, with what the excavators called a 'sala dei sedili' ('room of seats'), and a new temple was erected to Zeus (Figure 1.4). In an effort to squeeze this structure in, so that it faced directly onto the agora space, the new temple obliterated the entrance of the *nomophylakeion* building next to it (Bonacasa and Ensoli 2000: 66–9, 85).

In the second half of the second century BC, however, attention once again returned to the central space of the agora. Here, along the boundary wall that marked the division between the lower northern half of the agora and the higher southern half, a series of monumental bases was erected to accompany the exedra monument from the previous century (Figure 1.4). The largest ('alpha'), which was placed on the higher southern side of the divide, carried three statues, probably depicting members of the Ptolemaic ruling dynasty (Stucchi and Bacchielli 1983: 47–61).

The Ptolemaic period (301–96 BC)

In this period too, the well (Figure 1.4 'copertura del pozzo'), which had been built in the north-western corner of the agora in the fourth century BC, was covered with a tall pedimental roof supported by columns on three sides (and a solid back wall). As a result, it became a significant structure, impeding both line of sight towards and access to the northern half of stoa O3 (the distance between them was less than 2 m). In response, the northern entrance to that stoa appears to have been shut off, leaving only two entrances at the centre and southern end of the colonnade (Bacchielli 1981: 159–63).

Cyrene's position as the capital of the Ptolemaic 'Pentapolis' of Cyrenaica can explain the expensive elaboration of the city's agora in the first half of the second century BC. But given that Cyrene was in revolt against its ruler around the mid-second century BC, how should we understand the continuing enrichment of the city's agora between 150 and 100 BC? Laronde (1987: 438–45) has sought to explain it as part of an attempt by the Ptolemaic kings to win the favour of the people following their reinstatement with Roman help, particularly by focusing on civic construction rather than border protection, as some of the third-century BC kings seem to have done. But the tenor of that civic construction favoured the ruling monarchs more than it did the civic organs of the city (e.g. the honorific statues, the sidelining of the northern end of stoa O3 by the construction of a roofing structure for the well, and particularly the imposition of the temple of Zeus, which bulldozed part of the *nomophylakeion*). If anything, the ruling family, with Roman support, were making their power even clearer through their rearticulation of the city's agora.

But what of the agora's place within the wider city during this time (cf. Figure 1.1)? The addition of a temple of Zeus to the agora (and the rebuilding of Demeter and Core) only reinforced the central, key nature of this space. As Chamoux has argued (1953: 340) now processions to the three major border sanctuaries (Apollo, Demeter and Core, Zeus) could begin from their respective temples in the agora, creating a classic centre and periphery model of spatial dominance as described in De Polignac 1995. At the same time, it is important to note that, though the Ptolemaic period bore witness to the introduction of temples for Egyptian deities into spaces such as the sanctuary of Apollo, no similar introductions were made in the agora (von Habsburg 1985: 359). Thus, as the agora was strengthened in its role as the religious centre for the major Greek divinities worshipped around the boundaries of the settlement, it was also marked further as a very 'Greek' space in contrast to the increasingly multi-cultural worship going on in those same boundary sanctuaries.

34 *Inheriting and articulating a community: the agora at Cyrene*

   This continued embellishment of the agora should not distract attention from major building works going on elsewhere (Figure 1.1), in particular the addition of a spectacular gymnasium structure (also known as the Ptolemaium) to the east of the agora, linked to it by a long portico and served by the eastern extension of the main road arteries that went north and south of the agora (Luni 1990: 92; 2006: 37). This new civic structure, the marker of 'Greekness' par excellence in the Hellenistic Period, seems to have been a response to a general expansion of the city to the east, but may well have been constructed at the expense of a good deal of private habitation already in this area. It was by far the most impressive structure built at Cyrene in the Ptolemaic period, outshining the agora, and a marker of the beginning of a change of focus for the city as a whole.

FROM AUGUSTUS TO HADRIAN (96 BC – AD 150)

   In 96 BC, the Roman senate restored the liberty of the cities of Cyrenaica and took only the personal property of the last Ptolemaic ruler. Yet this light-handed solution only caused great civic unrest and instability in the region, as individuals fought to secure power within Cyrene, and cities wrestled for primacy in the region as a whole. In 74 BC, Cyrenaica was, as a consequence, declared an official Roman province, overseen by a sequence of Roman officials. In 27 BC, it was organised into a new province in conjunction with Crete and seems to have enjoyed a relatively stable and peaceful existence during the first century AD (Applebaum 1979: 63–8; Braund 1985; Bonacasa and Ensoli 2000: 23).

   The changes to the agora in this time were not as monumental as they had been in the third and second centuries BC, but they did signify a major shift in the political make-up of the city. The *gerousia* building on the west side of the agora was remodelled with curvilinear seating focused on a *bema* platform (Figure 1.6a), and it was in and around this building that several edicts of Augustus have been found inscribed on stone (Bonacasa and Ensoli 2000: 74). These edicts, dating to 7 – 6 BC and 4 BC, attest the close interest and involvement of Augustus in the political affairs of the city, which was, after all, supposedly within a 'public' province, and Augustus' desire to balance the needs of native citizens and Roman control (de Visscher 1965; Goodchild 1971: 63). Their placement, by one of the key civic buildings of the city (indeed not far from where the *Demiurgi* stelae were once erected), is evidence of the way Augustus exploited the key spaces and structures of the city in order to communicate his message.

From Augustus to Hadrian (96 BC – AD 150)

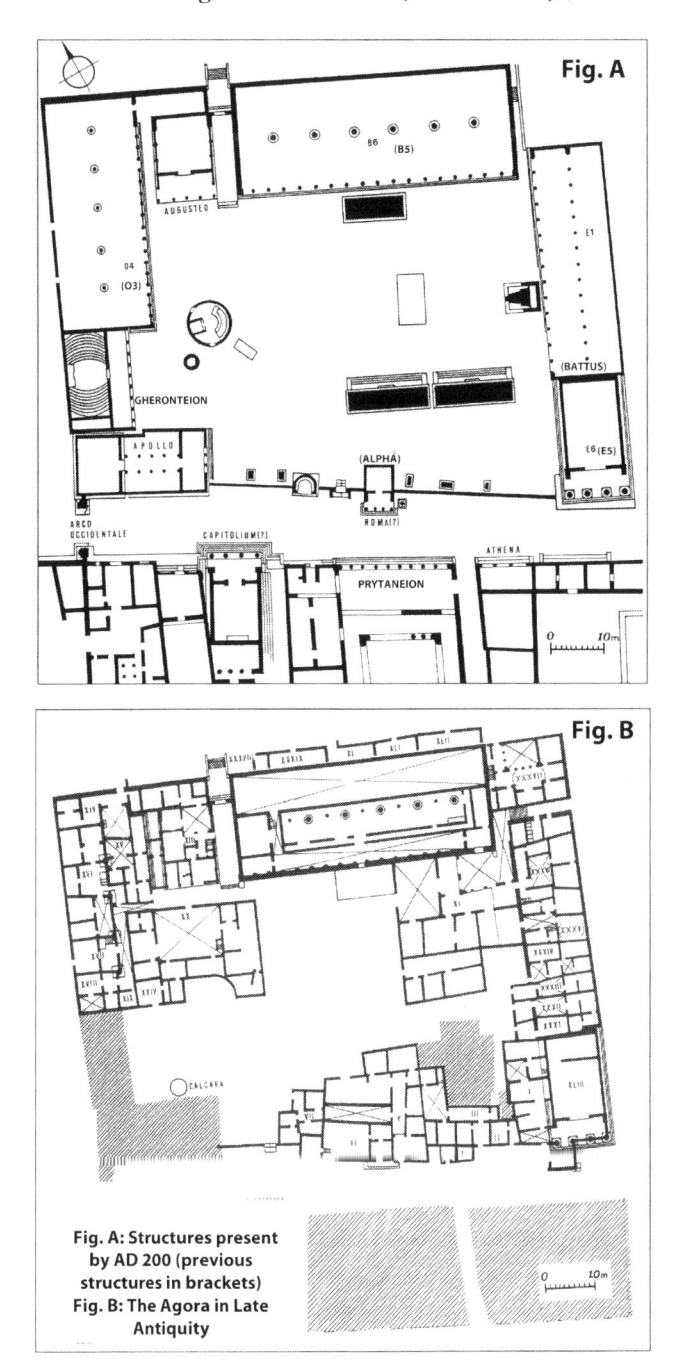

Figure 1.6 (a) The agora of Cyrene by the third century AD and (b) in late Antiquity

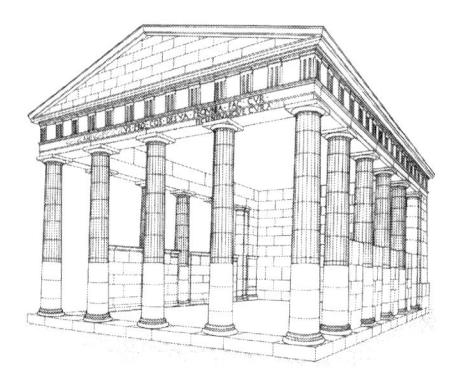

Figure 1.7 The Augusteum (former wellhouse) in the agora of Cyrene in the first century AD

It was in the reigns of Tiberius and Claudius, however, during the first century AD that the agora began to be reshaped through Roman influence. The monumental structure covering the well in the north-west corner of the agora was taken over, extended and converted into a sanctuary of the divine Augustus (Figure 1.7), with an official dedicatory inscription on the peristyle of its southern side facing out into the agora, accompanied by inscriptions on its side walls from individuals in honour of Augustus (Stucchi 1965: 207; Bacchielli 1981: 164–8; Laronde 1987: 445).

The choice of this structure can perhaps be explained by its dominating position within the agora, but perhaps also by the fact that it was the only temple-like structure in the agora without a previous ritual or civic history. It had originally been, after all, just a wellhouse (Figures 1.4, 1.6a, 1.7). As such, it allowed the Romans to signify a visible break with the religious observance and political mechanisms of the past, while at the same time not inciting criticism for having imposed upon/destroyed any of the city's traditional spaces of worship. Thus, though we might think of it as an insult that Augustus was worshipped in a former wellhouse, perhaps it was actually a particularly astute way for the Romans to avoid the damaging effects of impinging on civic and religious memory within this most charged of civic and religious spaces.

A similar delicacy can be detected in another monument erected at this time. Along the north–south dividing wall of the agora, in amongst the gathering number of honorific statues, was placed an acanthus column dedication with a statue of Demeter on top (Stucchi 1975: 142; Stucchi and Bacchielli 1983: 64–7). This was a unique monument in Cyrene, combining the acanthus, as the artistic symbol of the new Augustan peace, with a representation of one of the most important deities of the Cyrenean agora.

During the rest of the first century AD, several agora structures underwent repair (stoas O3 and B5 as well as oikos E4, which was rebuilt again in an elongated but still archaic format, as E5), although the temple of Apollo in the south-west remained untouched (Figure 1.6a). The stairs by stoa B5 were given a small propylon entrance way, and statues were set up within the stoa itself (Stucchi 1965: 208 (B5), 235 (E3/4); Bacchielli 1981: 167 (O3)). Yet through this process of renewal, the new dominance of Rome continued to be made clear within the space of the agora. Following its restoration, stoa B5's dedicatory inscription was recut to honour Zeus Soter, Roma and Augustus (*SEG* 9, 1, 127). Such an insertion of Augustus and Roma, coupled with the worship of Zeus Soter, neatly reflects the Roman balance between new construction and respect for the old; it achieved innovation through a process of restoration. It was followed by further similar inscriptions in the wake of other restoration projects, such as on the *nomophylakeion* before the end of the century (Callot 1999: 104).

Yet if, in the agora, the Roman emperors of the first century BC and AD attempted to walk a narrow line between the new and the old, they did not bother with such diplomacy elsewhere in Cyrene (Figure 1.1). The Ptolemaic gymnasium constructed in the second century BC was dramatically reconstituted as the Roman forum (or Caesarium) in the first century AD with the addition of a basilica containing statues of the imperial family (Luni 1990: 87–116; 2006: 115). This difference in treatment between the historic heart of Cyrene (its agora) and its newer monumental spaces signified not only the peculiar character and importance of the agora space within the city's mentality and memory, but also the gathering pace of the change in focus to the new 'business' section of the city.

The Jewish revolt in AD 115 destroyed much of Cyrene's agora, and its sanctuaries of Zeus, Demeter and Core and Apollo, as well as the newly built Caesarium (Applebaum 1979: 265; Polidori et al. 1999: 25–6; Bonacasa and Ensoli 2000: 186, 216). All the signs are, however, that the city recovered successfully through the rest of the second century AD, not least because the emperor Hadrian and later emperors Marcus Aurelius and Commodus appear to have put enough effort into the city's reconstruction. Cyrene was a member of Hadrian's Panhellenion (cf. Walker 1985: 98); indeed, Hadrian did enough for Cyrene to earn the title of Cyrene's 'second founder' (cf. Reynolds 1977: 55). Yet the rebuilding of the agora in the period up to AD 150 not only confirmed the change of focus from agora to Caesarium as civic centre, but seems also to have deliberately cut the city off from some of its most ancient structures, practices and forms of worship.

The western stoa O3 was rebuilt following damage during the Jewish revolt as O4 (Figure 1.6a). The small civic rooms, which had been added on the north side in the second century BC, were reincorporated and filled with statues of the Roman emperors. The stoa's columns were Romanised, and metal gates now completely filled the intercolumniations, cutting off the once open civic assembly structure even further (Bacchielli 1981: 168–79). The *gerousia* building to the south was also rebuilt following the revolt, inscribed to demonstrate who had rebuilt it, and a statue of Hadrian was installed on the *bema* platform, which at the same time remained the focus of the council chamber's curvilinear seating (Stucchi 1975: 279; Bonacasa and Ensoli 2000: 77, 84). The sanctuary of the divine Augustus was similarly restored and indeed further converted into the traditional style of a Roman temple with a strong frontal focus, pronaos and cella (Stucchi 1965: 241). The circular sanctuary of Demeter and Core in the open agora space survived the revolt, but the circular sanctuary of Aristaeus, which had stood in the agora since the first half of the fifth century BC, and had been destroyed in the revolts, was not rebuilt but simply covered over by the new paving (Figure 1.8) which spread across the whole of the agora (Bonacasa and Ensoli 2000: 83). Though not obviously damaged in the revolts, the temple of Apollo in the agora was significantly elongated by the construction of a peristyle courtyard and pronaos to its eastern side (Purcaro 2001: 89). To the north, there was some restoration work done to stoa B5, yet the tomb of Battus, which was destroyed in the revolt, seems to have been left unrepaired (Figure 1.6a). Unlike the sanctuary of Aristaeus, however, it was not covered over by the new paving, but its ruins were left visible for all to see, right next to apparently the only structure (apart from the Apollo temple) not damaged in the

Figure 1.8 The temenos of Aristaeus (Anax) covered over by paving in the second century AD

revolts: the still archaic-looking oikos of Orpheles/Asclepius (Stucchi 1965: 241–52).

On the central and southern sides of the agora, more restoration and elaboration took place. The temple of Zeus was given a new marble frontage and high podium in traditional Roman style, employing some marble from other parts of the agora, including particularly the monument 'alpha' (associated with honouring the Ptolemaic kings), which was moved from its original location and reused in the temple (Stucchi and Bacchielli 1983: 63). The temple was mostly probably rededicated as the Capitolium in this period, with statues of the imperial family placed inside it. All the civic buildings in this area (*prytaneion*, magistrates, 'sala dei sedili', *nomophylakeion*) were also restored, with particular attention paid to their facades (Bonacasa and Ensoli 2000: 76–89).

There was only one new building added to the agora after the Jewish revolt and that stood squarely on the central division between the lower northern and higher southern sides of the agora. It occupied the spot previously held by the large statue base (monument 'alpha'), which had now been moved into the Capitolium (Figure 1.6a). In its place was built a Roman-style temple (including the first use of the Corinthian order in Cyrene) dedicated simply to the goddess Roma (Stucchi and Bacchielli 1983: 74–95). In the middle of the agora, commanding both upper and lower terraces, and built in the place of a monument that had honoured the Ptolemaic kings, this ultimate Roman cult structure demonstrated more than anything else that the space of the agora, like the city itself, had been irreversibly altered.

It is interesting to note that, compared to other arenas of restoration across Cyrene, the agora seems to have been considered fairly important. The road from Cyrene to Apollonia, as well as the baths, were restored by AD 119 and the agora by AD 150 (cf. Figure 1.1). But restorations in the sanctuary of Apollo and Zeus, in contrast, were not completed until the end of the century (Bacchielli 1981: 168). The agora ranked below economic, hygienic and recreational facilities, but above the ancestral religious sanctuaries, which were, also in contrast to the agora, restored not to reflect the new Roman imperium but in old-fashioned, conservative, Doric style. The agora, however, did not rank higher than the Caesarium further to the east (Figure 1.1). The forum was rebuilt, a temple of Bacchus added at its centre, and the emperor Hadrian explicitly signalled his responsibility for the restoration, along with the addition of several statues of the imperial family and statues of Nemesis, Tyche and Themis (Applebaum 1979: 281, 282; Luni 1990: 116; Callot 1999: 315).

THE END OF CYRENE'S AGORA (AD 150–400)

Cyrene's recovery following the Jewish revolts continued from the end of Hadrian's reign well into the early third century AD, during which time it remained the capital of the region of Cyrenaica, briefly known as the Hexapolis rather than Pentapolis following new construction work by Hadrian (Goodchild 1976: 216–28). Throughout this period there were important changes made both to the space of the town as a whole, involving a rebalance in its focal areas, and to the agora itself.

Just after the end of Hadrian's reign, two monumental arches were constructed, one at the entrance to the agora on the south-west side, straddling the main processional road, and the other at the far end of this road as it passed the Caesarium (Figures 1.6a, 1.1). The road seems to have been shut off at this time to non-foot traffic. As such, it joined these two (previously competing) civic spaces into one larger unit within the city. At the same time, large houses (such as that of Jason Magnus cf. Figure 1.1) were constructed along this new pedestrian processional road (Luni 1990: 116–17). Yet within this new coupling, it was also clear that the Caesarium was the focus of people's attention. Opposite the Caesarium there was a 'construction fever' (Figure 1.1), the creation of a whole new complex consisting of temples, two theatres and houses (Callot 1999: 160; Luni and Mei 2006).

Yet within the city as a whole, it was also clear that, however important the Caesarium (and agora) may have been, it was not the focus of attention. In this period there was an enlargement of a new north–south road running along the eastern side of the Caesarium (which would become the Decumanus Maximus of the city), which itself crossed a new west–east road running straight from the sanctuary of Apollo along the northern edge of the settlement (Figure 1.1). It was along this new road, a good deal north of the agora and Caesarium, that Marcus Aurelius built his monumental archway, as did Septimius Severus in the early third century AD (Figure 1.1), nearby which were several new sanctuaries and a theatre (Luni 1990: 116).

Despite the increasing focus on the Caesarium, and indeed other parts of the city, some building did continue in the agora. The transformation of the monumental wellhouse into a typical Roman-looking sanctuary to the divine Augustus was finally completed. In the central space of the agora, restorations were made to the two monumental altars, and to the dividing wall between lower and upper terraces; additionally, a new monumental honorific base was planted to the east and a new embellished monumental propylon was constructed by the side of the new temple to Roma that straddled the north and south sides (Figure 1.6a), marking even further the transition between the two sides of the agora (Stucchi and Bacchielli 1983: 95). In the southern half of the agora, the *prytaneion* was given a Doric portico (Bonacasa and Ensoli 2000: 78). But it was the eastern side that saw the most significant changes. The tomb of Battus, left visibly in ruins since the Jewish revolt, was now completely covered over (Figure 1.6a) with the construction of a new stoa (E1), and the archaic-looking oikos (E5) was rebuilt as an enlarged Roman-style temple E6, perhaps even under the name of a new deity (Stucchi 1965: 278). The agora's Greek heritage, apart from the temple of Apollo, had all but disappeared.

The city was radically affected by the earthquake of AD 262. A decree (*SEG* 9,1,9) details how Probus, prefect of Egypt, on behalf of the Roman emperor Claudius Gothicus, repelled native Libyan tribes who took the opportunity to attack the city. In honour of his (and the emperor's) efforts to save Cyrene, the city was renamed Claudiopolis. However, his efforts to save the city, and to protect it in the future, had a devastating effect on its civic space. In the second half of the third century AD, a new fortress wall was hastily built using much spolia and material from previous structures. The wall joined up with the south-east walls of the Caesarium as the new limit of the protected city (cf. Figure 1.1). All housing outside this (such as the magnificent house of Jason Magnus) was abandoned or deliberately destroyed to aid the construction of the walls (Goodchild 1971: 144–5; Lloyd 1990b: 44). The city's misfortunes, however, continued. At the end of the third century AD, Diocletian split Crete from Cyrenaica, reforming the latter as the 'upper part' of 'Upper and Lower' Libya, and declared a rival city Ptolemais as capital of the 'Upper Libyan' Pentapolis. It was in Ptolemais that he built his own triumphal arch in AD 312 (Lloyd 1990b: 42).

As a result of this loss of status, the city of Cyrene and its agora suffered a quickening decline in the fourth century AD. The third-century AD Roma temple and propylon (so recently constructed) were taken over as private housing, as were the Apollo temple and stoa O4 to the west (cf. Figure 1.6b). To the north the enormous stoa B5 was blocked up, and housing occupied its lower shop area. In the east, the newly constructed stoa E1 was given over to housing and even a set of public latrines. Indeed, the only parts of the agora which continued functioning, and in some cases received restoration, were the monumental altars, the temple of Augustus, the Capitolium, the newly-built Roman-style temple E6 and the civic offices on the southern side (*prytaneion*, 'sala dei sedili', *nomophylakeion*).[6]

Cyrene was rocked by a further earthquake in AD 365, after which time even the sanctuary of divine Augustus in the agora became private housing, as did temple E6 and the temple of Zeus (Capitolium). The monumental altars were torn down, their material used in private housing and the *nomophylakeion* was completely destroyed (Figure 1.6b). Only the *prytaneion* shows signs of continuing in use (Bonacasa and Ensoli 2000: 79–80, 87). The letters of Bishop Synesius, who was bishop of Ptolemais in the Libyan Pentapolis, were written at the end of the fourth and early fifth century AD and they speak of a still functioning city at Cyrene, but one under constant attack from desert tribes and immeasurably cut off from the rest of the world, to the extent that some citizens apparently thought that Agamemnon was still alive (cf. Synesius letter 148.1549a–c; Bregman 1982: 41, 75). Synesius himself soon had to flee Cyrene for the safety of Ptolemais, after which time we know little of the city, except that the walls of the many agora buildings became the fortress walls of the city in its last years (cf. Figure 1.9).

Figure 1.9 The ruins of the agora of Cyrene as they stand today

---

[6] See Stucchi 1965: 294–306, Bacchielli 1981: 181–90, Stucchi and Bacchielli 1983: 111–13, Bonacasa and Ensoli 2000: 79, Purcaro 2001: 103.

CONCLUSION

How does this analysis of the spatial development of the agora from the seventh century BC to the fourth century AD enhance our historical understanding of Cyrene? What I hope it has done is add a good deal of texture to the picture of the rapidly changing political complexion of the city, and foster understanding of how the politics of the city were formulated, negotiated and perceived through a very particular (and important) space within Cyrene itself. In particular, this analysis has underlined how political changes in the seventh to fifth centuries BC could be articulated in several different ways: first, through the physical realignment of the agora's primary structures, for example after the intervention of Demonax of Mantinea; second, through the grouping and attachment of structures within particular zones as statements of particular kinds of ideology and outlook, for example the agro-pastoral north-western corner of the agora as reflecting the concerns of the citizen body and the occupation of the western side of the agora by civic structures as opposed to the eastern side with the founder's royal tomb, and the subsequent transition of all civic structures to the higher southern end of the agora; third, through the imitation of styles of architecture and spatial usage from other cities and political systems as a marker of Cyrene's political outlook, for example the fifth-century BC copy of the stoa of Zeus Eleutherius from Athens; fourth, through the mirroring, surpassing and usurpation of certain Cyrenean forms of architecture in support of the worship of particular Cyrenean deities and thus political allegiances, for example the circular temple of worship to the local deity Aristaeus in comparison to the circular tumulus of Battus.

In the fourth century BC and Ptolemaic period, such articulation of political change was accomplished in slightly different ways: through the changing occupation of the central open space of the agora; through the motif of monumental honorific monuments particularly of the Ptolemaic kings (e.g. the ship monument and monument alpha); through the subsequent reoccupation and association of monarchy with religious structures and space previously representing the citizen body (e.g. the rebuild of Demeter and Core); and through the reduction of openness in the architecture of particular structures and their physical accessibility as means of making visible the changing political system (e.g. the changes to stoa O3 and its subsequent blocking off by the monumental well covering).

In the Roman period, such changes were enunciated both through a subtle 'romanisation' of architecture, structures, spaces and worship (the adaptation of the wellhouse for the Augusteum, of the Zeus temple for the

Capitolium and of stoa B5 in order to honour a blend of Roman and Greek deities) and, later, by a more blatant erasing of previous 'local' structures and deities and the more forceful insertion of Roman structures and beliefs (e.g. the erasure of the temple of Aristaeus, and of the tomb of Battus, and the construction of the Roma temple).

At the same time, however, this analysis has revealed how the agora space as a whole was treated in comparison to other important spaces within the city. Its elaboration in tandem with the city's major sanctuaries has shown how the agora was a key civic space, indeed increasingly the central space of the city linked to the major boundary sanctuaries. But the agora also appears to have been increasingly linked with democratic sympathisers in contrast to the more aristocratic sanctuary of Apollo.

Yet the agora was not always the recipient of elaboration. In times of peace and prosperity, such as in the first half of the fourth century BC, the agora was hardly touched. But in time of political difficulty, such as the second half of the fourth century BC, it became a charged, contested and busy space. However, with the advent of the Ptolemaic gymnasium which became the Caesarium forum (and the development of newer plains and arenas of activity across the city as a whole), it seems clear that the agora's significance shifted slowly from that of being a economic/religious/civic centre to that of being a place of civic memory. That does not make it any less important: it is instructive that the Roman emperors (particularly Augustus and his immediate successors) were extremely careful to achieve a subtle balance of innovation and restoration, of local and Roman in the agora, but had few such qualms about employing a much more dominating stance in the (newer) forum area. In that role as a space of memory, it is fitting that almost the last building to be taken over by domestic housing was actually on the site of the agora's first and oldest: the oikos of Orpheles (E1–6).

CHAPTER 2

Networks of polytheism: spaces for the gods at Delos

INTRODUCTION

The island of Delos, despite its small size, enjoyed a critical importance in the ancient Greek and Roman worlds. In myth, it was the spot where Leto gave birth to Apollo and Artemis. In the Archaic and Classical Periods it was home to an increasingly important cluster of religious sanctuaries that became the centre of a series of international groupings including, most famously, the Delian League. In the Hellenistic Period its religious and commercial communities grew enormously, attracting divinities, worshippers and traders from all over the ancient world, making it one of the most cosmopolitan communities in the Mediterranean (cf. Figures 2.1, 2.2, 2.10). In the Roman world, its convenient midway location in the Aegean and accessible free port facilitated continued and increasing commercial success, as well as its eventual destruction due to ongoing pirate raids and invasions.

What makes Delos even more distinctive, however, especially for those studying the ancient world today, is the extraordinary breadth of the surviving evidence for its activities. Literary sources including the *Homeric Hymn to Delian Apollo*, Thucydides and Callimachus combine with a mass of epigraphical data as well as the plentiful archaeological evidence for the religious, athletic and civic landscape of the island (cf. Figure 2.1).[1] Above all, the picture presented to us by this wealth of evidence is of a Delos that became an increasingly cosmopolitan community over time, worshipping a combination of many local, Hellenic and foreign cults, assimilated and syncretised in an imaginative number of ways (Bruneau 1970; Bruneau and Ducat 2005: 49–53, 58–9, 64).

---

[1] Sadly we have also lost several of the literary works originally written about the island, such as Semos' eight books entitled *Delias*, or the Aristotelian *Constitution of the Delians*. For the bibliography surrounding the epigraphic and archaeological material, see the bibliographic essay in this volume. Much of the island is still to be excavated: Bruneau 1968: 633–4, Papageorgiou-Venetas 1981: 140–4.

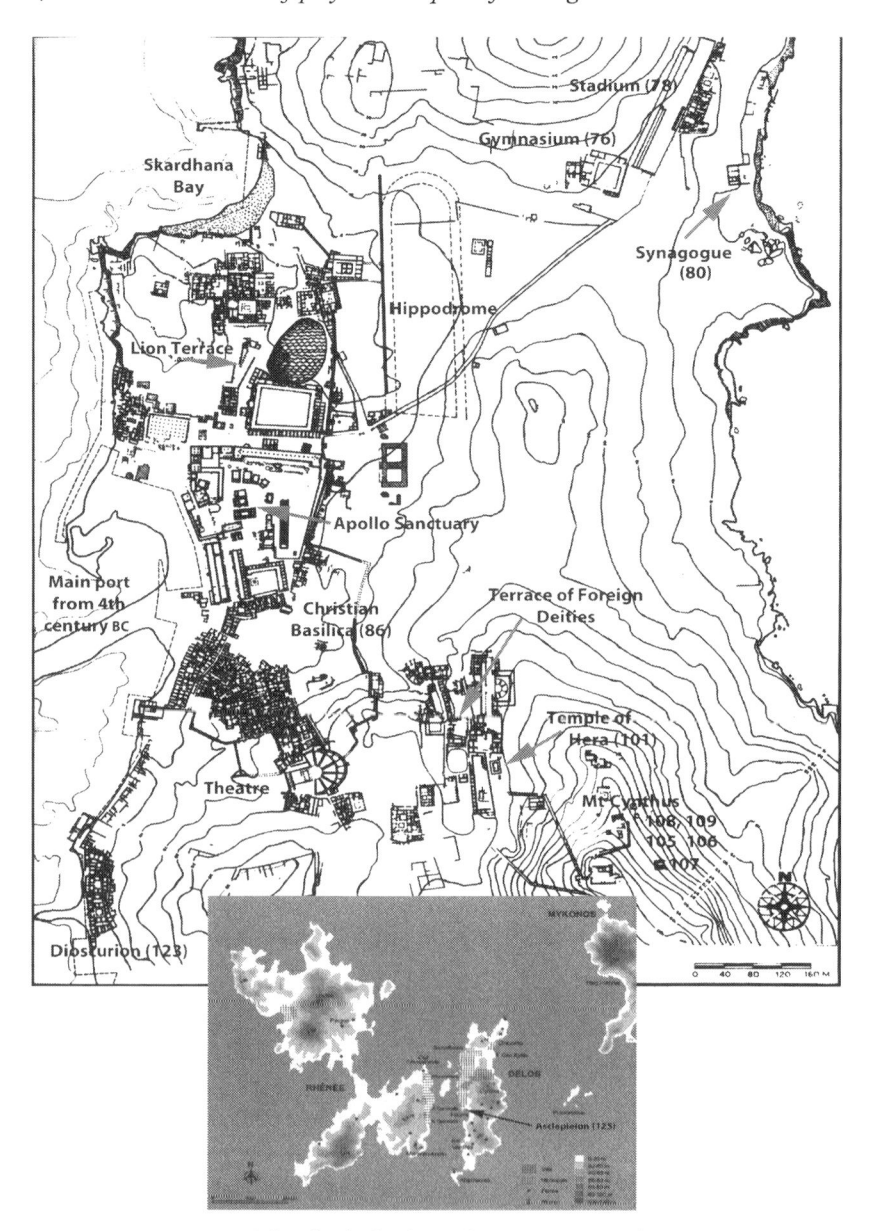

Figure 2.1 The island of Delos and its main excavated regions

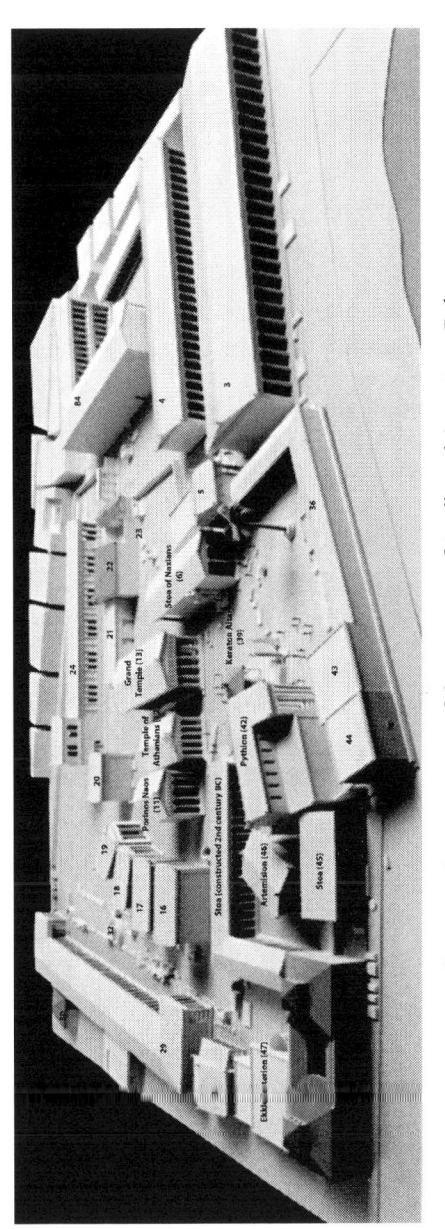

Figure 2.2 Reconstruction of the sanctuary of Apollo and Artemis on Delos

48 *Networks of polytheism: spaces for the gods at Delos*

Yet while much effort has been invested in studying the different surviving structures and linking the epigraphical and archaeological evidence in order to help identify them, not much thought has been given to how the physical spaces of the gods on Delos themselves created a network of spatial relationships which would have contributed to a visitor's experience and understanding of the integrated, cosmopolitan nature of Delian religious practice. In short, while we know how gods were syncretised through their epithets, linked through their positions on inscribed inventories and accounts, and worshipped by people from a variety of geographical origins, we have not thought much about how those relationships were actively managed and experienced in terms of the physical landscape.

In this chapter, therefore, I move from studying individual spatial structures within a civic space, as in Chapter 1, to focusing on the spatial relationships between sacred structures within the wider sacred landscape of Delos. My study will take the surviving material evidence in conjunction with the epigraphic and literary material to create a spatial picture of Delian 'networks of polytheism' as they developed over time. The purpose is to understand better how these sets of relationships were structured and perceived, and, in turn, how they impacted upon and were influenced by the island's changing identity within the wider Mediterranean world.

DEVELOPING THE NETWORK: 700–500 BC

Though there appears to have been habitation on Delos from the end of the third millennium BC, particularly on the high ground of Mt Cynthus (cf. Vatin 1965), it is only from the ninth century BC that we may gain some understanding of the religious landscape of the island (cf. Figure 2.1). During this period, in the area of the main sanctuary of Apollo and Artemis, on the lower ground of the island by the coast, a number of structures were built: one probably dedicated to Artemis (**46A$_c$**), a megaron H, a structure known as temple Γ (**7**), and probably two ritual tombs (**41, 32**) (Figure 2.3).[2] By 700 BC, however, this new, singular, spatial focus had been radically expanded. In the area of the sanctuary of Apollo and Artemis, a new Artemision had been erected (**46E**) over its predecessor and a new temple G (**40**) over the megaron H, which Vallois has argued (1944–78: 51–4) to be the cult place of Eileithyia. At the same time it appears that a second sanctuary to Artemis was begun on the neighbouring island of Rhenea, a temple to Hera (**101A**) was constructed halfway up Mt Cynthus

---

[2] All numbers in bold refer to monument reference numbers in Bruneau and Ducat 2005.

Developing the network: 700–500 BC

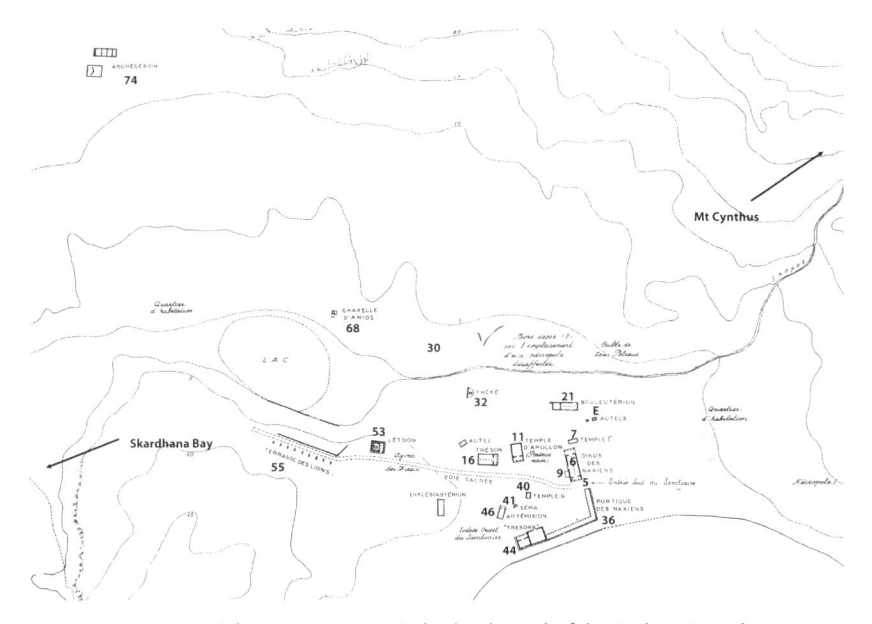

Figure 2.3 The sanctuaries on Delos by the end of the Archaic Period

Figure 2.4 View from the Apollo and Artemis sanctuary to Mt Cynthus, Delos

(Figures 2.4, 2.5), and cults to Zeus and Athena were begun on the mountain-top itself, reframing this original area of habitation as an arena of religious worship (Figure 2.1). Delos thus bears witness both to a process of monumentalisation by the end of the eighth century BC that predates

Figure 2.5 View from Mt Cynthus over Delos

what were to become the major panhellenic sanctuaries of Delphi and Olympia (cf. Constantakopoulou 2007: 41) and to an accentuated preference for female deities over male ones.

Several spatial relationships here are worth noting. The first is the presence of the two ritual tombs within the Artemis (and Apollo) sanctuary (Figure 2.3). One belonged (cf. Courby 1912: 63–74) to the virgins Laodice and Hyperoche (**41**) and the other to Opis and Arge (**32**), all of whom were reputed to come from Hyperborea, the region north of Thrace where Apollo was said to spend the winter. The proximity of these tombs to the shrines of Apollo and Artemis reflects their mythological involvement with these divinities, and their importance as part of the divine landscape is underlined by the fact that, in the case of Opis and Arge, there is evidence of continuous dedication from the late Helladic Period onwards. Moreover, both tombs would be architecturally embellished in the third century BC. This is despite the repeated purifications of the island, which demanded the removal of its dead, over the course of the sixth and fifth century BC (cf. Hdt. 1.64; Thucydides 3.104).

The spatial location of the new cults to Zeus and Hera is also important. A mountain-top site may seem perfectly suited to Zeus (cf. Scully 1969). But the location of the Hera temple – isolated halfway between the summit of Mt Cynthus and the main sacred space by the coast, with its entrance facing to the south and thus away from the Apollo sanctuary – has been linked to Delian mythology, which posits Hera as extremely hostile to the birth of Apollo and Artemis on Delos (cf. *Homeric Hymn to Delian Apollo* 89–114). The cult's estranged spatial relationship may thus reflect the Delians' difficult position: Hera was too powerful to be ignored, but equally could not be included in the new primary area of cult worship by the sea. The relative physical remoteness of Mt Cynthus, and yet its omnipresent visual dominance over the island, may thus have provided an ideal solution to the Delians' problem (Figures 2.1, 2.4). Moreover, throughout Delos' history, Papageorgiou-Venetas (1981: 108) has argued, the routes leading to the Cynthus mountainside were only ever accessible to people on foot, whereas roads in other parts of the island were accessible to wheeled transport. Throughout Delos' history, therefore, the Cynthus mountainside was rendered even more distant by the comparative physical effort and time it took to reach it. Such physical separation, specifically for Hera, is underlined even further in the epigraphic sources. Bruneau (1970: 254) noted that, though many deities are found receiving private worship in sanctuaries other than their own, the worship of Hera remains almost exclusively within the confines of her sanctuary.

In this early period of monumentalisation on Delos, therefore, there seems to have been a definitive move not just to create a religious (and divinely female) landscape reflecting Apollo and Artemis mythology, but more importantly to use the natural physical landscape to create specific spatial relationships between deities that were to have a lasting impact on Delian polytheism.

By the end of the seventh century BC (Figure 2.3), the balance between Artemis and Apollo within the central sacred area was equalised, thanks to Naxian investment in the island, and Delos' place at the centre of a burgeoning Ionian confederation was established. A structure (6), often thought of as the first temple of Apollo (although it would later be renamed as the oikos of the Naxians), was erected (Courbin 1980; Courbin 1987). It was accompanied on its northern side by the 9-metre-high Naxian *kouros* (9), made of Naxian marble, which itself faced west, towards the Artemision and Temple G. To the east were constructed the terrace and passageway of Lions (55), again fashioned from Naxian marble; this passed through an area which has been posited as an early site of burial before the purification of the island (Gallet de Santerre 1958: 277, 300; 1959).

These three structures bear witness to Naxian efforts to connect, and funnel people towards, what was for them the primary area of importance in the religious landscape (Vallois 1944–78: 21). The Lions terrace in particular is best understood as an elaborate processional alley, taking people from the original port for the island (before the development of the larger port directly by the Apollo sanctuary) to the central sacred area (Figures 2.3, 2.5). The marked processional way acted as an important guiding tool for visitors, who would not have been able to see the central sacred area on disembarkation, since the Schardhana hill was in the way (Gallet de Santerre 1958: 245; Papageorgiou-Venetas 1981: 104). The processional route from Schardhana bay via the Lions terrace may also help explain the location of the Archegesion (74), the temple of the legendary founder of the community on Delos, which was constructed in the north-east of the island in this period (Figure 2.3). It would have been a visible, and visibly linked, entity in this new religious processional landscape.

At the same time as the Naxians made links within the religious landscape, their efforts were also directed towards articulating more clearly the boundaries of the Apollo and Artemis sanctuary (Figure 2.3). By the end of the sixth century BC, a stoa (36) was constructed with Naxian marble decoration, which formed a border for the sanctuary on its south and west sides (Hellmann and Fraisse 1979); this was accompanied by a propylon entrance gate (5) in Naxian marble (indicating the movement of visitors through the Apollo and Artemis sanctuary to the southern parts of the island). It is also around this time that earlier habitation in this central area was deliberately cleared away (Gallet de Santerre 1958: 294). Such a privileging and articulation of the Apollo and Artemis sanctuary has been presented as evidence for the use of this space as the 'agora' of the Ionian Confederation (Martin 1951: 238; Gallet de Santerre 1958: 245). Such a network was in turn strengthened through the existence of a Delian sanctuary on Naxos, one of (so far) twenty-two known shrines to Apollo Delios around the Aegean, demonstrating the formal, perhaps island-led, character of the Confederation and the importance of Delos to it (Constantakopoulou 2007: 58).

Such international attention to the Apollo and Artemis sanctuary encouraged further investments there during the remainder of the sixth century BC (Figure 2.3). These ranged from an ornate well (30), to a luxurious marble treasury (44), tentatively identified as the treasury of the Parians or Delians themselves, and another (16), which has been identified as that of the Carystians of Euboea (but cf. Benchimol and Sagnier 2008: 53–4). It was also clearly in this central sacred area, and through supporting the primacy of Apollo, that the Athenians sought to impose themselves as their influence over the island increased. This is visible most clearly in a new construction dated to this time, the *'porinos naos'* temple to Apollo (11). Courby (1931: 210, 214–15) was the first to argue that the material (*poros* – a kind of limestone) was not native to Delos and indeed that it most probably originated from Athenian quarries. This new structure was most probably intended as a replacement for the early temple of Apollo (6), and its completion became part of the very

Developing the network: 700–500 BC

visible ascension of Athenian power at Delos at the centre of the Apollo and Artemis sanctuary (Vallois 1944–78: 22; Gallet de Santerre 1958: 288, 302; Bruneau and Ducat 2005: 68; Chankowski 2008: 72–4).

The growing strength of Athenian influence, not just over Apollo but also over arenas of local political activity and religious worship on the island, is also noticeable. Just to the east of the sacred central area, edifice Δ, normally identified as a *bouleuterion* (21), was constructed around the middle of the sixth century BC and was accompanied by an inscribed column to Athena Polias (*ID* 15). Surrounding the structure was a series of small altars, one of which was dedicated at this time to both Zeus Polieus and Athena Polias (altar E). Its dedicatory inscriptions (*ID* 2607 and 2608), however, made it clear that these altars were set up by Athenians; indeed, they listed the individuals involved (with their Athenian deme names).

The second half of the sixth century BC also bore witness to a renewed interest in constructing and elaborating other areas of cult (Figure 2.3). In the region of the Lions terrace processional way, in the space perhaps newly purified of graves, two new cults were founded. The first was that of Leto (Gallet de Santerre 1959). A small temple (53), facing onto the route indicated by the Lions terrace, was the focus for a cult whose goddess controlled a much larger open area of Delian land. Further to the east, en route to the Archegesion, another smaller temple-and-altar structure (68) has been identified as a second temple to the city's founder, this time named after him directly: Anios (Gallet de Santerre 1958: 270). The close proximity of the Leto cult to the Apollo and Artemis sanctuary reflects her role as their mother, and the proximity of the cults of Delos' civic founders mirrors the links between the religious and civic foundation histories of the island. The position of the founder cults perhaps also underlines a desire to make them visible to the increasing number of visitors to the island, who would have been frequenting this part of the landscape more than any other. Such a motive seems also to be behind the placement of a group of statues, all dating to the same period (*c.*500 BC), just to the south-west of the temple of Leto (Marcadé 1950; Gallet de Santerre 1958: 266; Bruneau and Ducat 2005: 95). These statues, comprising an Athena, Artemis, Leto, Apollo, Hera (one of her rare appearances outside her own sanctuary) and Zeus, created a veritable 'agora of the Gods' in this transitional zone between the sanctuaries of Leto and of Apollo and Artemis.

By the end of the sixth century BC, the spatial and religious focus was thus firmly on the Apollo and Artemis sanctuary, in no small part thanks to the actions of Naxos and Athens. The close relationship between the two central divinities was reflected in their physical proximity, yet the dynamics of that relationship had been in constant transition as the number of structures dedicated to each had equalised and subsequently increased in favour of Apollo. At the same time, the Apollo and Artemis sanctuary had been separated off from any surrounding habitation. Yet linked to them spatially were other mythological figures and divinities important to their story: Leto and the Hyperborean virgins. Capitalising on the increasing number of visitors to the island and the linked archaic processional way were also spaces for the Delian founding cults, the local poliad divinities and even a majority of the pantheon. Perhaps the rare presence of Hera outside her own sanctuary in this collection represents a softening of the mythological and physical distance between her and Apollo and Artemis, especially since it was also at the end of the sixth century BC that her sanctuary on the hillside of Mt Cynthus, untouched since the end of the eighth century BC, was substantially renovated (101 B) with a new temple, official *peribolos* and monumental altar.

II. RECONFIGURING THE NETWORK: 500–314 BC

Delos' history in the fifth and fourth centuries BC is known in general outline: from 477 BC Delos was at the centre of the powerful Delian league; the island was 'purified' for a second time in 426 BC (Thuc. 3.104), when the Athenians also began the Delia festival. The Delians were themselves expelled in 422 BC (Thuc. 5.1), but allowed to return in 421 BC thanks to the command of the Delphic oracle (Thuc. 5.32); they achieved brief independence in 404–394 BC and finally gained independence in 314 BC, with the assistance of Antigonus I, who created the 'League of Islanders', a federal organisation of the islands with Delos at its centre.

One of the major results of the increasing importance of Delos in this period was the continued articulation and separation of the Apollo and Artemis sanctuary from its surroundings through the addition of structures primarily dedicated to social functions associated with their cult (Figure 2.6). In particular, a series of small peristyle courts (**48**), which seem to have acted as a banqueting house for the sanctuary complex (Roux 1973), and a structure for the display of paintings (**35**) were added to complete the line of buildings defining the sanctuary on its north-west side.

At the same time, the structures associated with Apollo were improved and added to. It is to the fifth century BC that we can securely date the marble elaboration of the main altar of the sanctuary, the *keraton* (**39**), towards which nearly all earlier Apollo-related structures had been orientated, so that these

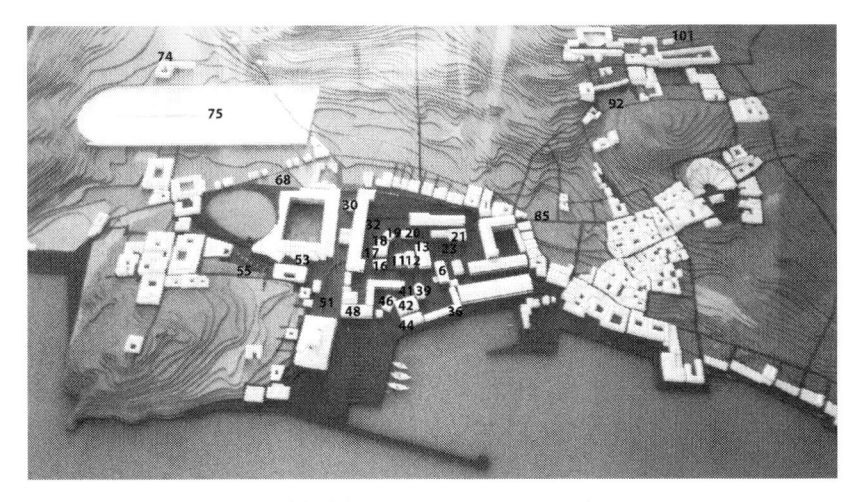

Figure 2.6 Model of the main sanctuaries on Delos 500–314 BC

structures had faced west, consequently distinguishing them from the traditional orientation of many Greek temples (Bruneau and Fraisse 2002). The so-called 'Grand Temple' (13) of Apollo, begun soon after Delos became the centre of the Delian League, was completed up to the level of its frieze, but was left abandoned after the transfer of the league's treasury to Athens in 454 BC, and remained unfinished until the third century BC. Yet in the last quarter of the fifth century BC, the Athenians did complete a smaller temple (12) in the space left vacant next to the *porinos naos* (11). This temple (12), known in the fifth and fourth century in the inscribed inventories as the 'Temple of the Athenians', was smaller than the Grand Temple (13), but it was carefully constructed in Pentelic marble and housed seven statues placed on a curved podium (one of which represented Apollo).

Yet as a result of this continued building, very different attitudes towards Artemis and Apollo were put on display (Figures. 2.6, 2.2). Whereas Artemis' temples were built one on top of the other, destroying their immediate predecessor in the process, no Apollo temple was destroyed (although some were declassed over time and some not finished), as each was instead built next door to one another (Courby 1931), fanning out around Apollo's altar. The continued (and increasing) worship of Apollo (particularly by Athens) was visibly on display in contrast to that of Artemis, thanks to these different attitudes to the destruction/accommodation of previous structures. This focus on Apollo at the expense of Artemis was further underlined by the construction of a series of treasuries during the fifth and early fourth centuries BC, which fanned out around the back of the Apollo temples (17, 18, 19, 20), although their attribution to particular cities is not possible. As a result, the continuing swing in emphasis away from female deities (Artemis, Leto, Eileithyia) within this central sacred area since the sixth century BC was perceivable spatially and architecturally in the landscape, as Apollo became more and more the dominant focus.

This investment in Apollo by Athens was accompanied by an investment in structures for use in the Delia festival celebrated every four years: a hippodrome (75) area was laid out in the north-east of the island in the last quarter of the fifth century BC (Figures 2.6, 2.1). Yet if access was being encouraged to one part of the island through the replication of cult places for well-established deities and the development of athletic facilities, it was simultaneously being cut off for others. The Archegesion (74), in the north-east of the island, was, according to a fifth-century inscription found there (*ID* 68), banned to everyone except local citizens. As Delos became more international, the religious network became more differentiated, not simply in terms of which gods were worshipped, but also of who could worship them, reflecting the increasingly bitter relationships between local Delians and their Athenian masters.

There was also renewed interest in cults on Mt Cynthus during the fifth century BC (Figure 2.1). At least one new sanctuary, that of Artemis Lochia (108), was constructed during this time, hidden from view on the far side of the Cynthian mountain. An inscribed rock (*ID* 64) also proclaimed itself the boundary stone of a temenos of Leto (109). During the fifth century therefore Mt Cynthus, which had been the relatively remote preserve of problematic deities such as Hera and deities with epithets specifically associated with their remote location (Zeus and Athena Cynthia), now had new cults introduced to them, mirroring those of the major sanctuaries by the coast (Plassart 1928). This move may have been instigated in part to counter the increasing marginalisation of these deities (particularly of Artemis) in the central sanctuary. The important absence from this mirroring effect, however, was that of Apollo: no cult attestation for Apollo, the deity par excellence of the island, has been found on the summit of Mt Cynthus. The irony is that the best view of the central sanctuary, indeed of much of the sacred landscape of Delos, was from Mt Cynthus (Papageorgiou-Venetas 1981: 127). It was here, at the island's most isolated point, that the balance of relationships within this polytheistic landscape could be most easily perceived (Figure 2.5). Certainly it seems to have been a popular enough destination: one private Athenian monument (85) was erected on the road leading up from the Apollo sanctuary to the Hera temple and another (92) on the pathway to the summit in this period (Figure 2.6).

In the fourth century BC, the continuing Athenian influence at Delos pushed the balance between Apollo and Artemis even more in Apollo's favour. The *keraton* Apollo altar (39) was again remodelled, and right next to it, between the altar and the Artemision (46), a vast building was introduced (42), identified as the Python for the cult of Apollo Pythius from Delphi (Bruneau 2006c: 954). This structure not only invaded Artemis' space (the boundaries of the two buildings practically touch), but also physically isolated and marginalised the Artemision from the rest of the sanctuary (Figures 2.6, 2.2). At the same time, the Athenians introduced the worship of the most warlike gods yet to be seen on this otherwise 'neutral' island on a grand new altar (23C): Apollo and Athena Paeon ('of the war cry') (Bruneau 1970: 165–6), placed in amongst the local poliad divinities around the *bouleuterion* (21). They also added a further series of altars a little further east from their 'agora of the gods', in between the sanctuaries of Artemis and Apollo and Leto. The inscription of altar C (51) in this region has survived, revealing the joint worship of 'Athena, Zeus and Hera' (*ID* 2471).

Relationships between divinities were undoubtedly fundamentally reconfigured through Athenian influence on the island during the fifth and fourth centuries BC. Primarily, this took the form of an increasing separation and articulation of the main Artemis and Apollo sanctuary, coupled with a particular emphasis on Apollo at the expense of Artemis. This was experienced not just in the addition of new Apollo cults (e.g. Apollo Paeon), nor simply in the imposition of new structures for new deities that physically marginalised Artemis (e.g. the new structure for Apollo Pythius), but also through the very different strategies of worship for these two divinities. Apollo gained more and more structures in his honour that fanned out around his aggrandised altar, whereas any improvement to structures associated with Artemis' worship involved the destruction of their predecessor. At the same time, introducing the worship of Apollo under different epithets, including Pythius, and associating him with Athens' primary deity, Athena (as in Apollo and Athena Paeon), involved the Delian religious network securely in a much larger one, connecting the island through its divinities to both Athens and Delphi. Yet at the same time as Delos was being drawn into this wider network, its own network of divinities was being refashioned to look increasingly like a microcosm of the larger one. The addition to the 'agora of the gods' of more altars for Zeus, Athena and Hera, coupled with the mirroring on

58   *Networks of polytheism: spaces for the gods at Delos*

Mt Cynthus of cults from the central sacred area, ensured that Delos looked and felt every bit the international sanctuary it had become.

MAKING SPACE FOR A WIDER WORLD: 314–166 BC

Delian predominance over the religious landscape

The political change marked by the period of Delian independence was also very visible in the changing physiognomy of the religious landscape of the island (Figure 2.7). To the north, the worship of the founder Anios (**68**) increased substantially in this period (Bruneau 1970: 658). Equally, the Athenian dominance over the central sacred area and particularly the worship of Apollo was challenged. While it is uncertain who undertook the rebuilding of the Artemision (**46D**) in this period (Hellenistic monarchs or the Delians), it was definitely the Delians who took it upon themselves to finish the Grand Temple (**13**), which had been left unfinished by the Athenians since the mid-fifth century BC, when they moved the money in the sacred treasury from Delos to Athens (cf. Bruneau 1970: 658). This temple, while less monumental than those built at Delphi or Olympia, gained an imposing quality from the way in which visual access to it was hindered for approaching visitors until they were in its immediate vicinity

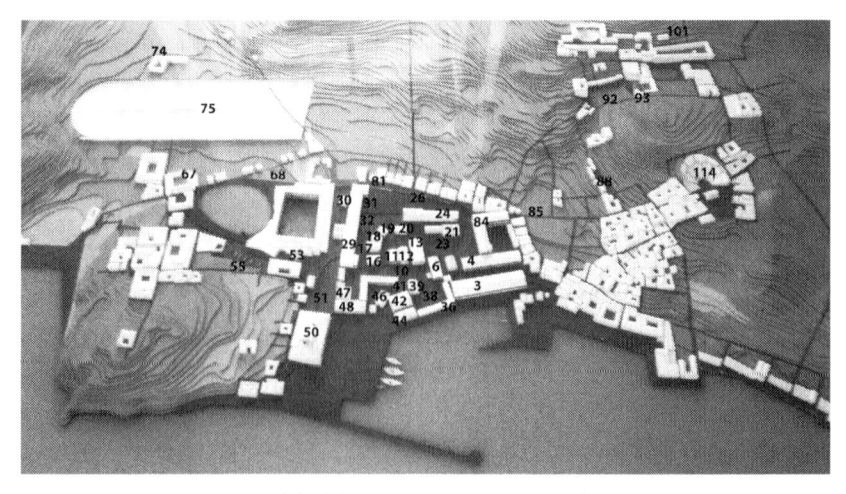

Figure 2.7 Model of the main sanctuaries on Delos 314–166 BC

Making space for a wider world: 314–166 BC

(cf. Figure 2.2); this gave it a dominating appearance which suddenly filled their whole view (Papageorgiou-Venetas 1981: 50).

Following its completion, early in the third century BC, the surrounding (and competing) temples of Apollo either had their status as temple revoked or their Athenian ownership denied. The *porinos naos* (**11**) was now recorded in the inventories of 282 BC as the '*porinos oikos*'. The Temple of the Athenians (**12**), likewise, would later be recorded in the inventories simply as the 'temple of the seven statues' (Courby 1931: 107–205). If all this was not clear enough, the *keraton* altar to Apollo (**39**) was also remodelled at the end of the fourth century BC. Indeed, Callimachus (*Hymn to Delos* 312, 321) would, in the third century BC, attest its ownership by the divinity 'Delos' (Bruneau 1970: 23–4).

While demonstrably taking control of the worship of Apollo on Delos, the Delians were also responsible for broadening and monumentalising the Delian pantheon. In the third century BC the largest religious structure to be built on the island was undertaken by the Delians, outside the northwestern corner of the Apollo and Artemis sacred area (Figure 2.7). Here a hall (**50**) was built measuring 56 m by 34 m, inscribed on its south side as an offering from the Delians (*IG* 11, 4, 1071). Its purpose seems to have been to act as the setting for the banquet during the annual Posideia festival and its position may have marked the location of much of the island's worship devoted to Poseidon. Just to the south of the hall has been found a series of small altars dedicated to Poseidon (e.g. *ID* 2483; Jacquemin 1985), and the hall itself was often known in the inventoried accounts simply as the 'stoa by Poseidon' (Leroux 1909; Vallois and Poulsen 1914; Bruneau 1970: 259, 263–4).

Individual Delians were also busy enlarging the polytheistic network. There was an increasing focus on the worship of Dionysus in the northeastern corner of the Apollo and Artemis sanctuary after 314 BC (Bruneau 1970: 296; Moretti and Fincker 2008), especially by Delians (for example, the choregic monument in the shape of a phallus acting as an altar for Dionysiac worship set up by the Delian Carystius (**81** [*IG* 11, 4, 1148]). To the south of the Apollo and Artemis sanctuary, an individual Delian, Stesileos, archon in 305 BC, consecrated a private cult to Aphrodite (**88**) on hitherto virgin ground at the end of the fourth century BC (Figure 2.7). This private cult, with expensive marble temple and statues, was the counterpart to a public cult situated somewhere (its exact location is unknown) in the Apollo and Artemis sacred area. The location of Stesileos' private cult may well have been influenced by the fact that the principal arrival point to the island was now the port just to the west (cf. Figure 2.1; a row of shops was also constructed just by the harbour in this period; cf. Bruneau and Ducat 2005: 165). Yet his choice of cult also reflects the growing popularity of Aphrodite in contexts of private worship, which continued throughout the Hellenistic Period. Indeed, in terms of number of appearances in statues, statuettes, mosaics etc., Aphrodite became the most popular divinity, far outstripping Apollo, who, despite his official importance, in fact appeared infrequently in contexts of private worship.

The location of Stesileos' sanctuary, however, may equally have been influenced by the fact that this south-western corner was also the main route through to new areas of Delian expansion on the southern half of the island, particularly around the routes to Mt Cynthus and in the area of the theatre (**114**), which was itself under construction from the end of the fourth century BC (Figures 2.7, 2.1). The focus in these areas was not simply on commerce and civic space but also on religious worship. Beyond the area of the theatre lay the *dioscurion* (**123**); the cult of the Dioscuri, begun in the seventh century BC, had withered down to the fourth, but their shrine was now rebuilt and enlarged (Figure 2.1). Further south, on the remoter west side of the island (Figure 2.1), a new sanctuary was begun, which clung to the water's edge: the Asclepieion (**125**). Its remote construction here may have been because its cult was a focus for the sick, coupled in particular with the purified nature of Delos and the regulation that no one could be born or die on the island (Robert 1952; Bruneau and Ducat 2005: 61). Its liminal location away from the main sanctuary thus enabled it to continue its business while at the same time providing a convenient spot from which to evacuate quickly those who were about to die to nearby islands. Bruneau has in fact pointed out (1970: 373) that this side of the island is the most sheltered from winds, ensuring safe sea passage in almost all weathers.

At the same time as expanding the pantheon worshipped on Delos, the Delians were also heavily engaged in building in order to furnish Delos with the commercial, social and athletic spaces it needed. At the southern end of the Apollo and Artemis sanctuary, construction began on what, during the course of the third and early second centuries BC, would become a multicolonnaded agora of the Delians (**84**), accompanied by a dedicatory exedra from the Delian people (Figure 2.7). Further afield, Delian efforts during the third century BC were concentrated on supplying Delos with the permanent athletic facilities necessary for its religious festivals (especially the Apollonia). In the third century, these were being celebrated in the works of Callimachus (Bruneau 2006d), and may have been attracting ever larger numbers of people. Both the stadium (**78**) and parts of the gym by the lake (**67**) were constructed in the north-east end of the island

(Figures 2.1, 2.7; Delorme 1961), near to the increasingly popular cult-place of the founder (74 – which was of course banned to foreigners).

The epigraphic record reflects this increasing physical monopolisation of the island by the Delians as well as their willingness to utilise their resources and capitalise on their developing position as a commercial hub. The preamble to their honorary decrees, for example, now began by underlining that the recipient had done good for 'the sanctuary and city of the Delians' (Vial 1984: 92). Vial has also pointed out (1984: 276) that the Delians did not object to blurring the lines between civic and religious financial funds during this period. It is interesting to note too that houses rented out by the different priesthoods around the island, the rents for which are recorded in the surviving inscriptions, saw a massive hike in rates after 246 BC, perhaps attesting to the priesthoods' decision to capitalise on the increase in business (Molinier 1914: 89).

Hellenistic rulers and the Apollo and Artemis sanctuary

Delian construction in the late fourth and third centuries BC indicates the beginning of a new phase for the Delian religious landscape, thanks to its developing role as a cosmopolitan emporium during the Hellenistic Period, which would witness the arrival of many wealthy individuals of increasingly varied geographical origins (Bruneau and Ducat 2005: 59). In contrast, however, to the Delian interest in the religious landscape of much of the island, the focus of the Hellenistic rulers was almost exclusively the central Apollo and Artemis sacred area and its immediate vicinity (Bruneau 1970: 583). A new and enormous monument, the Neorion (24), was constructed just to the east of the *prytaneion* and *bouleuterion* area (Figure 2.7), probably dedicated by one of the early Hellenistic kings (Demetrius Poliorcetes or his son Antigonus Gonatas). Antigonus Gonatas was certainly responsible for a 21-metre-long statue base, on which were placed bronze statues of his ancestors (31). Antiochus III, Seleucid king of Syria, was honoured with a statue on top of a column (38), and Philetaerus, founder of the Attalid dynasty of Pergamon, was honoured with a statue group (10) by Sosicrates. Other parts of the Apollo and Artemis sanctuary benefited from this intense focus as well, although we don't know who exactly was responsible for their elaboration (Figure 2.7): the *ekklesiasterion* or 'assembly-room' (47) was built, while the boundary wall of temple G (40) and boundary wall of the archaic tomb of the Hyperborean virgins (41) were remodelled, and the Artemision (46 D) underwent its final rebuild at this time.

Hellenistic ruler interventions also began to alter fundamentally the relationship of the central sacred area to its surroundings. In the south-western corner, between the central sacred area and the main port, a stoa (**4**) was built, probably by Attalus I son of Philetaerus (statues of his generals and monuments to his victory over the Galatians also lined the front of it). In the third quarter of the third century BC, another stoa (**29**), this time funded by Antigonus Gonatas (with dedicatory inscription), was set up along the long northern side of the central sacred area. This formed (along with a *peribolos* wall (**26**) built along the east side, probably also by Antigonus) part of a solid line of structures that now encased both the north and west side of the central area (Figure 2.7), cutting off the long-standing visual and processional links with the sacred area of Leto and the archaic Lions terrace (Courby 1912). Similarly, at the southern end of the area, the stoa erected by Attalus I (**4**), was paralleled by another stoa (**3**), set up by Philip V of Macedon, which formalised the new processional way (the 'dromos') into the sacred Apollo and Artemis area (Vallois 1923). This dromos quickly became a popular area for family exedra dedications (particularly directly outside the propylon of the Apollo sanctuary), which, at least until after 166 BC, seem to have been formally controlled and regulated with regard to both position and style of dedication (Dixon 2011).

The Hellenistic rulers were also active in the immediate vicinity of the Apollo and Artemis sanctuary. To a Hellenistic ruler should be ascribed the construction of a formal temple and altar for the *dodekatheon* (**51**), over the area previously established as an 'agora of the gods' by the Athenians (Will 1955b). Yet, despite the formalisation of the worship of the twelve gods in this area, it was noted by Bruneau (1970: 440) that this official cult did not ever attract individual dedicators: no ex votos to the twelve gods have been found. The cult, though physically central and official, was not part of the popular religious landscape.

Spaces for foreign deities in the religious landscape

On the slopes of Mt Cynthus, at some point in the later fourth century BC, the north section of the Samothraceion (**93**), for the Cabirioi or 'Great Gods' of Samothrace, was constructed (Figures 2.1, 2.7, 2.8). Gods from Samothrace hardly qualify as 'foreign deities', yet the location of their sanctuary on Delos speaks volumes about the way these divinities were perceived. It may also have been determined by the almost simultaneous construction of a large water reserve (**97**) just next door, built to contain and channel the flow of the Inopus river, which rose on the south flank of

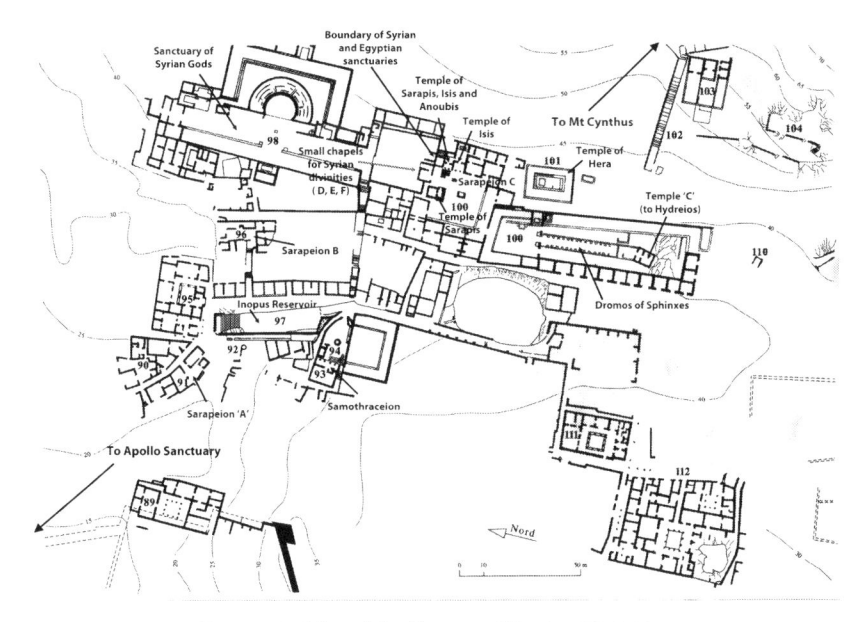

Figure 2.8 Map of the Terrace of Foreign Divinities

Mt Cynthus (Figure 2.8). As a result, the Samothraceion was able to benefit from easily-accessible water for ritual and other purposes (Chapouthier 1935). But apart from this, the sanctuary was also constructed on the rear of the theatre hillside, facing towards Mt Cynthus, in a natural mini-valley (cf. Figure 2.5). The sanctuary was thus rendered completely invisible from the main Apollo sanctuary and indeed from most of the island (cf. Figure 2.4). Samothracian deities may thus not have been technically foreign, but they were located on Delos in such a way as to be cut off from the rest of the visual religious landscape. They both were, and were not, part of the Delian network of polytheism.

It was at the end of the third century and the beginning of the second century BC that the vast majority of truly foreign cults were given cult spaces on Delos, all of which were positioned on the terraces leading up to Mt Cynthus near to where the first part of the Samothraceion had been constructed (Figures 2.4, 2.8). It was here, still invisible from the Apollo sanctuary, that the foreign deities of Egypt, for example, were installed in the late third century BC. The process was inscribed and publicised in detail (*IG* 11, 4, 1299).[3] In the early third century, the priest Apollonius brought

---

[3] For commentary: Roussel 1915–16, Engelmann 1975: 71–83; Moyer 2011: 142–79.

the cult of Sarapis to Delos. In *c.*220 BC, his grandson, on the god's orders, began the process of building him a sanctuary (for about eighty years, therefore, the cult worship of Sarapis seems to have been mobile, without permanent physical location, taking place wherever possible). The god himself, pushed by his priest, who was said to have been worried that there would soon be little space left for a permanent sanctuary (*IG* 11, 4, 1299.52–3), was reported to have asked to be placed in an area which was '*korpos*' (often translated as 'smelly', but probably better translated as 'bustling' – the hillside was a busy commercial area in this period). The final location may also have been thought suitable, however, because of the nearby Inopus river, which was in fact channelled directly into the sanctuary and made accessible through a cistern (Roussel 1915–16: 30–1). The placement required careful negotiation with the civic authorities: terrain was purchased, but, due to a technical issue, permission for this private cult was temporarily withheld and only subsequently granted (Bruneau 1970: 658; Bruneau and Ducat 2005: 268; Moyer 2011: 142–79, 194–207).

The first of these Egyptian sanctuaries, Sarapeion A (**91**), in which the chronicle of these events was inscribed on an architectural column, was eventually built in just six months (*IG* 11, 4, 1299.23), and, although not very different in its architectural style and use of space from those associated with Hellenic deities, still clearly catered for a different set of rituals and required a different relationship to its surroundings (Roussel 1915–16: 68–9). It was set apart from the road by a marble sill and set of stairs leading down into the sanctuary, and consisted of a reunion hall, a small crypt, three altars and several other covered spaces (Figure 2.8). A second Sarapeion sanctuary (Sarapeion B (**96**)) was built further up the path leading through this area of the hillside, its entrance staircase squeezed in amongst a series of shops; it was thus even more cut off than Sarapeion A (Roussel 1915–16: 33).

In contrast, however, the third Sarapeion (Sarapeion C (**100**)) was instituted as an official cult in 180 BC. It was also, perhaps intentionally, the first sanctuary of foreign deities to be located higher up Mt Cynthus in a position visible from the Apollo sanctuary and surrounding landscape (cf. Figure 2.4). Molinier has argued (1914: 71) that the granting of an official cult (and visible position) should be seen as a move by the Delians to buttress foreign support against resurgent Athenian interest in the island. If so, it did not work very successfully: though some of the earliest structures here, such as the temple of Sarapis (**100** F) and the temple of Sarapis, Isis and Anoubis (**100** H), may have been built at the time of its adoption as an official cult (Figure 2.8), much of the building in this sanctuary would take place only after the reassertion of Athenian control in 166 BC (Bruneau 1970: 465–6).

Above the temple of Hera (101), which was enveloped by the developing Sarapeion C, there were never any official Delian cults (Bruneau 1970: 402). But that did not mean the higher parts of Mount Cynthus were undeveloped in the third and early second centuries BC – in fact, just the opposite. A sanctuary dedicated to *Agathe Tuche* ('Good Fortune') and/or particular Hellenistic monarchs (103) was constructed, as well as the 'cave' of Cynthia (104), most probably a place of cult worship for Heracles (cf. Bruneau 1970: 411–12), not far from the summit (fig 2.1). Almost at the summit an amalgamation of smaller structures known as the Cynthion (105) was created, which housed, amongst other divinities, Zeus Cynthius and Athena Cynthia, along with spaces for ritual dining (Plassart 1928; Bruneau 1970: 476).

A changing network of polytheism

The period of Delian independence thus bears witness to four key changes in the Delian religious landscape. The first is a Delian emphasis on de-Athenianising Apollo, potentially reasserting Artemis, and reducing the location of Apollo's worship to one temple (the Delian temple) by reclassing other previous efforts by other cities. Such a move to reassert Artemis in particular is underlined by the huge popularity of statues of the goddess in the houses of Delos (some eighty-five statues have been found). The second key change is the Delian interest in the worship of a range of other deities, some of which were located close to the Apollo and Artemis sanctuary (Dionysus, Aphrodite, Poseidon), as well as others (Hermes, Dioscuri, Asclepius) who found their homes in other expanding athletic, commercial and civic parts of the island. Hellenistic rulers, in contrast, were interested mostly in associating themselves with the Apollo and Artemis sanctuary, and their most major contribution to the religious network of the island, the formalisation of the 'agora of the gods' into a *dodekatheon*, seems never to have become a popular place of worship.

The third major change was the arrival of a number of foreign deities, first of all in very mobile form (e.g. the eighty-year period of worship of Sarapis before his sanctuary was constructed). The placement of their eventual sanctuaries was due to a combination of practical factors (e.g. the presence of water), the god's request (for a 'bustling' place), and most probably a Delian civic concern to 'nail down' these increasingly popular cults and keep them at a distance from the main sanctuary – indeed, for the most part, in a location in which they were invisible from the rest of the island (cf. Figure 2.4). Despite the arrival of so many deities from wide swathes of the Mediterranean, however, Bruneau noted (1970: 478–80) that some well-known non-Greek deities, such as Bendis and Adonis, were never worshipped on Delos. Such absence stands in contrast to their incorporation in other cities and sanctuaries around Greece, as in the Piraeus in Athens (Rhodes and Osborne 2003: No. 91), and underlines the particularity of the Delian religious landscape within the wider picture of the Greek world.

The fourth and final change was the slow death of the worship of some divinities, particularly Leto. Her cult area, which had extended over a vast part of the north side of the island, began to wither in the Independence Period. Leto received no specific private offerings during the entire Hellenistic Period, and was mentioned little in the inventory lists, and a (rather small) stele dating to 202 BC (*ID* 69) specifically had to remind people not to throw rubbish into her temenos (Laidlaw 1933: 157; Bruneau 1970: 210–18, 305; Bruneau and Ducat 2005: 56, 61, 63–4). Her fall in popularity may well have been due to the change in the location of the main arrival port, from Schardhana bay to just by the Apollo and Artemis sanctuary, which must have decreased the numbers visiting the temenos of Leto (cf. Figures 2.1, 2.5); the increasing architectural articulation and separation of the Apollo and Artemis sanctuary, to which Leto had in the past been linked, would have had the same effect. More importantly, however, her downfall must be due to her overwhelmingly local, rather than Hellenic, importance (Bruneau 1970: 210), which failed to strike a chord within an environment that was increasingly cosmopolitan.

NETWORKS OF POLYTHEISM IN A CHANGING WORLD: 166–69 BC

Athenian efforts to change the network

In 166 BC the Roman Senate gave Delos back to the Athenians, who promptly expelled the local population and settled the island with their own colonists. The Athenians' attempts to reimpose themselves on the island are manifest. They resurrected the Delia festival and introduced the Theseia, Athenaia and Romaia festivals (Roussel 1916: 199–200; Baslez 1982: 150–78), built a new gymnasium (**66**) to the north of the Apollo sanctuary (Figure 2.9), and embellished the pre-existing gymnasium by the lake next to it (**67**), as a result of which the worship of Hermes greatly increased (Delorme 1961; Bruneau 1970: 350–1).

Their impact was also particularly clear in the Apollo and Artemis sanctuary. They rebuilt the monumental propylon entrance to the Apollo

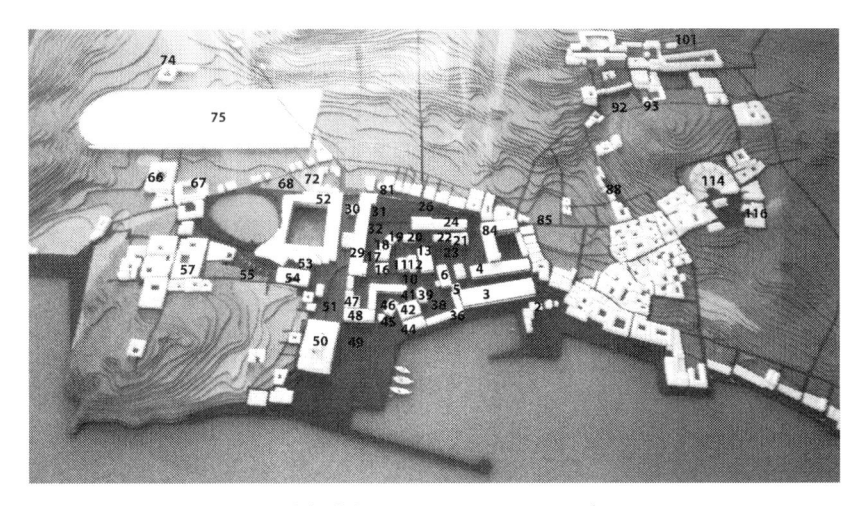

Figure 2.9 Model of the main sanctuaries on Delos 166–69 BC

sanctuary (5) and added the cult of Demos and Roma to those already worshipped in the nearby *prytaneion* (22), such as Hestia (Roussel 1916: 222; Laidlaw 1933: 219). The importance of this new trio of divinities (Demos, Roma and Hestia) is underlined by the fact that they were placed second in the hierarchical list of Delos' official priesthoods in 158–157 BC (Laidlaw 1933: 219). At the same time the Athenians also marginalised the older, polis-focused cults of Zeus Polieus and Athena Polias by placing a new, larger altar nearby, this time dedicated to Zeus Soter, reflecting the wider popularity of Zeus Soter and Athena Soteria across the island (and indeed the Greek world) in the later Hellenistic Period (Roussel 1916: 228; Bruneau 1970: 235).

The Athenians moved to lessen the importance of Delos' founder by renaming the archaic Archegesion (74) simply as the sanctuary of Anios (denying him the founder title) and later associating him with Nike (Roussel 1916: 239; Bruneau 1970: 421). The hall (50) to Poseidon, whose dedicatory inscription had so clearly ascribed the construction to the Delians, was altered so that it was dedicated by the Athenians (*IG* II, 4, 1971). The worship of Pythian Apollo was encouraged within the Pythion structure (42), which was built by the Athenians in the early fourth century near the *keraton* altar (Bruneau 1970: 125–9). Finally, the arrival of the Athenians may have brought about the abandonment of the *dioscurion* (123), which had only recently been enjoying renewed vigour (and physical embellishment) in the Independence Period (Robert 1952; Bruneau 1970: 385–6, 393–4, 660).

The central sacred area of Apollo and Artemis continued to receive Athenian attention into the second half of the second century BC (Figure 2.9). The *keraton* altar (39) was surrounded with new paving (Bruneau 2006c). The Artemision (46), newly rebuilt in the third century BC, was also now 'encircled' by two new stoas. The first surrounded the north and east sides of the Artemision, which in turn meant the destruction of temple G (40), itself also only recently rebuilt in the third century BC. The second stoa (45), in blue marble, faced the west side of the Artemision (Figure 2.9). As a result, the Artemision, though seemingly embellished, was actually cut off from view: by the Pythion to the south, by a stoa and the *ekklesiasterion* to the north, and by stoas to the east and west, to such an extent that Roussel (1916: 215) labelled Artemis as an 'enslaved precinct' in the Apollo sanctuary (cf. Figure 2.2). Laidlaw too argues (1933: 219) that Artemis loses her priestess in this period. But here the physical evidence may mask what is not an absolute decline of Artemis but a diversification in terms of her place in the religious landscape. Bruneau has argued (Bruneau 1970: 174–206) that not only did Artemis have several sanctuaries (including one of the nearby island of Rhenea (cf. Bruneau et al. 1996: 26)), but also that dedications to Artemis with varying epithets are found all over Delos (particularly in the Egyptian sanctuaries), in addition to her popularity as exemplified by statues in private houses. As a result, while the central Artemision may have become little more than a treasury for offerings moved from other sanctuaries in this period, the worship of Artemis continued to flourish in other locations and forms.

Yet more construction during this Athenian period also furthered the physical decline of other cult locations. To the north of the Apollo sanctuary, in the area of the *dodekatheon* (51) and Leto (53), a new structure, the 'granite monument' (54), was constructed; its exact function is unknown (Figure 2.9), although it probably religious (Gallet de Santerre 1959). Its construction invaded the sanctuary of the *dodekatheon*, destroying part of its *peribolos* (boundary) wall, and significantly impinged on the territory of Leto, whose western entrance door (facing onto the granite structure) was blocked up at around the same time (Bruneau and Ducat 2005: 223). Reflecting its impoverished physical structure, the cult of Leto continued to fade in the second and first centuries BC (Roussel 1916: 221; Bruneau 1970: 210–18).

The impact of cosmopolitanism

Delos' position within the wider ancient world at this time continued to improve, particularly as a central emporium between the burgeoning

Roman Empire to the west and the traditional trading routes in the east (cf. Figure 2.10). This position strengthened further after the destruction of Corinth in 146 BC and the declaration of Delos as a free port (Molinier 1914: 72; Baslez 1982: 150–78; Rauh 1993: 101–4; Étienne 1996: 81; Bruneau and Ducat 2005: 59). Its users became increasingly international, and its population rapidly expanded (by 90 BC approximately thirty thousand residents), with housing and commerce increasing rapidly both in the older habitation area of the theatre and in amongst the foreign deities on the sides of Mt Cynthus, as well as in newer areas such as to the north of the new granite monument (cf. Bruneau et al. 1996: 37).

The implications of this were threefold. First, there was a significant increase in the number of divinities worshipped by this cosmopolitan population, not least in the private sphere of their own homes, which often bear witness to a heavily rural cult focus despite their urban surroundings (Roussel 1916: 199, 276; Bulard 1926: 414, 422, 428–9, 436; Deonna 1948), and to a change in ritual practice as altars for divinities

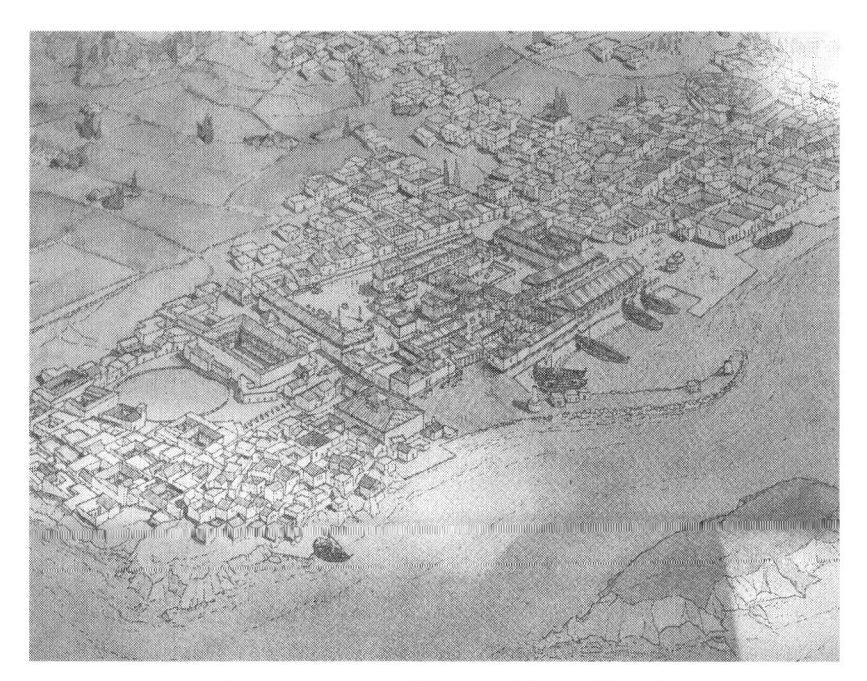

Figure 2.10 Watercolour reconstruction of the area of the Apollo and Artemis sanctuary, Delos in the first century BC

traditionally worshipped in the street outside the home were brought inside, perhaps due to the impractical nature of street worship in such a bustling community (Bulard 1926: 439).

The second implication was a massive investment in and expansion of the number of private and official sanctuaries dedicated to foreign deities, particularly on the flanks and summit of Mt Cynthus (cf. Figure 2.1), increasing the sense of the compartmentalisation of different areas of the island allocated to the worship of Hellenic and foreign divinities (Bruneau and Ducat 2005: 40). But this was at the same time mitigated both by the complex ways in which sanctuaries of foreign divinities interrelated and by the high rate of syncretism between Hellenic and foreign deities worshipped within different sanctuaries.

The massive expansion of the worship of foreign deities was clear to see, particularly on the top of Mt Cynthus (cf. Plassart 1928). A new cult space of Zeus Hypsistus (Ba'al) was begun in this period (**106**), associating two divinities (the Greek Zeus and the 'Master' ['Ba'al'] divinity worshipped in the semitic Levant) whose cults demanded a mountain-top location. Similarly Philostratus created a sanctuary for the gods of Ascalon (**107**) near the summit in honour of his homeland. On the western side of the mountain-top, a series of thirteen small cult spaces was also built, entirely for non-Greek deities (Bruncau and Ducat 2005: 289). Further down from the summit, in the Cynthion (**105**), the cult space of Zeus Cynthius and Athena Cynthia was renovated and extended as a space of eastern cult worship (Roussel 1916: 227). In particular, new purity regulations were introduced at the end of the second century BC, which responded to the use of this area for Eastern deities and their worshippers (no keys, iron rings, belts, shoes, purses; worshippers to be dressed all in white, having abstained from meat and sex and presenting themselves 'with a pure soul': *ID* 2529 (Sokolowski 1969: 113)).

Other spaces for the worship of divinities who were much less foreign were also expanded, for example the Samothraceion (**93**), which now included spaces for the worship of Heracles and the Dioscuri, and so, potentially, was taking over from the defunct sanctuary of the Dioscuri (**123**) on the coast (Roussel 1916: 230–3; Bruneau 1970: 398–9).

Such syncretism of Heracles went beyond sharing a cult location with the gods of Samothrace. After 166 BC, cults of Heracles are found in a new cult foundation by the Heraclists of Tyre (*ID* 1519), on the summit of Mt Cynthus (*ID* 2308, 2433), and in the cult areas of Sarapis (*ID* 1417). Heracles' persona was ideally suited to this cosmopolitan world (Bruneau 1970: 411–12). Nor was Heracles the only one to flourish thanks to processes of syncretism.[4] Cults of Zeus, for example, particularly that of Zeus Cynthius, attracted a large number of dedications from a wide variety of foreigners at Delos (Bruneau 1970: 230). At the same time, Bruneau (1970: 221–47) has demonstrated how Zeus cult syncretised with a wide variety of foreign deities worshipped across the island, creating cult epithets such as Zeus Hypsistus (the syncretisation of Zeus and Ba'al, who, as we saw above, had his own sanctuary on Mt Cynthus: *ID* 2306), Zeus *Ktesios* in Sarapeion C (*ID* 2186), Zeus *Hadad* in the Syrian sanctuary (*ID* 2262), Zeus *Ourios* by the hall of Poseidon (*ID* 1754), Zeus *Sabazios* (*ID* 2417, first century AD), and even bilingual dedications to Zeus *Du*[*sares*] in Nabatean and Greek (*ID* 2315). Other Greek deities gave themselves over almost entirely to syncretised forms of worship. After 166 BC the Greek Poseidon, for example, does not seem to have been worshipped at all (Bruneau 1970: 266), but was well represented as Poseidon of Beirut (near the shrine of Leto, *ID* 1519), and of Ascalon (with his own shrine (**107**) on Mt Cynthus (*ID* 1720)).

Spaces of worship for the Egyptian deities provide a slightly different model of development in this period. Sarapeion A (**91**), despite being the first Egyptian sanctuary to appear in Delos, was not embellished at all after its initial construction. It remained a private cult, as did Sarapeion B (**96**), and there were concerted attempts by the Athenians to close them down (Roussel 1916: 250; Laidlaw 1933: 217). Indeed, the majority of offerings in these two cult locations (still invisible from the rest of the island) were made by non-Egyptian foreigners, particularly from either Arabia/Phoenicia or Phrygia and Mysia (Bruneau 1970: 243).

Sarapeion C (**100**), on the other hand, became an official cult after 180 BC (although last in the inscribed lists of official priesthoods on the island in 153–152 BC (Roussel 1916: 220, 347–50)); it grew substantially and received a good number of Athenian dedications (Figure 2.8). The temple of Isis (**100** I) was dedicated by the people of Athens in 130 BC (*ID* 2041), as was the cult statue of Isis inside (*ID* 2044). The artistic style of the statue was another kind of witness to the syncretism of deities in this period: Isis' appearance resembled that of the Greek figure Tyche (Bruneau and Ducat 2005: 101–10). By the side of the Athenian temple of Isis was perhaps another temple (H) to Sarapis, Isis and Anoubis (cf. Bruneau 2006a; 2006b). The sanctuary was at some point also extended to the south along the terracing wall of the Hera sanctuary, creating complex pathways of movement so as to ensure that the approach to a further, pre-existing,

---

[4] Most Greek gods were syncretised on Delos in this period: the only exceptions being Leto, Hera, Eileithyia and Anios, who had specific local associations: Bruneau 1970.

temple (C) was via a dromos of sphinxes, a typical feature of Egyptian cult spaces, and the most 'Egyptian' example of religious architecture on Delos (Roussel 1915–16: 52–3, 68–9; Bruneau 2006e). Interestingly, within this very 'Egyptian' extension to Sarapeion C were placed not only further Athenian statues (e.g. *ID* 2096), but also dedications to a whole range of Greek deities, most of all Apollo (Laidlaw 1933: 225).

The architectural extension of the approach to temple C in Sarapeion C via the dromos of sphinxes is perhaps to be understood as representing a desire to compete with the extensive sanctuary to the Syrian gods placed to the north (**98**). This sanctuary, first attested epigraphically in 128–127 BC (*ID* 2226) and made an official cult in 112–111 BC (and, like Sarapeion C, visible from the rest of the island), was extremely prosperous by the end of the second century BC (Will and Schmidt 1985). It was reached by a staircase leading up to the terrace on which the sanctuary was built, and, though its 'chapels' are small and unelaborated (D, E, F), there were also large spaces for banquets, a theatre which could seat approximately 500 people, and a long stoa whose back wall shielded from external view all cult activity taking place inside the sanctuary (Figure 2.8), in keeping with many Syrian sanctuaries across the East (Roussel 1916: 260). Originally dedicated as a cult to *Hadad* and *Atargatis*, after it had been granted official cult status, its worship was also directed to *Hagne* Aphrodite. However, unlike Egyptian-related cults, which are found in this period spread out across the island, the worship of Syrian cults outside the sanctuary of the Syrian gods was extremely rare (Bruneau 1970: 473). Moreover, though the Syrian and Egyptian sanctuaries are spatially very close together (indeed, they shared a boundary: Figure 2.8), there are no crossover dedications between the two (Roussel 1915–16: 13; 1916: 255). Egyptian and Syrian cults, though both could be mixed with Greek cult, remained entirely separate from one another, and Syrian cult influence was almost entirely confined to the Syrian sanctuary itself.

The third implication of the increasingly cosmopolitan nature of Delos' population during the second century BC was the establishment of several 'agoras', each of which acted as a central focus for specific populations and/or religious associations. This was not new to Delos: the agora of the Delians had been established since the end of the fourth century BC. But by the end of the second century BC, the central sacred area of Apollo and Artemis was ringed by a series of such structures (Figure 2.9), all of which placed themselves at major arteries and intersections of movement around the island (Rauh 1993: 76–80). The earliest of these was the structure for the association of Poseidoniasts of Beirut (**57**), composed of businessmen from the area (*ID* 1774, 1520). This building was actually begun in the last decades of Delian independence within the expanding habitation quarter to the north of the Apollo sanctuary. It was simultaneously a place to gather, centre of commerce, hotel and sanctuary, comprising a series of small cult rooms dedicated to Poseidon of Beirut, Astarte and the goddess Roma (Picard 1921; Bruneau 2006f).

Just to the east of the Poseidoniasts' structure was the agora of the Italians (**52**). This was the largest built complex on the island, with a double internal courtyard and double-storey stoa (Lapalus 1939; Coarelli 1983). While there were dedications here from a series of religious associations (Bruneau 1970: 587), in contrast to all of the other agoras, the agora of the Italians probably had a series of principally secular functions (Rauh 1993: 81; Müller and Hasenohr 2002), which may have allowed its Italian users a certain exclusivity compared to other people on the island (Rauh 1993: 210). But its construction also had a negative impact on the already endangered cult of Leto. The agora took over what must have been part of the temenos of Leto and was built perilously close to Leto's temple itself (indeed, public latrines were built in the agora at the closest point to the temple); in response to the agora's construction, the east wall of the temple of Leto had to be rebuilt.

On the western side of the Apollo and Artemis sanctuary, not far from the hall of Poseidon, was the agora of Theophrastus (**49**), of which we know very little, except that Theophrastus, the Athenian administrator of the island, had had the agora constructed after having expanded the capacity of the harbour's docking facilities through landfill in 126–125 BC (*ID* 1645), for which he was thanked by Roman and foreign businessmen (Rauh 1993: 77). On the opposite side of the Apollo and Artemis sanctuary, by its monumental entrance, was founded the agora of the Hermiasts or Compitaliasts (**2**) in the second half of the second century BC. The stoas already in place (dedicated in the third century BC) were incorporated within this agora and filled, as was the processional space in-between them, with dedications almost exclusively from Italian dedicators. As a result, along the official entrance path to the sanctuary of Apollo at Delos, small cults sprang up to gods such as Mercury and Maia, as well as the Lares Compitales (which welcomed slaves as well as citizens) and other divinities (Rauh 1993: 101–4, 110, 122). It would have been a fitting introduction for visitors to the cosmopolitan (but Italian-dominated) island that Delos had become.

Nothing could have been more shocking to this vibrant and diverse community than the raids of Mithridates VI, king of Pontus, in 88 BC which destroyed much of the island. In the first twenty years of the first century BC, the inhabitants had been busy building a new gymnasium

(**76** (cf. Audiat 1970)), new sanctuaries of Heracles on the nearby island Rhenea and of Artemis Soteria (**72**) by the agora of the Italians, along with a series of small sanctuaries by the theatre to Apollo (**116b**), to Artemis-Hekate (**116a**) and to Dionysus, Hermes and Pan (**116c**) (Figures. 2.1, 2.9). Following the raids, the population was severely reduced and many of the cult spaces permanently destroyed. Only nineteen years later, in 69 BC, the island was hit again with raids by pirates, and its function as a commercial hub went into decline. The theatre was abandoned, for example, and even the sanctuary of the founder Anios was built over by a defensive wall. The only major cult areas to survive into the first century AD were the Apollo sanctuary, Sarapeion C, and some of the cults on the summit of Mt Cynthus.

The most critical result of the study of the century 166–69 BC is to demonstrate how the material and epigraphic evidence works in harmony to give texture to the nature and experience of the polytheistic network on Delos. In some cases the epigraphic material alerts us to subtleties not revealed by the archaeology (e.g. the absence of worship for Bendis and Adonis). In other cases, they reinforce one another (the decay of Sarapeion A and B, for example, or that of Leto). In other cases, the combination of the archaeological and epigraphic material underlines the differing perceptions of divine relationships on view. The complete absence of epigraphic dedicatory crossover between the Syrian and Egyptian sanctuaries, for example, must have been made all the more acute, and startling, by the spatial proximity and indeed architectural connectedness of the two sanctuaries (cf. Figure 2.8), and should perhaps be attributed to a difference in outlook between those 'organising' the space (Delians thinking that Syrian/Egyptian divinities were similar and thus should be close spatially) and those 'using' the space (worshippers purposely keeping their distance). In other cases still, the archaeological material shows us the diversity of ways in which the relationship between cults could be experienced. So, while in Sarapeion C there are numerous examples of syncretism between Greek and Egyptian deities attested in the epigraphic evidence, and while the style of the surviving cult sculpture shows that Egyptian deities were being represented in Greek sculptural form, the imposition of particularly Egyptian-style architecture and use of space (e.g. the dromos) in this period distanced the experience of this space of cult from its Hellenic surroundings.

Delos was by no means deserted after 69 BC; however, its continuing history will be sketched only briefly here. Delos continued to be a natural stopping-place for Romans passing across the Aegean (including Cicero) and important for the corn supply to Rome, as is shown by the *lex Gabinia*

Calpurnia of 58 BC, which praised Delian sanctity and privilege (cf. *ID* 1511; Nicolet 1980). There was also one new religious addition to the landscape in this period. Using blocks from the abandoned gymnasium (**67**) a synagogue was constructed in the remoter northern quarter of the island (**80**) (Figure 2.1), a testimony to the new cult practices of the reduced community which made its home within the ruins of the former emporium (cf. Bruneau et al. 1996: 18). In the first century AD more defensive walls were constructed, more of the remaining small sanctuaries, such as the Aphrodision of Stesileos, were purposely destroyed to provide material for habitation, and only one new cult is attested, that of Zeus Sabazius on Mt Cynthus. By the third century AD, Delos once again bore witness to the changing religious landscape with the establishment of a small Christian community on the island, and in the fifth century AD a basilica (**86**) was built in the corner of what had been the Apollo sanctuary (Figure 2.1).

CONCLUSION

This chapter has focused on following the development of sacred space on Delos from the eighth century BC to the first century BC. In doing so, it has argued for the existence of a network of polytheism on this extraordinary island which constantly reflected and constructed, influenced and was impacted by Delos' entwined religious, social, political and economic life. It has explored a range of motivations for particular spatial relationships: practical, mythological, those related to the dynamics of visitor movement, site visibility, and expressing control over the island. It has exposed a variety of types of relationship between divinity and space: deities with a single 'spatial catchment area' such as those from Syria; those omnipresent (e.g. Zeus); those with certain no-go areas (e.g. Apollo, who was everywhere except on the summit of Mt Cynthus), those who were, for a long period of time, entirely mobile (e.g. Sarapis), and those who were always spatially vague (e.g. Dionysus). It has highlighted the constantly changing relationship between divinities within the network as expressed through their relative spatial and architectural proximity or distance and interaction. It has investigated how different cities and individuals, as well as the wider entities of Greek and Roman culture, interacted with this network and sought to change it.

Most importantly, it has analysed how the different networks of relationships represented in the literary, epigraphic and material evidence could reinforce and contradict one another, as well as deepen our understanding of the complex nature of the ancient perception and experience of the different networks of polytheism simultaneously on view. While the material and epigraphic evidence, for example, shows that official cults of Artemis were 'enslaved', her popularity as a figure of cult in private houses, as witnessed through the surviving artefact record, seems to have increased substantially. Equally, while the official gods such as Apollo were given large spaces of public cult, Apollo in terms of the total number of his appearances in mosaics, frescoes, statues and statuettes was actually one of the least popular divinities (the most popular being Aphrodite). Such comparisons and insights bring out clearly the usefulness not only of adopting a spatial approach but also of combining the pictures provided by the different types of evidence in trying to understand better the complex nature of the changing religious landscape of Delos throughout its long history.

CHAPTER 3

Spaces of alienation: street-lining Roman cemeteries

INTRODUCTION

There is an immense array of scholarship on death and burial in the Roman world, covering a wide range of investigative approaches and types of evidence. In particular, previous scholarship has highlighted both a series of overarching factors affecting and a conventional development timeline for the design and location of Roman tombs. Those factors range from the changing preference for inhumation or cremation and the changing rules surrounding burial to the acculturation of different styles in different parts of the Roman world. The timeline charts a move from modest graves in the early Republic to more showy and ornate tombs located in arenas of high visibility peaking in the late Republic, followed by an even wider diversity of communal tomb forms (columbaria) in the early Empire. The popularity of stone monuments tails off from the end of the second century AD, and even columbaria gradually give way to the use of underground catacombs in the third and (particularly) fourth centuries AD as the role of the cemetery and the importance of tombs as display markers shifted (cf. Bodel 2008; Hope 2009: 162).

Yet even scholars who have published widely in this area highlight the need for more work to be done, especially that which places these tombs fully within their spatial environment (e.g. Koortbojian 1996: 211; Jaeger 1997: 26; Larmour and Spencer 2007: 7; Hope 2009: 153, 159, 186). This is an opportune moment at which to respond to such a call. There has recently been a renewed interest in understanding the complexities of urban space and how it was perceived (e.g. the importance of mobility, procession and other kinds of action within urban space: Hope and Huskinson 2011; Laurence and Newsome 2011; O'Sullivan 2011). Equally, the importance and meaning of the major Roman roads along which these tombs lay have recently been re-emphasised, with a special focus on their spatial dimensions as connectors between different arenas of activity (e.g. Jackson 1984:

26–7; Dyson 1992: 148; Lomas 1998; Laurence 1999: 157–8; Hope 2009: 155; Spencer 2010: 55). Most importantly, the 'suburbs' of Roman cities, where many of these tombs were located, have also recently been under the spotlight, revealing the much more complex interplay between social, economic and political activities, as well as the way in which they mediated the wider relationship between city and countryside (e.g. Purcell 1987; Hope 2000c; Patterson 2000; Coates-Stephens 2004; Graham 2005; Gray 2006; Rosen and Sluiter 2006; Hope 2009: 154–5, 176–7).

In this chapter, which will focus on tombs at Ostia, Pompeii and Rome, my interest is not so much in each individual tomb, but in the spatial development over time of tomb groups along different roads leading from these cities. What were the particular (and differing) perceptions and insights that these tomb groups offered to visitors arriving at the city from each different direction? How did these tombs thus contribute towards their city being 'presented' (both actively and passively) both at any one time and over time in a multitude of ways to those who came there? To what extent would a visitor, resident, Roman and non-Roman have engaged with the identities put forward by these tomb groups? Most importantly, given the scholarly acceptance of the centre and periphery model for Roman society which presupposes a tendency to copy the actions of Rome as the central city and thus create a cultural unity across the system, what roles could these tomb communities play in collectively offering a welcoming or alienating experience for visitors of different kinds moving from city to city within the Roman world? To what extent could they therefore contribute to, or undercut, the wider sense of Roman community that the centre and periphery model is supposed to have created?

OSTIA

The city of Ostia served as the port of Rome and has often been characterised as a city frequented by international traders, imperial officials and artisans (Figure 3.1). Sacked in 87 BC by pirates, the city was later rebuilt and fortified (Hermansen 1981: 4), with settlement expansion towards the east. Most of the east side of the city served as *horrea* (grain-storage facilities), particularly after AD 42, when Claudius began construction of a new harbour nearby at Portus, which was itself finished in AD 64 and expanded again under Trajan (ruled AD 98–117) (Hermansen 1981: 6; Keay et al. 2005; de la Bédoyère 2010: 1). It was during the second century AD that Ostia reached its climax of activity. From the second century onwards, Portus gradually developed as an independent town, to which Constantine I

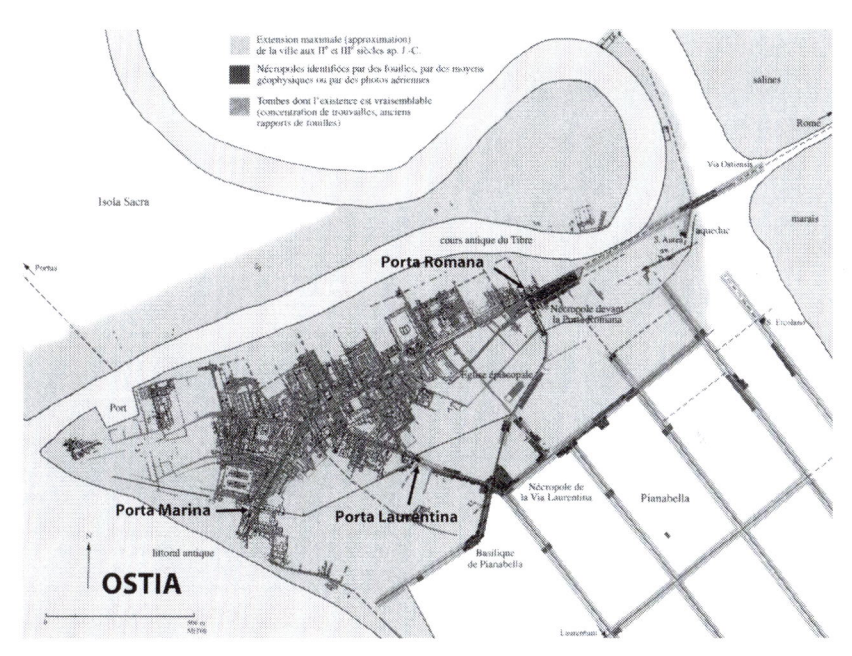

Figure 3.1 Map of the city and surroundings of Ostia with main burial areas marked

transferred Ostia's civic rights in the fourth century AD, after which Ostia went into terminal decline (de la Bédoyère 2010: 12). The geography of the landscape around Ostia was thus crucial both to augmenting its civic development and to limiting it (Figure 3.1). On the one hand, the close presence of the sea and the Tiber guaranteed its important position as a port community and defined the nature of much of its civic construction. On the other hand, as a result, the physical development of the city was tightly limited by the sea to the south, by the Tiber to the north and by marshland to the north-east, which prevented further building in that direction (Heinzelmann 2001: 373).

Four main areas of excavation have revealed tombs in the region around Ostia (Figure 3.1, although all excavators realise that these are only a part of a wider picture). The first is a very small burial area outside the Porta Marina looking towards the sea. The second is on the road leaving Ostia at the Porta Laurentina, which joined a regularised road system, laid out under Augustus, providing access to the available land to the east (Heinzelmann 2001: 373). The third lies directly outside the Porta Romana along the Via Ostiensis heading towards Rome. The fourth is the burial area of the Isola

Sacra on the road between Ostia and Portus. The Isola Sacra burials, however, will not be discussed here, because they appear to have been administered not by Ostia but by Rome (perhaps because Isola Sacra served as the principal burial ground for Portus rather than Ostia). Fines for tomb desecration at the Porta Laurentina and Porta Romana cemeteries, for example, went to Ostia, but at Isola Sacra to the treasury at Rome (Thylander 1952: A245, B210).

Porta Marina

At the Porta Marina (Figure 3.1), there are two isolated burials, both dating from the first century BC, and both respected throughout Ostia's building history, even when the city extended past them towards the beach. The first, and older, is on the right-hand side of the road at a lower ground level equal to that of the old city gate. Fashioned in carefully carved travertine and decorative marble, this is an exedra tomb with carved images of Augustan ships. The second, further towards the beach area, preserves its epitaph, which tells that the tomb was for C. Cartilius Poplicola, a senior magistrate (*duumvir*) of the city eight times and one of Ostia's most famous citizens from the second half of the first century BC. Again built in travertine and marble, it is decorated both with ship imagery and with representations of the magisterial fasces (Hermansen 1981: 108). These burials stand out at Ostia. At the time they were made, the main civic centre of Ostia extended from the *castrum* area towards the Porta Marina (Figure 3.1). The burials were thus given pride of place in the city's living landscape, facing out towards the sea – the chief source of both the dead occupants' and the city's importance and wealth. The honour paid to these two burials is especially marked, since most of the other early burials at Ostia (150–0 BC) were well away from the civic centre in the area around the (later) Porta Romana (Heinzelmann 2001: 376–7).

In the following half-century, however, Ostia was dramatically expanded towards the east as well as to the north-east towards the Porta Romana. The Porta Marina area does not appear to have been subsequently used as a burial ground in the rest of the city's history. These burials, once thus honoured at the 'centre' of the city, were subsequently separated off from the city's future burial areas, and yet remained important enough to the city for them to be respected for at least the next three centuries. The Porta Marina burials thus may have come to symbolise not just important individuals, but the earliest foundations and civic identity of Ostia.

Porta Laurentina

Burials on the roads outside the Porta Laurentina offer a very different picture.[1] Interest in the Porta Laurentina area seems to begin only after the rebuilding and expansion of the city following its sack in 87 BC. Yet throughout its history of use, as yet no identifiable graves of magistrates, town councillors or Roman knights have been found (Meiggs 1973: 455). Instead, the burials seem to have been of small traders, craftsmen and ex-slaves.

The development of this area over time has been carefully studied by Heinzelmann (Heinzelmann 2000; 2001), who emphasises the increasing importance of a visible position (Figure 3.2). The first datable monumental burial in this area (A1), for example, was positioned exactly at the crossroads of the Via Laurentina and XV street, facing towards the city gates. Subsequent building in the early-middle Augustan period was similarly squeezed in along the roadsides at the crossroads (A3a, A4a, B1, B3a, L2a). A comparable pattern can be discerned for the middle and late Augustan periods: regularised construction along the roads (e.g. B4a, A5a) was coupled with a move closer towards the city gates (e.g. K4), and the occasional decision to move back from the roadside to obtain more space (e.g. E1).

A second wave of building took place in late Augustan to early Tiberian times (Figure 3.2), with more regularised building along the roadside where available (e.g. L3a–8a) and the occupation of a second tier, which sacrificed visibility from the road in order to be part of the central burial area (A2, C1, C2, C3a, C4a); this was coupled with several much larger and more ornate tombs constructed further back again (e.g. E2, D7). Heinzelmann (2001: 380) argues that all of these belonged to freedmen, often artisans, and many from the Augustan period belonged to those coming to the city as immigrants from Rome (e.g. A3a, B3a, C2, K4).

A preference for group burial increased in popularity at Ostia with the adoption of columbaria under Tiberius. During the Tiberian period, such group tombs were added along the roads, particularly closer to the city gates (e.g. K2a, K3a) and at the crossroads (e.g. D5a, E3). In contrast, several burials opted for distance from others (e.g. F7, F8). In the Claudian and Neronian periods, older tombs were converted into columbaria (e.g. E2 becomes E4, and L3b and L4b are rebuilt), although some earlier tombs were elaborated, perhaps still under continued family supervision (e.g. C1). Many of the columbaria tombs also show evidence of provision for festivities (including

---

[1] Tomb numbers (in the text and maps) for Ostia follow those in Heinzelmann 2000. The original excavation report is Squarciapino 1955.

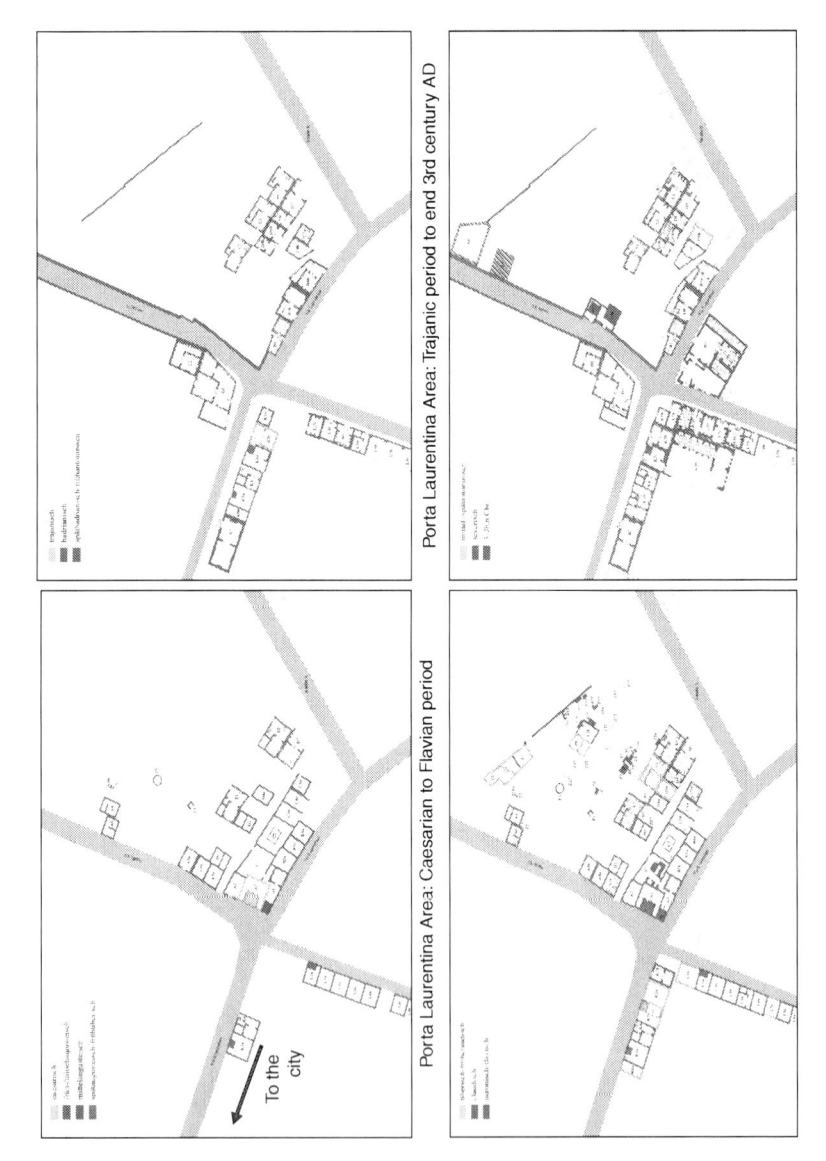

Figure 3.2 Burials at Ostia in the Porta Laurentina area

wells dug within the tomb), and often have a more modest exterior compared to a more luxurious interior (Heinzelmann 2001: 380; Graham 2005: 138).

In the early second century AD during the Hadrianic period (Figure 3.2), however, there was an abrupt destruction of tombs associated with a rearticulation of the road system (tombs A3a, A4a, A5a, B2a, B3a, B4a were destroyed). Some tombs were the casualties of road-widening, but some may simply have fallen out of use. The collective tomb B3a, for example, was destroyed and quickly replaced with a new, much larger, tomb (B3b), and L2a, L3b and L4b were rebuilt (L2b, L3c, L4c). In addition, new, much larger columbaria were constructed (G1, G2) at the crossroads. By the end of the second century AD, new tombs not only were more obviously luxurious, but even jutted out onto the new road layout (A4b, A5b). Yet almost nothing was built in this area from the third century AD onwards. From the fourth century AD, there is in fact much evidence for the pillaging and reuse of tomb material within the city (Meiggs 1973: 466).

Porta Romana

The Porta Romana area contains the city's oldest burials. All are modest and show no interest in a highly visible position (in comparison to the two rare burials at the Porta Marina), although they were for fairly wealthy and socially important people (Squarciapino 1955: 11–14 (tomb f–rich but distant from the road; tombs a, b, c, d, e – poor but close to the road); Heinzelmann 2001: 376–7). After the sack of the city and its rebuilding in 87 BC, that pattern changed abruptly (Figure 3.3). Visibility was now key, with the earliest tombs being built either at the first crossroads of the Via Ostiensis (e.g. A22, B21), or closest to the city gates (e.g. A1). The Porta Romana area was also the preferred area in this period for those who held important civic positions in the town (Meiggs 1973: 455; de la Bédoyère 2010: 92). Yet it is crucial to note that, taken overall, very few highly elaborate tombs were constructed in the immediate vicinity of the Porta Romana. In fact, the most elaborate tomb to be found in the Ostian area was at Acilia, some 5 km away (Meiggs 1973: 456). As a result, it is possible that at Ostia itself the richest sought distance rather than visibility.

There were fewer tombs built at the Porta Romana during the Augustan period than around Porta Laurentina, though those that were built tended to be more individual in their style (circular tombs, large monumental facades, etc), or for particular groups such as the Praetorian soldiers (buried in B4). Under Claudius and Nero some older tombs were converted into columbaria (A7a, A9a, B50), and a second row of tombs was begun behind those situated along the Via Ostiensis (Figure 3.3).

Porta Romana Area: 1st century BC to Flavian period

Porta Romana Area: Trajanic period to end 3rd century AD

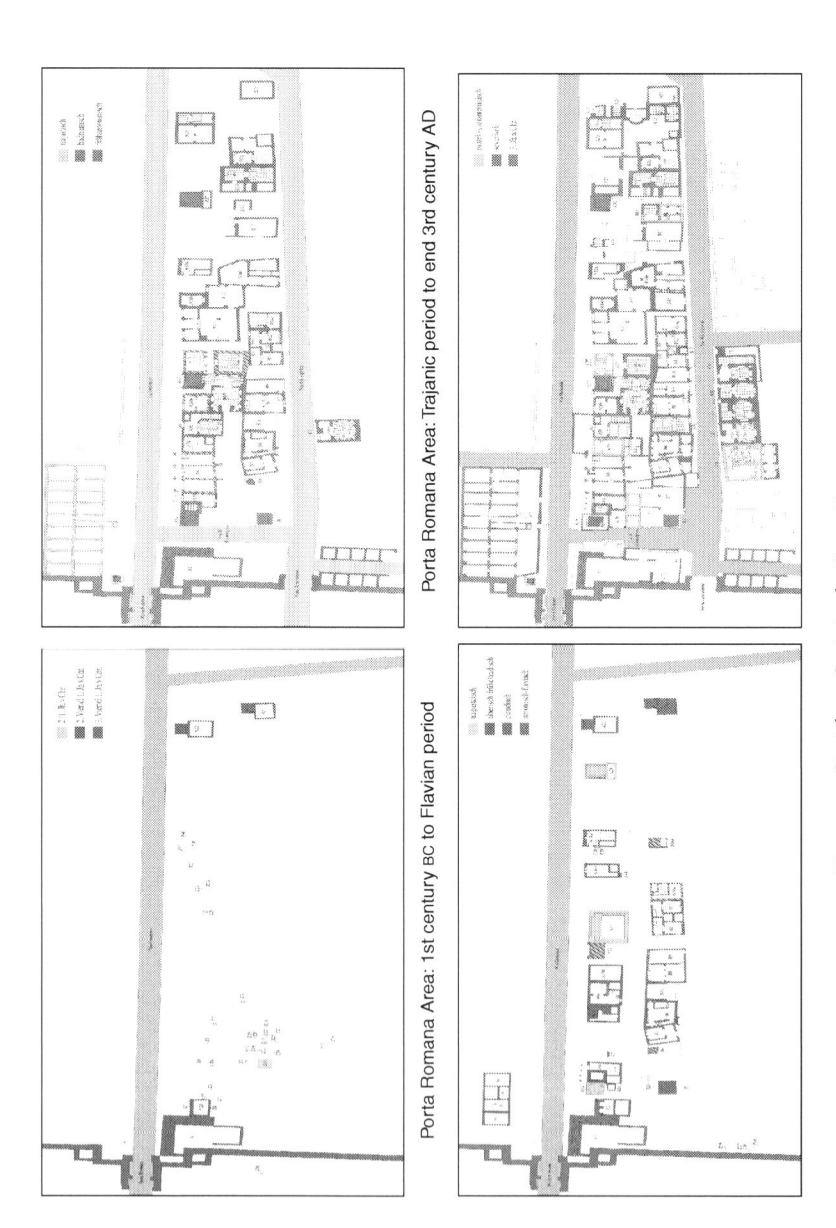

Figure 3.3 Burials at Ostia in the Porta Romana area

The continuing expansion of Portus, particularly after the beginning of the second century AD, completely changed the picture at Porta Romana (Figure 3.3). The Porta Romana became the premier space for burial (far more burials have been found here than in the Porta Laurentina area). Space along the road was at an absolute premium, as tombs jostled for space with taverns (e.g. A5a, A6, B3, B9, B10), a *stabulum* (A15) and even an apartment block built by Trajan, which was itself built over a whole series of old tombs (D1–4). Tombs were also destroyed (e.g. A2, A14) to make space for new tombs and connecting roads. A parallel city gate and road (Via dei Sepolcri) were also constructed at this time; this offered a second visual front for new tombs and became the site for the most expensive monuments in the whole necropolis (C1–6).

Such building also brought a social revolution to the area. Most of the new tombs from the second century AD were for newly immigrant freedmen whose descendants would go on to hold civic posts (e.g. C. Domitius Fabius Hermogenes in A3b, who also had an equestrian statue in the forum, but also B7b, C1, C2, C3, C4). Equally, a significant number of tombs were destroyed and built over during the course of the second century AD (A3a, A7a, A9a, A16a, B4, B7, B16a, B21); their replacements were luxurious and individualised (e.g. A7b, A23), often copying styles from Rome, a trend culminating at the end of the second century AD (A3b, C6), with particular focus on a prime individual within the tomb (e.g. C3, cf. *CIL* 14.396). As at the Porta Laurentina, in the third century AD there was an almost complete shutdown; only one new tomb was built (C6).

Approaching Ostia through its tombs

This examination of the development of communities of tombs surrounding the different gates at Ostia highlights the different perspectives on the city each community would have offered (cf. Figure 3.1). At Porta Marina, it was unchanging: two small monuments to important individuals selected for separation from other burials and subsequent incorporation within the city, which were respected perhaps because they were understood to be an important part of the city's history and identity.

Until the second century AD, the area immediately outside the Porta Romana was the space for civic officials (it was after all the road leading to Rome), as well as for groups particularly associated with the rule of Rome (e.g. the Praetorian guard). Though graves were more individualised here, Porta Romana was not the busiest space around the city for burial (indeed, those wealthy enough may have avoided it in preference for places much further away). In contrast, the area around Porta Laurentina, always avoided by civic officials, was the busiest burial area, popular with artisans and traders (some of whom were freedmen), and particularly those newly arrived in the city. As a result, the Porta Laurentina area supported a community of the dead which most accurately reflected Ostia's international and trading population. Porta Marina thus symbolised Ostia's past, Porta Romana the official side of the city, but Porta Laurentina represented its everyday character. Yet, at that time, all the tomb communities at the different gates of Ostia seem to have had little interest in providing for future generations: the burial areas of both Porta Romana and Laurentina show very few tombs which sought to provide space for future family members (Meiggs 1973: 458–61). The horizon of interest in the future at Ostia appears much more limited.

From the second century AD, however, the dynamics changed dramatically. A large number of rich freedmen were buried at Porta Romana (in contrast to its earlier 'civic official' focus). At the same time (and perhaps as a result), Porta Romana became the main focus for construction, and this created not only a more diverse tomb community sporting a much higher degree of luxury, but also a much more socially diverse civic space for both the living and the dead (with the addition of taverns, flats, etc.). Both tomb communities, even though they suffered continued tomb destruction and conversion, also displayed more interest in providing tomb space for the future. Such increased interest may have been the result of witnessing at first hand the short lifespan of destroyed tombs, but it may also have been to do with a social revolution in the composition of the city's citizenry, which (particularly in terms of the rise of freedmen whose descendants would occupy civic positions) demonstrated the existence of a population much more settled in the city with an outlook much more focused on their long-term future (cf. Heinzelmann 2001: 375).

POMPEII

The city of Pompeii had its origins in Greek and Samnite culture. But it suffered during the Social War, and was made into a Roman colony in 80 BC, with a resulting decline in Samnite and Oscan traditions (cf. Cic. *Sull.* 62). The city flourished in the late Republican and Augustan periods, then suffered an earthquake in AD 62 or 63, before its famous final destruction in AD 79 (cf. de la Bédoyère 2010: 13–20). Funerary monuments have been excavated around several, but not all gates of the city (Figure 3.4: Herculaneum, Vesuvian, Nolan, Nucerian and Stabian gates with burials, but not the Marina gate), and scholarship has been at pains to stress both the incomplete nature of our knowledge of burials at each of these gates and the

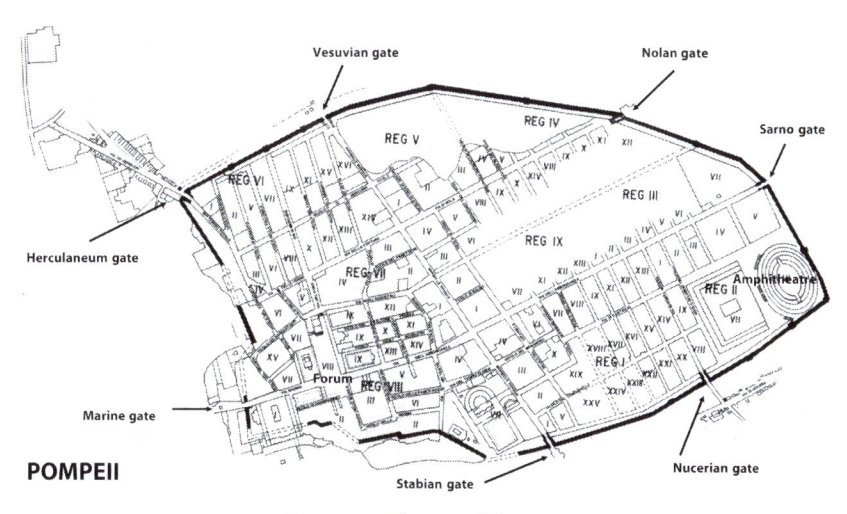

Figure 3.4 The city of Pompeii

extreme diversity of the tombs that have survived (cf. Toynbee 1971: 118; Emmerson 2011: 164, 168; forthcoming).

Stabian gate

At the Stabian gate, several examples of Samnite-Roman burials have been found (Figure 3.4). One in particular, situated about 500 m from the Stabian gate, is a *c*.400 sq.m. burial plot (G1–3) enclosed by a wall, containing 44 Samnite inhumations dating from the fourth to the second centuries BC; it included one monumental tomb, a feature that is seen in Samnite burial culture only outside Samnium itself (Davies 1977: 14).[2] In addition, there were 119 Roman cremations in the same area up to AD 79. The whole area seems to have belonged to the Epidii family, a notable family at Pompeii from Oscan times (cf. Cooley and Cooley 2004: 138), and the burial plot provided not just for the family members, but for their freedmen (cf. tomb G1) and even perhaps for their dog. In addition to this long-serving burial plot at the Stabian gate there were several tombs which were granted special placement near the walls of the city by decree of the town councillors (*decurionum decreto*): those of Marcus Tullius (G6), M. Alleius Minius (G7) and Gn. Clovatius (G8) all date to the Augustan period.

---

[2] Tomb number references for the Stabian, Nolan and Vesuvian gates are those in Cooley and Cooley 2004.

These were expensive tombs for people who had held important civic offices and performed civic deeds (Tullius, for example, had built the *Aedes Fortunae Augustae*). Those building Clovatius' tomb underlined his munificence in life by decorating it with scenes of gladiatorial fights and beast hunts (cf. Coarelli 2002: 390). Crucially, the known Stabian gate burials were all of people from Pompeii. This civic connection is underlined by the particular burial (complete with typical Pompeian herm grave marker) of one member of the Praetorian guard (tomb G69) who was from Pompeii, in contrast to three other Praetorians who were not from the city and who were instead buried outside the Nolan gate. Yet this intense civic connection at the Stabian gate did not guarantee longevity: Tullius' and Minius' tombs had been abandoned well before AD 79, and rubbish, including other funerary inscriptions, dumped in them (Cooley and Cooley 2004: 139).

Nolan gate

The graves of the three Praetorians buried just outside the Nolan gate formed a single line (G66–68), perhaps occupying public land and thus buried there only with civic permission (Figure 3.4). All had tomb markers, which, while common from other parts of Italy, were exceptional at Pompeii. All indicated their tribe or hometown of origin in their epitaphs (cf. De Caro 1979). They were clearly outsiders, but well-respected and honoured outsiders.

Yet the Nolan gate also bore witness to monumental tombs for Pompeian residents. M. Obellius Firmus was buried here (tomb G12), by the authority of the city council, to whose funeral, his epitaph proclaims, the 'inhabitants of the country district' also contributed money and precious goods (Dyson 1992: 149; Cooley and Cooley 2004: 141). This rectangular enclosure with a high wall all around (it could only be entered by means of ladders) contrasted with the other later (Tiberian/Claudian) major tomb at this gate: a seat-tomb (G5) erected by N. Herennius Celsus for his wife (again with the authority of the city council). The seat-tomb encouraged passers-by not only to look but also to sit down and pass time at the grave. Indeed, at Pompeii at least, the seat-tomb is argued to have been particularly appropriate (perhaps even reserved) for those granted public honours (for a contrary view see: Richardson 1988: 256). As a result, the tomb style both reflected the service rendered by the dead person to the city and allowed them to go on providing a 'service' (as a seating area) for visitors and residents.

Yet the area around the Nolan gate was by no means reserved exclusively for respected outsiders and wealthy honoured Pompeians. Discovered along the pomerium line between the Nolan and Sarnus gates were some of the humblest burials ever found at Pompeii: 38 cinerary urns buried in the ground (Coarelli 2002: 91–2). The identities of those buried in the urns were inscribed not on the urn or on any monument over the burial, but instead in short funerary epitaphs written directly onto nearby city walls (G56–8).

Vesuvian gate

Only a limited number of tombs have been identified at the Vesuvian gate, and it is interesting that they are all for, or set up by, women (Figure 3.4). Tomb G9 belonged to Arellia Tertulla, wife of a prominent magistrate in the town; she died c.AD 26, and her plot and funeral expenses were sanctioned and paid for by the city council. It was again a seat-tomb, decorated with winged-lion paws on either end. A slightly earlier tomb, again for a woman (Septumia), was set up by her daughter (Antistia Prima), after the *duumvirs* had granted the space and funeral expenses (G10). This was not a seat-tomb, but instead a high podium supporting a column. This tomb, however, was neglected after the earthquake of AD 62 or 63: its base was covered in graffiti, and debris from the destruction was heaped casually around it (Richardson 1988: 257). Yet while this tomb was neglected in the period AD 62–79, another new tomb was built at the Vesuvian gate in the same period. Tomb F88, belonging to C. Vestorius Priscus, states in its epitaph that the funeral was paid for (and the location of burial sanctioned) by the city, but the tomb itself by his mother (cf. de la Bédoyère 2010: 26–7). This was another rich and individualised tomb, with paintings on the internal walls of the enclosure, and the whole edifice was topped by an altar.

Nucerian gate

The limited number of surviving tombs at the Stabian, Nolan and Vesuvian gates is in sharp contrast to the plethora of tombs outside the Nucerian and Herculaneum gates. At the Nucerian gate, the excavated area is not along a road running away from the city, but instead along a road running parallel with the city walls in the direction of the Stabian gate to the west, and in the direction of the amphitheatre to the east (Figure 3.5). With the exception of two possible late Republican/early Augustan tombs on the stretch from the Nucerian gate towards the amphitheatre (28 EN and 44 EN), the earliest tombs discovered are all to the west, between the Nucerian and Stabian gates (the oldest Republican tombs in this stretch

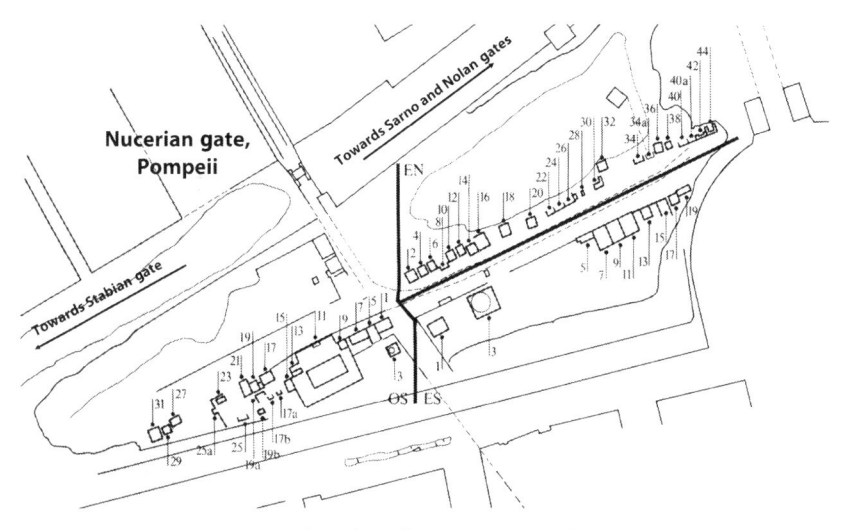

90 *Spaces of alienation: street-lining Roman cemeteries*

Figure 3.5 Burials at the Nucerian gate, Pompeii

are 9 OS and 13 OS).[3] Such a predisposition for older burials in this area connects perhaps with the old Samnite/Roman family tomb directly outside the Stabian gate itself.

Yet this section of road also made clear the changing nature of Pompeian society and politics after its conversion to a Roman colony in 80 BC. Tomb 29 OS was for a *duumvir* (L. Caesius) from the time of the conversion. The tomb actively highlighted the presence of Roman power through the depiction of fasces on its facade. Alongside is evidence for Pompeii's changing population. Tomb 31 OS belonged to the Stronii family, from a tribe outside Pompeii and seemingly part of the early immigrant population brought into the city. Tomb 17 OS is similarly for the Tillii family, who migrated to Pompeii from Arpinum in the second half of the first century BC, and whose first three generations of burials were marked pointedly with records of their public service in their previous home town.

While this western section of the road contained some freedmen burials, freedmen from the Republican period normally preferred a place nearer the Nucerian gate itself (e.g. P. Flavius Philoxenus and Flavia Agathea in burial 7 OS). Indeed, the richest of all Republican tombs at Pompeii is that of a freedman at the Nucerian gate. L. Ceius Serapio, a freedman who made his

---
[3] Tomb numbers at the Nucerian gate refer to De Caro 1983.

money as a moneylender, set up a tholos tomb for himself and his wife directly on the Nucerian road (3 OS), at the point where the ground rose up, giving this extremely individual and elaborate tomb extra visibility (Figure 3.5).

Under the Julio-Claudians, there was an increasing number of types of tomb that expanded on both sides of the Nucerian gate: arch tombs (e.g. 2, 6, 12 EN), aedicular tombs (e.g. 23 OS), double-storey tombs (e.g. 34a EN), more tholos tombs (e.g. 3 ES), and house tombs (e.g. 9 ES, 13 ES). Some matched or surpassed earlier ones (e.g. tholos tomb 3 ES stands almost opposite the earlier tholos 3 OS, similarly occupying the higher ground but much larger). Yet by far the largest tomb here, indeed in all Pompeii, was that of Eumachia (11 OS). Built in the early first century AD between the two oldest Republican tombs in this area, this tomb (in total 14 m deep and 13 m wide) had at its heart a semi-circular seat (Figures 3.5, 3.7). Eumachia was a public priestess but also a successful businesswoman, whose commercial building, just off Pompeii's forum, was dedicated to Augustan Concord and Piety and was one of the city's largest private structures (cf. Figure 3.4; *CIL* 10.959; 10.811). The tomb structure was built for her and her son. Yet it is curious in two respects: first, the seat-tomb – normally designed for people to relax on – was in fact locked off by an enclosure wall (Figure 3.7; perhaps because Eumachia's tomb was not sanctioned by the city council (*decurionum decreto*) and thus, according to some scholars, did not officially merit a seat-tomb – see the discussion of tombs around the Nolan gate above); second, and more importantly, Eumachia's family did not use this tomb for long. By the mid-first century AD, it was being used by another family, that of Cn. Alleius Nigidus. The largest tomb in Pompeii thus also functioned as a clear marker of the dynamically changing nature of Pompeian (tomb) society.

Around the middle of the first century AD, C. Munatius Faustus, a freedman and one of a group of wealthy benefactors involved with the imperial cult (*augustales*) at Pompeii, erected tomb 9 ES for himself and his wife at the Nucerian gate (Figure 3.5). The tomb's location was sanctioned by the city council, and took the form of a house tomb, one of a series of equal-sized tomb slots built along the road between the Nucerian gate and the amphitheatre. Faustus' epitaph described him as a 'country-dweller', and other epitaphs discovered in the enclosure reveal that other members of his household (tomb 9 ES nos. 3–8), both free and slave, were buried with him. The only person missing is his wife. To find her, we have to look to an entirely different tomb community.

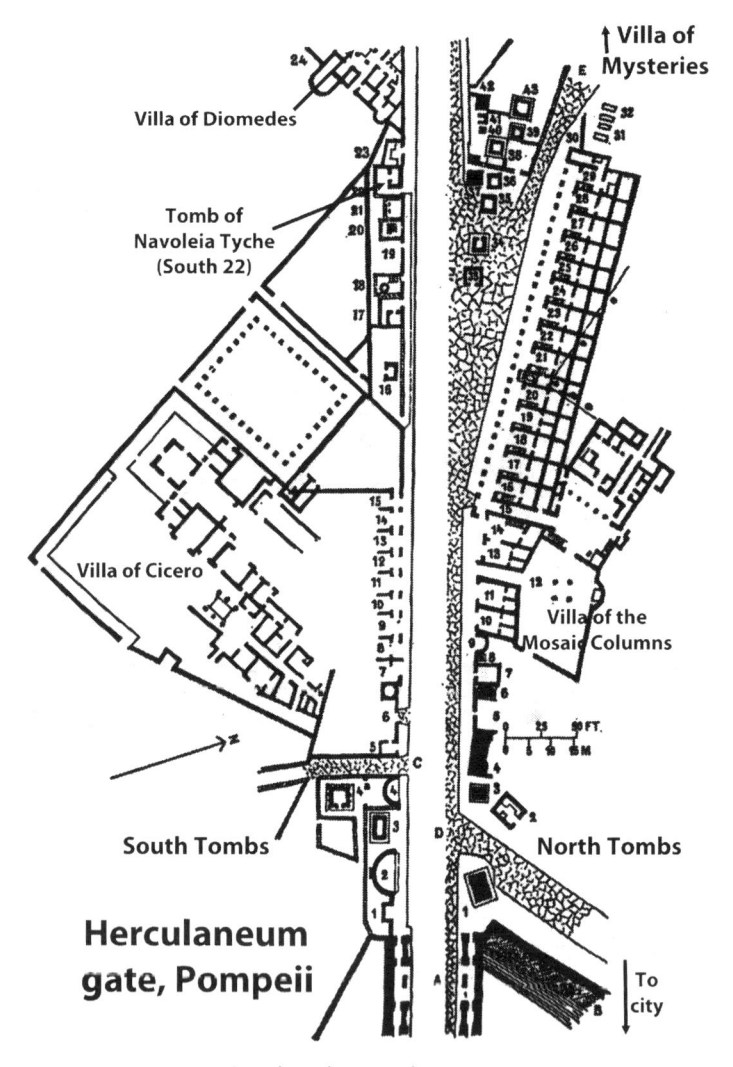

92 *Spaces of alienation: street-lining Roman cemeteries*

Figure 3.6 Burials at the Herculaneum gate, Pompeii

Herculaneum gate

Navoleia Tyche, wife of Faustus, was buried at the Herculaneum gate as part of the 'street of tombs' leading directly away from Pompeii (Figures 3.6, 3.7). The tomb she set up (South 22), technically in honour of her husband, took the form of an altar tomb, with the altar raised up high to ensure its visibility

Pompeii 93

Above: Tomb of Eumachia (11 OS), Nucerian Gate, Pompeii. The curved seat-tomb is cut off from use by an enclosure wall.

Left: Tombs South 22, 21, 20 from the Herculaneum gate, Pompeii. Tomb 22 belongs to Navoleia Tyche (with image of a ship on side)
Above: Tomb South 22 (Navoleia Tyche) front.
Below: Tomb South 22 (Navoleia Tyche) side with *bisellium* seat carving.

Figure 3.7 Tombs of Eumachia and Navoleia Tyche, Pompeii

from the street.[4] Tyche's altar underlined not only her husband's civic position (through the depiction of a *bisellium* (double-width honorific chair) on the side of the altar pointing towards the city, the image of a ship on the other pointing towards Herculaneum, and a relief of Faustus distributing grain on the front: Figure 3.7), but also her own status: a bust of herself accompanied that of Faustus (cf. Koortbojian 1996: 224). The pride in their freed status, their new-found wealth and the fact they now had their own freedmen and women were all underlined in the epitaph itself (*CIL* 10.1030).

Tyche's tomb, while extravagant in its detail, was very much in keeping with the style of other tombs at the Herculaneum gate (it was in fact part of a line of altar tombs, like that of C. Calventius Quietus (South 20), another *augustalis;* cf. Figure 3.7). This area of the street of tombs, furthest away from the city gate, was popular with rich successful freedmen (e.g. tomb South 21 for N. Istacidius Helenus, North 42 for M. Arrius Diomedes, North 43 for P. Sittius Diophantus, South 20 for C. Calventius Quietus, who highlighted his '*munificentia*' in his epitaph). Yet, as a result of the similar styles of tombs in this area, those of rich freedmen and those of freeborn citizens were,

---

[4] Tomb numbers at the Herculaneum gate follow those in Kockel 1983.

architecturally at least, indistinguishable (e.g. the tomb of L. Ceius Labeo (North 39), who was *duumvir*, was almost identical to that of the freedman Diophantus in the tomb next door (North 43)).

This section of the street of tombs was also, like the Porta Romana at Ostia, a very diverse area accommodating both the living and the dead (Figure 3.6). The tombs here were book-ended by private villas (villa of the Mosaic columns, villa of Diomedes, villa of Cicero, and, further away, the villa of the Mysteries), and faced by a potters' establishment (North 30), a large inn (North 17–29), shops (North 10–14), and another villa (North 15). Perhaps as a result, this area continued to be popular for tombs right up to the moment of Pompeii's final destruction (tombs North 33 and 35 were unfinished at the time of the eruption). More importantly, it seems to have been an area in which people felt it was important to keep their tombs in good order. The tomb of Quietus (South 20), for example, seems to have been subsequently enhanced in its grandeur, perhaps as part of his descendants' ambition for further public recognition, or indeed desire to match the grandeur of later constructions (Kockel 1983: 96–7).

At the city-gate end of the 'street of tombs' was another section of tombs lining both sides of the street (Figure 3.6). The oldest Republican tombs were placed here (as previously older Samnite tombs).[5] The first was that of M. Porcius (South 3) built about 20 m from the gate.[6] Dated to the middle of the first century BC, this altar tomb was set within an enclosure measuring c.2.3 sq.m. (a size specified in the accompanying epitaph), and the plot was allocated by the civic authorities. Porcius was responsible for the *Theatrum Minus* and the amphitheatre at Pompeii (Richardson 1988: 184). Visitors to his tomb may well thus have been able to see the tops of his creations dominating the Pompeian skyline from the site of his tomb, as they would have been able to enjoy the superb views of Vesuvius and the coast (Coarelli 2002: 382). It was a commanding position for a man who had done much to shape the civic landscape of Pompeii.

In the Augustan period, Porcius' tomb was surrounded by two bench tombs (Figure 3.6). The first (South 4) was that of Mamia, *sacerdos publica*, which had its epitaph cut in highly visible letters into the seat's back. Mamia had built the Temple of the *Genius Augusti* in the forum, and her tomb's location was sanctioned by the city council. Slightly later, closer to the city gate, A. Veius was awarded a bench tomb (South 2), *decurionum decreto*, for

---

[5] See tombs 31-2 in Kockel 1983.
[6] Von Hesberg believes that the Tomb of Ghirlande (North 6) preceded that of Porcius: von Hesberg 1994: 39.

his services as *duumvir* and *tribunus militum a populo*. In the late Augustan/ early Tiberian period, a new and elaborate tomb for the Istacidii (South 4a) was placed on a terrace newly constructed behind that of Mamia, in which 19 burials have been found. It was a quadrangular podium structure enclosing the burial chamber, with a tholos above (Coarelli 2002: 384–5). In the Neronian period, in contrast, a smaller square tomb (South 1), still with benches, was squeezed in even closer to the city gate for M. Cerrinus Restitutus, whose tomb plot had also been granted *decurionum decreto*.

Approaching Pompeii through its tombs

We are still missing much of the various *necropoleis* of Pompeii, as the discovery of 50 unidentified tombs 80 m east of the amphitheatre shows (Cooley and Cooley 2004: G59). Yet we can say something about how these different *necropoleis* contributed to creating an impression on visitors coming to the city, of which there must have been many, as Laurence's work on the way Pompeian street design responded to the influx of visitors has demonstrated (Laurence 1994; 1995).

Those approaching the Marina gate saw, it has recently been argued, no street-lining tombs at all (Emmerson 2011: 164; forthcoming). Those approaching Pompeii via the Stabian gate, or perhaps walking around the city between the Stabian and Nucerian gate, would have been greeted with a sense of the history of the city dating back to its Samnite roots and would have been confronted with a picture of continuity in Pompeii's population thanks to the tombs for particular families stretching over many generations (Figures 3.4, 3.5). If instead visitors entered directly by the Nucerian gate, or strolled between that gate and the amphitheatre, the changing nature of Pompeii's history and population would have been much more apparent (Figures 3.4, 3.5). Equally, under the Julio-Claudians, the diverse architectural collection of rich freedmen tombs at this gate would have underlined the dynamic social structure and successful economy of the city, as well as its continuing social turnover (particularly through the handover of Eumachia's grand tomb to another family after such a short period). Such a full spectrum of the city's social structure was also on display by the Nolan gate, whereas at the Vesuvian gate the surviving evidence highlights in particular the powerful role of women in the city (or at least in Pompeii's city of the dead). At all of these four gates, visitors would have been reminded of the multicultural nature of its population by funerary material ranging from monumental Samnite grave markers, to rare non-Pompeian grave markers for Praetorians from other cities, to epitaphs of newly immigrated families who still chose to commemorate their civic service in their previous home town.

The experience gained through arrival at the Herculaneum gate, for which we have the most evidence at Pompeii, shifted radically over time (Figure 3.6). The early phases of tombs in its immediate vicinity made it a place for citizen celebration – celebration that often linked itself (both visually and through the epitaph) from the tomb to structures within the city (amphitheatre, temples, etc.). The visitor as a result was prepared for the kind of city they might find; they would appreciate the role of its citizens in making it, and would be encouraged to admire what rewards such *munificentia* could bring. Over time, particularly in sections further away from the gate itself, the 'street of tombs' became a favoured spot for rich freedmen and women. For Navoleia Tyche, there was clearly a social benefit to being buried at the Herculaneum rather than Nucerian gate, enough for her to desert her husband's tomb at the latter and to build him (and herself) another one at the former. Yet by the time Pompeii was destroyed, that distinction between freedmen and freeborn citizen, at least in terms of the spatial and architectural disposition of tombs, was almost imperceptible. Not only were the tombs of freeborn and freedmen citizens built side by side and almost identical in their architecture along the course of the street of tombs, but a freedman *augustalis* could be buried close to the city gates in amongst the tombs of major citizen civic benefactors, indeed in the closest position to the city gate.

ROME

Rome is a city far too complex to cover in any great detail here (cf. Figure 3.8), and that coverage is in any case made more difficult by the irregular survival of tombs, the typological approaches of previous scholars and the ongoing piecemeal publication of tombs (as well as increasing numbers of unmonumentalised burials for the members of the *plebs urbana*) surrounding the city (cf. von Hesberg 1994: 48; Catalano 2008; Hope 2009: 153; Gowland and Garnsey 2010; Liverani and Spinola 2010). As a result, this section will examine some of the different areas of burial at Rome, not gate by gate, but instead chronologically from the third century BC to the second century AD, in order to highlight the different dynamics at work in different *necropoleis*. Between them, they laid out a story of Rome's changing sense of self and its relationship to the world around it, as a result imposing a series of varied impressions on visitors.

Figure 3.8 Map of Rome

Up to the first century BC

The evidence for early Rome (Figure 3.8) demonstrates the existence of a cemetery in the forum area, as well as the funerary use of the Esquiline hill (some tombs here date back to the ninth century BC). Such tombs were simple, yet should not be considered to represent the poor (Davies 1977: 16). Indeed, Cicero would claim in the first century BC that the Esquiline was still an appropriate place for men of noble ancestry to be buried, when advocating the burial there of Servius Sulpicius Rufus (Cic. *Phil.* 9.17). Early Rome thus looked (or was later constructed as looking) to the tombs atop the Esquiline with a degree of respect and admiration. This area was also home to the sacred grove of Libitina, the goddess of funerals (cf. *CIL* 6.3823). Much recent discussion has focused on the concept of viewing Rome (e.g. Larmour and Spencer 2007), and in particular on the opportunities and disadvantages brought by viewing Rome from its hills. In the first century AD Martial (4.64.11–12) claims to be able to '*aestimare*' Rome from the Janiculum (cf. Vout 2007). Such positions offered a sense of both the whole of the city and of alienation from it. The association of the Esquiline with Roman noble burial in the early period of Rome's history provides a complex example of this viewing relationship. The Esquiline, as a hill within the city, was always visible as an enviable destination after death. Equally, looking from the Esquiline towards the city offered an opportunity to gain an overview of its physical extent. At the same time, however, viewing from the Esquiline situated the viewer in amongst the city's most important (ancestral) burials, creating a potential sense of alienation both through being physically removed from the city and through being placed specifically within a city of the dead rather than of the living.

During the third and second centuries BC, the spatial layout of tombs at Rome, as well as the city itself, changed dramatically. The Esquiline area in this period was in heavy use, particularly for poorer burials: excavations have produced seventy-five trenches of poor *puticuli* burials (Davies 1977: 17; Robinson 1992: 125; Malmberg and Bjur 2011: 364), as well as for other purposes, such as public executions, informal markets and certain religious festivals like the Vinalia (Malmberg and Bjur 2011: 364–8). This would no doubt have had an impact on how the Esquiline was viewed from Rome and the opportunities it offered for viewing Rome, a change perhaps indicated by the fact that Cicero later felt the need to insist it was *still* a place worthy for nobles in the first century BC. At the same time, Rome's landscape was changed significantly by the building of its major roads connecting it to different parts of Italy (Figure 3.8). The Via Appia, constructed between 313 and 308 BC, for example, linked Rome to Capua, and in 220 BC the Via Flaminia was built, creating a physical connection between Rome and its colonies in central Italy (for discussion, see Laurence 1999: 13, 21). These roads were, as a result, visible demonstrations of Rome's increasing power and influence over the wider landscape. The Via Appia in particular, as it was named after the individual who created it, became something of a 'deathless monument' to its creator (cf. Diod. Sic. 20.36; Livy 9.29; Stat. *Silv.* 2.2.12). It was perhaps this monumental nature, coupled with the visibility such roads provided as the main access routes into the city, that attracted tombs to them, particularly those of the wealthy and powerful.

One of the earliest, placed between the Via Appia and Via Latina, was the tomb of the Scipios (Figure 3.8). The first burial here took place in 298 BC, not long after the construction of the Via Appia, and the tomb remained in continuous use until 130 BC; two burials were added in the first century AD. It was a fascinating tomb, hollowed out of the natural tufa rock, and offering a simple architectural pattern. While facing the Via Appia, it could be accessed only through a side path rather than directly from the road (Toynbee 1971: 103). The tomb of the Scipios has been characterised as having been built in the era 'before display' (Purcell 1987: 27). To an extent this is true. Rome (and all Latium) was something of a backwater in terms of tomb opulence in comparison to Apulia, Campania and Etruria before the time of the late Republic (Davies 1977: 18; Heinzelmann 2001: 383). Yet it would be misleading to understand the tomb of the Scipios as lacking the intention to display. The Scipios were in fact among the first to understand the display potential of the new major roads leading into Rome, and continued to care for the display they provided (the tomb was later embellished to keep pace with its surroundings).

The first century BC

During the first century BC, the use of the Esquiline hill for burials was officially restricted (cf. *CIL* 6.31615), although still possible (as Cicero indicated); its use as a marketplace, recreation and habitation area was increasing (Malmberg and Bjur 2011: 375). Important civic burials took place instead in the Campus Martius (cf. Figure 3.8): Sulla was buried here (Plut. *Vit. Sull.* 38), and later so too were Aulus Hirtius and C. Vibius Pansa, following their deaths in battle against Mark Antony (Hope 2007: 160). The period of the late Republic is characterised as one of the most frenetic and elaborate periods of tomb-building in the city's history, particularly along the roads leading out of the city. This activity included the area at the back of the Esquiline hill, later to be dominated by the Porta Maggiore (Figure 3.8). At this junction of two roads leaving the city, the Via Praenestina and Via Labicana, where there was a sanctuary of Spes Vetus, recent reinvestigation has highlighted the intense tomb-construction of the late Republican period, particularly by a varying range of 'middle classes' (including prosperous freedmen, one of whom, Q. Pompeius Sossus, is commemorated on the first attested epitaph in this area, from 70 BC), as well as for the slaves of senatorial families, such as those of Aulus Allienus and the Arruntii (Coates-Stephens 2004: 11), and for *collegia* (such as the *societas cantorum graecorum*: *CIL* I² 2519). It is not without irony that this popular region for burial was also the point at which all Rome's earliest aqueducts reached the city, an area known as '*aqua conclusa*'. This nodal point in the city's landscape thus provided a place that brought together Rome's life-giving water, evidence of its mortality and a representation of its dynamic social mix.

In 50–20 BC, the most famous of Rome's tombs was added to this area: the tomb of Eurysaces the baker (Figures 3.8, 3.9). Notable for its extremely

100 *Spaces of alienation: street-lining Roman cemeteries*

Figure 3.9 Tombs of Caecilia Metella, Cestius and Eurysaces on the roads outside Rome

visible placement at the junctions of the Via Praenestina and Via Labicana, and its use of travertine and marble on a scale unparalleled in the area, the tomb enshrines the career of a wealthy freedman (cf. Toynbee 1971: 128–9). But what recent investigations make clear is that there may well have been a working flour mill (*pistrinum*) in this area, using both water and animal milling (perhaps Eurysaces' own). There have also been a number of epitaphs discovered, testifying to a whole community of *pistores* buried in this area (Coates-Stephens 2004: 21–30). Eurysaces' tomb style thus reflects not only his life, but also its immediate environment, blurring the line between workshop and tomb, between life and death, within an area which was itself not just a zone of the dead, but indeed semi-industrialised.

What visitors entering or leaving Rome perceived in the Porta Maggiore area was thus something of a snapshot of Roman society: a spectrum ranging from wealthy freedman through to humble mill worker, *collegia* and senatorial slave. At the same time what was also on view was the potential for advancement and wealth that Roman society brought. The slave could become the wealthy freedman, and the means to achieve that (the working mills), as well as the people to whom this message perhaps meant most, surrounded the funerary testimonies of those who had achieved it. While this message may have been welcome to those of lower status, the effect on Roman citizen elite visitors travelling past Eurysaces' tomb was most probably quite different. The construction of such ornate tombs set up by freedmen (and women, as we saw in Pompeii) during the course of the Republic (cf. Pliny *Natural History* 33.135) could have deterred Roman citizen elites from choosing the same form of burial commemoration (Zanker 1975; Duncan-Jones 1982: 127–31; Hope 2000b: 159; 2001; 2009: 164). This zone could thus have been a source of both inspiration and exasperation for those with different stakes in Roman society, located at the junction of two roads, which were specifically associated with the bringing of provisions and foodstuffs from the fertile eastern hinterland of Rome (Malmberg and Bjur 2011: 364).

Not all roads leading into Rome offered such a snapshot of vibrant urban life. Recent work on the *necropoleis* that lined the Via Triumphalis (Figure 3.8), on the other side of the Tiber from the Campus Martius, has shown how Republican tombs lined the first stretch of this road, which passed through a very inhospitable, marshy, uncivilised landscape (Liverani and Spinola 2010: 142). The very opposite impression to that of the Porta Maggiore was thus created: a reminder not of the economic success and dynamic society of Rome, but of Rome's continuing struggle to dominate and overcome the difficulties surrounding it.

At the same time, Rome's increasing investment in tombs further and further away from the city within more hospitable parts of the landscape, together with its increasing suburban development, look like signs of growing Roman confidence in the security of its hold over the wider landscape (cf. Purcell 1987: 32, 40; von Hesberg 1994: 157; Mouritsen 1997). An observant foreign contemporary, Dionysius of Halicarnassus, remarked how the endless extent of Rome's tombs along its roads mirrored the endlessness of the Roman world itself (Dion. Hal. 4.13.4–5, cf. Ov. *Fast.* 2.684). No tomb displays this sense of power and connectivity more visibly than that of Caecilia Metella, from the mid-first century BC, on the Via Appia. Her tomb, on a 7-metre-high square base, which had a cylindrical tower tomb above with a diameter of 29 m and height of 11 m, stands not at any random point on the Via Appia, but very particularly on the crest of a hill which the road passes over about a mile away from the city of Rome (von Hesberg 1994: 40). Such a position not only guaranteed the tomb visibility for itself, but also placed it at a point on the road at which the visitor was best able to get a glimpse of the city ahead (Figure 3.9).

Roads provided space to be travelled through, and the natural landscape through which they passed, by rising and falling, added 'moments' of greater and lesser perspective (cf. Juvenal's description of the 'hilly' Via Latina: Juv. *Sat.* 5.5). Caecilia Metella's tomb stands at one of those 'moments' in which a traveller along the road may well have been able to glimpse Rome along the 'tunnel' created by the increasing number of tombs lining the Via Appia, which opened up into the city through the gap between the Aventine and Caelian hills. Thus this tomb, while distant from the city, was, through its particular location, actively connected to it. With the addition of further circular tombs along the Via Appia over time (both before and after Metella's), and of course in Rome itself, particularly Augustus' and Hadrian's mausolea, that sense of connection only increased. The visitor was drawn into the city through being provided with 'moments' of increased perspective twinned with recognisable architectural links between centre and periphery.

After Augustus

The burial of Augustus in his mausoleum on the Campus Martius (cf. Figure 3.8) had profound effects on burial at Rome (cf. von Hesberg and Panciera 1994). Many scholars have pointed to the drop in tomb elaboration, as well as the avoidance of prominent areas in Rome such as the Campus Martius, and even of Rome altogether, as evidence of the inability/ lack of desire to compete with the emperor. Elites chose more frequently to be buried away not just from Rome but indeed from cities more generally, preferring instead their own estates (cf. Bodel 1997; Hope 2009: 178; Várhelyi 2010: 170), as had indeed always been an option (e.g. Scipio Africanus: Dyson 1992: 144). Some competition did, however, continue, both in Rome and across the Empire, either through emulation of the emperors' own tomb choice (e.g. Toynbee 1971: 143, 156; Davies 1977: 18), or through the *cursus honorum* recorded by elites (particularly senators) on their epitaphs (Eck 1998: 38–40; Várhelyi 2010: 175).

Yet certain tombs in Rome continued to stand out, on what Davies has termed 'the lunatic fringe' (1977: 18). The most interesting of these is that of Caius Cestius, whose pyramid tomb was constructed near the Porta Ostiensis in AD 11–12 (Ridley 1996; Várhelyi 2010: 168). At 36-metre-high, and without access to the internal funeral chamber, Cestius' pyramid was a monument to be seen rather than used for later funeral commemoration (Figures 3.8, 3.9). It provided a very different impression of the city from that of the Porta Maggiore area: a city where inspiration for Cestius' pyramid tomb architecture reflected Rome's increasing power in far-off areas of the Mediterranean. Nor was Cestius' the only pyramid tomb in Rome; another (known as *the Sepulcrum Scipionis* although its actual owner remains anonymous) was constructed in the same period in the area of the Vatican *necropoleis*, near the Via Cornelia and Via Triumphalis (Liverani and Spinola 2010: 18).

At other routes into the city, this sense of Roman power was also on display. Along the Via Portuensis (Figure 3.8), the bodyguard of the Julio-Claudian emperors were buried as part of an intentionally united tomb community, since all the burials conform to a standard tomb design (Hope 1998: 192; 2000a: 111). It was perhaps no accident that the Via Ostiensis and Via Portuensis, both leading to Rome's port and port town, held monuments underlining both Rome's foreign trading connections and its military strength. Yet Rome's military pride was also on view at the Via Tiburtina (Figure 3.8), where twenty tombstones have been found commemorating members of the Praetorian guard in what may have also been a military burial area (Durry 1938: 60–3; Hope 1998: 192). Such a position, not far from the *Castra Praetoria* in Rome, again brought a particular community together in life and death, representing a particular flank of Roman society to those using that particular road to enter Rome.

Other paths into Rome changed in character under the influence of Imperial Rome. The tombs around the Via Triumphalis (Figure 3.8), which, during Republican times, had clung to the road surrounded by marshy inhospitable ground, began, in the Augustan period, to be placed just below the hill summit of the Galea area, giving them greater panoramic visibility (Liverani and Spinola 2010: 142–5). More and more burial areas were begun on the different slopes of the hills around the Via Cornelia and the Via Triumphalis, nestled in between the *Horti Agrippinae* and *Domitiae* (Liverani and Spinola 2010: 142, 161–4, 197–212, 214–228). These burial areas required terracing of the hillside, and were as a result rather haphazardly spaced. The area was used mainly by working-class Romans, as well as the freedmen and slaves of the Julio-Claudian family (particularly the Santa Rosa area: Liverani and Spinola 2010: 216, 228).

With the development of this area under Nero, and particularly the construction of his circus, the number of tombs here continued to increase. Yet the whole area remained extremely unstable. The tombs, particularly those clustered onto the hillsides, were sometimes catastrophically affected by landslides, which, certainly in the Flavian period, entirely destroyed large parts of the different *necropoleis*. They were subsequently not reconstructed, but levelled and built over by new burials (Liverani and Spinola 2010: 164, 216). This area may thus have offered visibility for the lower classes of Roman society, but it came at the price of uncertain longevity. To visitors arriving at Rome here, what was on display was not just a much less 'organised' and regularised Rome, but a much harsher one, in which both nature and man destroyed and built over the tombs of the city's previous occupants.

Other tombs at other roads, however, had no such problems with longevity. The earliest tombs, which had clustered at the junction of the Via Appia and Via Latina, were all for important Republican families, including the Scipios, the Claudii Marcelli, Servilii and Metelli (cf. Cic. *Tusc.* 1.7.13). Throughout the period of the Roman Empire, such tombs were not forgotten, but only increased in importance as places of pilgrimage and reflection on an idealised notion of Rome's past (Sen. *Ep.* 86.1; Livy 38.53). Nor was the Via Appia the only place for an encounter with history: other tombs, like that of the Crassi at the Porta Salaria (Figure 3.8), survived in the Roman landscape. Yet the connection to the past at the Via Appia proved attractive for the emperors: several columbaria within the Aurelian walls near this location were reserved for people connected with the imperial family (Toynbee 1971: 113).

At the Porta Maggiore (Figure 3.8), the once full burial grounds of the Esquiline were eventually covered over by up to 4 m of earth excavated from Trajan's forum (Robinson 1992: 125) and reformed as *horti* (cf. Hor. *Sat.* 1.8.7–16, where he jokes that the gardens of the rich used to be the burial ground of slaves). At Trajan's Forum, Trajan would eventually himself be voted burial at the base of his victory column in a strong break with normal funeral tradition (and funerary architecture). Subsequent construction at the Porta Maggiore entailed imperial confiscation of the area (including the *horti*), as well as destruction of at least one large Republican tomb in the area; it also entailed the requisitioning of columbaria once used by aristocratic families, such as the Statilii and Arruntii, for imperial slaves from the time of Claudius onwards (Coates-Stephens 2004: 20, 60–107). This area, once the flagship of freedman entrepreneurial success, now boasted both Eurysaces' baker tomb and the tombs of the community that served the emperor. The sea change in power over the course of Rome's history was thus manifestly on display.

The second century AD onwards

In the second century AD, the *Horti Agrippinae* near the Via Cornelia and Via Triumphalis were closed (Figure 3.8) and given over to funerary use, as were the *Horti Domitiae*, in the middle of which Hadrian built his Mausoleum. The number of tombs in this area expanded massively as a result (Liverani and Spinola 2010: 42). Yet, in contrast to the Via Appia, where successive emperors had commandeered previous structures, here the same thing happened to those of the Emperor Nero. During the second and third centuries AD, his Circus was built over by tombs, including one monumental tomb 30 m in diameter (Liverani and Spinola 2010: 19, 42).

The perception offered by the tombs at the different entrances to the city of Rome continued to change, most dramatically with the construction of the Aurelian wall from AD 271 (Figure 3.8). It has been calculated that up to 10 per cent of the Aurelian wall was composed of earlier structures which it had incorporated (Richmond 1930: 11), including several monumental tombs. Tomb monuments were built into the gates at Porta Salaria, Nomentana, Flaminia and Appia. At the Porta Maggiore, Eurysaces' tomb was now completely hidden from view, as it was turned into a central gate tower (Todd 1978: 28). The history of this area as a place of enterprise and social dynamism was thus completely rewritten. No longer were both stories – those of freedman entrepreneurship and of imperial power – on display. This area could now be perceived only as a place of burial for the imperial household dominated by imperial construction. The pyramid of Cestius at the Via Ostiensis (Figures 3.8, 3.9) was also enclosed within the walls, although its great height ensured that it still remained visible as part of the wall structure (even after the walls were increased in height in the fifth century AD). Here, the resulting perception must thus have been different from that at Porta Maggiore. Rome's 'lunatic fringe' burial history was still very much on view, even if now employed as a defensive structure, finally incorporated into an imperial monument (cf. Day 2011: 79).

Approaching Rome through its tombs

Such a brief survey of Roman tombs is necessarily incomplete (in terms of both its chronological and its geographical frame). Recent discoveries, for example, of several thousand unmonumentalised graves of the *plebs urbana* dating between the first and the fourth centuries AD, predominantly located on the east side of Rome, between the Via Appia and the Via Tiburtina, have done much to correct our focus on, and impression of, Rome as a city only of monumental tombs, and in turn to contextualise the experience of visitors who were confronted with such a wide spectrum of commemoration (cf. Catalano 2008; Gowland and Garnsey 2010). We may never be able to comprehend the full effect on visitors of walking past so many tombs along the roads to Rome (Figure 3.8). Nor indeed were the roads the only places to find them: the Tiber too was called the 'river of tombs' (Plin. *Ep.* 8.17). Yet what is clear is that arrival along a particular path into the city could create a particular perception of Rome for the visitor, an impression that changed over time as the *necropoleis* themselves changed. Different flanks of Rome's identity and place in the wider landscape were highlighted by the particular collections and dynamics of tombs at, and leading to, a particular gate. Depending on where (and when) you arrived, Rome could be a city of enterprise and social dynamism, a place of historic longevity and heroic simplicity, a place of supreme, 'lunatic' architectural elaboration, a place in which the memory of powerful individuals could be eradicated, a place which struggled to dominate the natural landscape and in which even tombs were subject to destruction by natural and human forces, or a place that comfortably portrayed its power both over far-flung parts of the Mediterranean region and closer to home. Nor, as has recently been emphasised, would these impressions have applied only to people leaving, and arriving in, the city: streets were, after all, often a 'destination in their own right' (Holleran 2011: 251) for inhabitants of the city. Moreover, the particular locations of many of these 'snapshots', especially those of Rome's power, were often not, I would argue, accidental. The destination of roads like the Via Ostiensis and Via Portuensis, for example, given the kinds of visitors who would, as a result, be using them, meant that a demonstration of Roman power at these entrances to the city was particularly appropriate. Equally, the fact that the bodyguard of the Julio-Claudian emperors were buried at the Via Portuensis, while the freedmen and slaves of that dynasty were buried around the Via Triumphalis, suggests that Imperial families may have sought to spread different parts of that unit in death around the city, creating an impression of their omnipresent involvement with every aspect of the city of Rome. The location of Rome's tombs at its different entrances thus not only reflected the different flanks of its identity as a city, but also actively articulated particular kinds of identity to particular visitors in particular places.

CONCLUSION

This chapter has argued that, while all tombs were subject to a series of wider trends already identified in tomb scholarship (burial regulations, burial pattern changes, periods of increasing elaboration and competition and the development of different tomb styles), a study of the location of tombs shows how the trajectories of development and the character of tomb communities could be perceptibly different as between the various entrance ways into a particular city. As a result, a single community offered up, through its numerous *necropoleis*, multiple aspects of its identity to visitors arriving at different points; such characterisations were sometimes actively and indeed purposefully linked to the destination or origin of that particular road.

Conclusion

In turn, these different 'flanks' of identity put forward through different spaces at a particular city also contributed to a sense of overall difference between cities. That could be achieved through something as straightforward as a particular city tomb style, but more importantly such differences could also be enunciated through different spatial dynamics of tomb development. So, for example, tomb elaboration took hold most quickly at Pompeii, followed by Ostia and finally by Rome. Equally, the social 'mixing' of elite, freedman and city immigrant happened faster at Pompeii (particularly in the case of their integration outside the Herculaneum gate) than outside the Porta Romana at Ostia (where the 'social revolution' did not occur in full until the second century AD). In addition, the provision of space for future generations of a family within tombs became the norm at Pompeii and Rome much earlier than it did at Ostia (again, not until after the second century AD). As a result, subtle distinctions – not just in their architectural funerary styles, nor simply in their relative pace of civic development, but also in their particular social dynamics and attitudes – could be gleaned through their *necropoleis*.

The centre and periphery model, which posits a tendency to imitate Rome as the centre and thus achieve a portrait of cultural similarity across the Roman world, has been widely accepted amongst scholars of Roman culture. To what extent were the differences between tomb communities commonly perceptible and to what extent did they support or undercut a wider sense of unity and similarity across the Roman world? A lot depended on not only the nature of the tomb space but also the visitor. Many visitors would perhaps have paid little attention to these tombs as they pressed on to the city, or engaged with them only enough to have perceived their general similarity (they are all tombs, after all); many would have seen enough of a city to know about the different aspects of its identity offered at its different entrances and thus be able to contextualise each particular characterisation within a more general pattern of similarity. Equally, the similar underlying dynamics of tomb style, epitaph and sculpture will have generated for many a sufficiently well understood 'way in' to reading the tomb communities at different cities, and that, in turn, would have contributed to a sense of their general similarity and a perception of unified 'Roman' culture. That similarity will have been reinforced in certain cases by the ways in which tombs linked themselves to other tombs, to spaces and structures within the city they surrounded, as well as occasionally to styles of tombs from other cities, particularly Rome.

On the other hand, such *necropoleis* could be very alienating and frightening spaces, both for residents and visitors, Romans and foreigners (Figure 3.10). For those entirely foreign to Roman *necropoleis* (e.g. new

Above: view of tombs from outside Nucerian Gate, Pompeii.
Right: view of tombs from far end of street leading to Herculaneum Gate, Pompeii

Figure 3.10 View of 'alienating' streets of tombs at Nucerian and Herculaneum gates, Pompeii

members of the Empire, outsiders visiting etc.) that alienation could have been generated simply from the crushing mass of tombs, particularly on the roads to Rome; this must have overwhelmed visitors, especially those only newly made aware of the military power of Rome and now confronted with a whole society of its dead crowding round them. Tunnels of vision through to the city of the living were punctuated by 'moments' of greater perspective thanks to the undulating nature of the landscape, which in turn only gave a greater impression of the mass, power and wealth of Rome (cf. Dion. Hal. 4.13.4–5; Ov. *Fast.* 2.684)

Yet that sense of alienation, I would argue, could also have applied to Roman citizens. Tombs provided important physical spaces not only in which to return to honour dead relatives (e.g. at Parentalia or Feralia festivals), but more generally for people to reflect on their own lives (cf. Petron. *Sat.* 61–2; Cic. *Leg.* 2.4). But *necropoleis* existed, after all, also within liminal, dubious, physical locations stretching away from cities through the suburbs and countryside (cf. Mart. *Epigrams* 1.34.8). They were physically dangerous places,

Conclusion 109

where you could be robbed or killed. They reminded you threateningly of your mortality (cf. Varro *Ling.* 6.49). They were places that, thanks to their overwhelming sense of death and foreboding, may have undermined your desire to undertake military service and civic duties (cf. App. *B. Civ.* 1.43). These were clearly not, thus, always welcoming places, even for Romans.

Moreover, especially for Roman visitors arriving at different cities who were well versed in reading tombs, who chose to engage with them, perhaps by taking up many tombs' invitations to sit and pass time amongst them, the differences between different entrance points into a city and between cities could have resulted in a heightened sense of alienation from that community. Not simply would visitors have seen things being done differently (they may well have expected that). But, as tomb communities developed large numbers of more insistently individualised tombs and groupings that reflected more strongly the particular social dynamics of that community, visitors were reminded more and more that they were not part of that community. As the identities presented by these tombs became more crystallised, their communities more defined, complex and individual, the more was the visitor alienated from them (cf. Figure 3.10). Unlike the community of the living to which they were journeying, in which visitors could carve themselves a role, this stone community of the dead was closed off to them unless they became not only a fully fledged part of that living community but also rich enough to merit and afford – or worthy enough to be honoured with – a place among its tombs (Figure 3.10).

Recent scholarship has suggested that we need to understand Roman funerary art more as putting distance between the living and the dead than as interlinking the two (Vout forthcoming), and has encouraged us to focus on the emotional impact of cities (Betts 2011: 118). As a result, I would argue that the spatial development and dynamics of tomb communities at different cities need also to be understood not just as offering a recognisably 'Roman' pattern of societal behaviour, but also potentially as contributing to a sense of alienation and distance between not only the living and the dead, between the city and its surrounding city of the dead, but also between Romans and non-Romans, and, even more importantly, between citizens of the Roman world itself. As has recently been emphasised, walking in the Roman world could be a process of learning (O'Sullivan 2011: 97–115). So, in commemorating their dead so insistently within spaces that had to be traversed in order to reach the cities of the living they served, the Romans created a recognisably Roman landscape, which, at the same time, forced them to learn about the many divisions that still lay within it.

CHAPTER 4

A spatial approach to relationships between colony and metropolis: Syracuse and Corinth

INTRODUCTION

The case-studies so far have focused on particular kinds of physical space (civic, sacred, funerary). This chapter, in contrast, outlines a significantly different conception of space as something both physical and perceptual. Its focus is on how we can understand the changing proximity or distance of the relationship (the perceptual 'space') between particular physical spaces. This is to be done by examining not only the way in which that perceptual space is constructed in the literary, epigraphic and material sources, but also how the nature and experience of each physical space themselves contribute to the texture of the spatial relationship between them. The case-study here will be one of the most often discussed relationships between poleis in the ancient world, that of metropolis and colony.

Studies of colonisation have advanced dramatically in the last three decades. The traditional portrayal of colonisation (cf. Bérard 1957; Mossé 1970) as a series of dramatic events occurring in the eighth to sixth centuries BC when mainland Greek cities, often pushed by land overcrowding or some kind of internal stasis, sought a solution (often in conjunction with a consultation of the oracle at Delphi) in the colonisation of a new settlement around the Mediterranean, has been severely criticised. In 1998, Osborne argued that the term colonisation should be abandoned (Osborne 1998), and in 2005 Purcell commented that 'colonization was a category in crisis' (Purcell 2005: 115). The resulting rethink has led to a much more dynamic interpretation of both the context and the process of founding colonial settlements (and subsequent further foundations made by the colonies themselves), as well as of the role that the concept of 'colonisation' played in literature and later Greek history.

The scholarly characterisation of the relationship between metropolis and colony has evolved, particularly with regard to western Greek colonies, from a unidirectional one, seeing the colony as a mirror image of the metropolis (Hüttl 1929; Dunbabin 1948: 17, 49, 267; Woodhead 1962: 17), to expressions of caution over such a blanket description (Graham 1983), to the acceptance of different kinds of relationships between different metropolis/colony pairings (Finley 1979: 20). The result, however, has been to make such relationships very unfashionable as a subject for study (cf. Morel 1983: 124). As a result, despite some discussion of the impact of the colony on developments in the mother city (cf. Malkin 1987: 263; 1994a: 2; Antonaccio 1999: 113), the tendency has been to downplay the importance of the relationship (e.g. Salmon 1984: 394). As Snodgrass put it in 1994, 'the description of, say, Syracuse as a Corinthian city, need mean little more than that the oikist and his immediate entourage came from Corinth' (Snodgrass 1994: 2).

The spatial approach in this chapter seeks to reinvigorate studies of the metropolis–colony relationship by offering a new way into the complex dynamics involved in the construction of that relationship over time. I will examine how the two spaces of colony and metropolis were defined, characterised and enunciated through time in terms of their material culture, inscriptional output and literary characterisation, and, how, as a result, this created a perception of similarity and difference between them as spaces within the wider landscape. In addition, I will examine the ways in which different kinds of links between the two spaces were actively constructed (and denied) at different points. As a result, I will investigate the extent to which both these passive and active constructions of similarity and difference changed the understanding of the perceptual space between the two poleis, and in turn fed into (and impacted on) wider networks of relationships present across the Mediterranean. My case-study in this chapter will be that of Corinth and Syracuse. This is chosen not only because these two sites have a good range of different kinds of sources covering their history from the eighth century BC to the second century AD, making a closer investigation of their continuing relationship possible, but also because this colony–metropolis pairing is often cited as a key example in the debate over such relationships.

SYRACUSE AND CORINTH IN THE ARCHAIC PERIOD

Urban layout

Syracuse was founded by Corinth, according to the later literary sources (e.g. Thuc. 6.3.2), in 733 BC (for some discussion on the date of foundation see Miller 1970). Traditional representations of the colonial foundation process characterise it as the imposition of a new settlement onto a 'virgin' landscape, or one populated only by indigenous groups (cf. Figure 4.1). The reality for Syracuse, however, was more complicated. Archaeological evidence points

112 *A spatial approach to relationships between colony and metropolis*

Figure 4.1 Syracuse and the surrounding region

not to an empty landscape, nor to one inhabited solely by an indigenous population, but instead to a landscape in which much of the peninsula around and to the north of it had acted as a trading station from the Bronze Age onwards, involving contacts ranging from Greece to Syro-Palestine. As a result, it was home to a much more cosmopolitan community (Holloway 1983: 264; Leighton 1999: 234–68).

At the same time, excavations on Ortygia (Figure 4.1: the small island which formed the centre of ancient Syracuse) have revealed areas of Greek settlement which seemed to have been violently thrust into (and built on top of) previous communities (Holloway 1983: 269; Malkin 2002: 201). In particular, the sacred area of the later Athena sanctuary was imposed over the remains of 'native oval' huts: a 'self-willed, deliberate choice, probably based on a criterion of centrality' (Malkin 1987: 177). This strong investment in, and imposition on, the landscape by Syracuse' founders underlines the 'unprecedentedly planned, deliberate and calculated nature of the movement to settle in the west ... it was building to last and building for success' (Snodgrass 1994: 1). Indeed, it is possible that such strong settlement development at Syracuse provided a spur towards urban development in its mother city, as part of the wider argument that colonies affected polis development in 'Old Greece' (cf. Mertens 1996: 322).

Yet to what extent can the early urban spatial development of the settlements of Syracuse and Corinth be compared in the century after Syracuse's foundation, and if they can, how similar or different were they? The first problem with undertaking such a comparison is the state of our evidence. We have little idea of the form of settlement space in Corinth in this period (cf. Figure 4.2), not only because of the city's destruction in 146 BC, but, more importantly, since it was not fully urbanised before the seventh century BC (cf. Salmon 1984; Malkin 1994a: 1; Mertens 1996: 322). Morgan has argued, however, that the wealth of objects found at the Corinthian sanctuary of Hera at Perachora (Figure 4.2), dating back to the ninth and eighth centuries BC, should be understood as underlining early Corinthian wealth (Morgan 1988: 336), and that Corinth's later urban expansion presupposes 'a range of domestic difficulties and aspirations' associated with, amongst other things, significant earlier pressure on land (Morgan 1990: 164).

What of Syracuse? Normally, the availability of space in which to expand at the site of a new foundation allowed for a much wider, more regularised and more egalitarian urban plan to be put in place than is in evidence for many metropoleis which in contrast emerged gradually within a more competitive landscape (see the regularised settlement patterns at Megara Hyblaia: Malkin 2002; see also Selinus: Mertens 2010). Yet the degree to which Syracuse's early urban space complies with this model (and thus its similarity to and difference from both other Sicilian colonial foundations and its mother city) is hotly debated.

On the one hand, some scholars argue that Syracuse's earliest houses were grouped together in naturally commanding positions, which allowed them to hold sway over a much wider area. Such an urban structure would make it, while very different from other nearby 'colonial' foundations, very similar to the way in which its metropolis Corinth is thought to have developed (e.g. Di Vita 1990: 349). On the other hand, van Dommelen has argued that Syracuse's earliest settlement actually followed a very similar pattern to Megara Hyblaia, with a regularised urban town layout, incorporating both housing and cultivation within a regular street plan, as opposed to the much denser, more truly urban, spatial style of Phoenician settlements seen, for example, in Sardinia (van Dommelen 2005: 154).

This wide divergence of opinion on what early Syracuse looked like is in part due to the fact that much of the earliest civic settlement at Syracuse remains unexcavated beneath the modern city. As a result, it is difficult to put forward a view with any degree of certainty regarding the extent to which Syracuse's urban spatial layout linked it either to the many neighbouring colonial settlements constructed in the eighth to

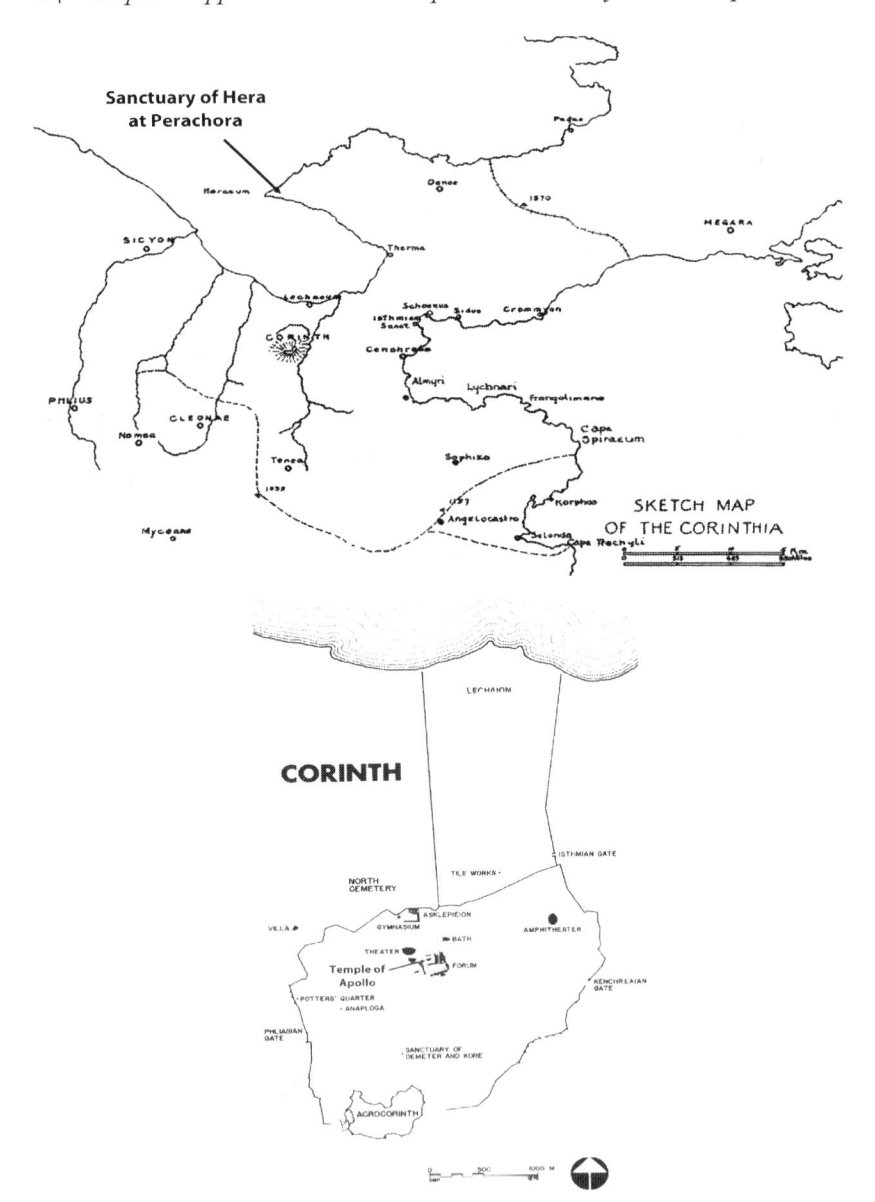

114 *A spatial approach to relationships between colony and metropolis*

Figure 4.2 Corinth and the Corinthia

sixth centuries BC, or, rather more unusually perhaps, to the spatial development of its metropolis.

Architecture, art and trade

If the urban spatial layout of Syracuse and Corinth does not prove to be an arena in which satisfactory comparisons can be made, what can we say about the varying conceptions of architecture and architectural space developed in the two cities? The geographical region around Syracuse is renowned for the fact that it produces a limestone that closely resembles Greek *poros* stone (cf. Mertens 1990: 374). While this may well, as a result, have produced built structures that had a greater visual affinity with their Greek mainland counterparts, there were also several crucial points of difference between Syracuse's architecture and that of its metropolis that would have impacted on the sense of distance between them.

In contrast to the Doric temple of Apollo constructed at Corinth soon after the middle of the sixth century BC (Dinsmoor 1927: 87), at Syracuse, through to the end of the sixth century, a very 'Syracusan' style of architecture developed. For example, the style of much of the surviving archaic revetment material from the early sixth century BC is unique to Syracuse (Barletta 1983: 71). The temple of Apollo, constructed on Ortygia *c*.565 BC (Figure 4.1), shows an 'independence from rigid specifications of mainland Doric models' (Barletta 1983: 73). Coulton has moreover argued for the creation of a specific 'Sicilian rule' for the design of the temple stylobate in contrast to the rule for the Greek mainland (Coulton 1974: 82–3). In addition, Sicilian builders made a particularly emphatic use of stone: the stone columns are huge and accompanied by a dedicatory inscription in which, uniquely, the architect specifically responsible for the columns boasts about them as 'beautiful works' (Berve and Gruben 1963: 416; Mertens 1990: 378). During the course of the sixth century, the Eastern Mediterranean influence on Syracusan architecture increased substantially. The temple of Zeus Olympius (*c*.555 BC), the stepped altar of Athena in the Athenaion on Ortygia (550–525 BC), along with the never-completed Ionic temple parallel to the later temple of Athena (525–500 BC), all demonstrate significant Eastern, particularly Samian and Ephesian, influences (Barletta 1983: 78, 86–8; Holloway 1983: 271; Cerchiai et al. 2004: 206).

It is not only the style of the architectural elements that creates this very individual Syracusan look, but the overall conception of architectural temple space as well. The internal architecture of the temple of Apollo at Syracuse, for example, was so arranged as to maximise open space (Mertens 1990: 379), in a way very different from that seen on the mainland (Mertens 1996: 324), and particularly in the temple of Apollo at Corinth (cf. Figure 4.2). Yet this may be more than simply a 'willingness to accept external influences' (Mertens 1990: 383). Such a change in the architectural space of the temple has been explained by a possible difference in ritual practice from that of the mainland (Barletta 1983: 75). It has also been attributed to a subtle shift in the purpose of monumental sacred architecture. Whereas monumentalisation in mainland Greece arguably signalled the central importance of these settlements for the surrounding region (Snodgrass 1991), such monumentalisation in the colonies is likely to have been more associated with 'colonial self-representation and the narrow local focus of the settler community' (cf. Morgan and Hall 1996: 214–5; van Dommelen 2005: 163).

The difficulty with much of this comparative evidence is that such traits are often presented as representative of 'Sicily' and the Greek 'mainland', rather than being specific to Syracuse or Corinth. Yet Barletta (1983: 95) has argued that 'such diversity in the method of expression of the ionic component in Sicily is nowhere so marked as at Syracuse'. Syracuse may, therefore, have been, during the sixth century BC, a space in which it was particularly easy to perceive a difference in style, as well as approach to architecture and architectural space, from those adopted in mainland Greece and, in turn, from Syracuse's metropolis.

Architecture was not the only arena in which a greater dissimilarity and distance can be noted in the perceptual space between colony and metropolis in the sixth century BC. The distinguishing Ionian influence, which begins to wane in Syracusan architecture after the end of the sixth century BC, continued strongly in other realms of visual art (Barletta 1983: 91), for example in the creation of draped kouroi statues. Graham (1983: 13) once argued that Syracuse's artistic output was almost totally influenced by Corinth, but Bookidis, in her recent discussion of Syracusan and Corinthian archaic sculpture, both underlines the difficulty of making an accurate comparison because of the lack of examples and claims that Syracuse's artistic style demonstrates 'less emphasis on [Syracuse's] colonial roots and greater freedom from the motherland' (Bookidis 1995: 256).

A similar picture of distance between metropolis and colony is also emerging as regards the general trade in material goods between Syracuse and Corinth in this period. Dunbabin originally postulated that Syracuse imported much Corinthian material and was heavily dependent on Corinth (Dunbabin 1948: 61). Yet both Finley and Shepherd have argued for a mutual flow of goods (in particular the export from Syracuse of particular types of fibulae), as well as for much less dependence of Syracuse on her metropolis, which was receiving only as much Corinthian pottery as Gela, a settlement founded by

Rhodians (Finley 1979: 33; Shepherd 2005b: 32). In contrast, though, Corinthian pottery did continue to be imported and used in Syracuse for much longer than in any other of the Western Greek cities (Sakellariou 1996: 183). It is impossible to know whether this should be interpreted as indicating a greater attachment to those forms of pottery, or perhaps a greater emphasis on the need to continue business with their metropolis. Yet the overall indications provided by the architecture, other visual art and trade patterns of Corinth and Syracuse in this period do create an impression of easily perceptible difference between the physical nature and 'lived' character of the two poleis, which in turn suggests a much more distant physical and perceptual spatial relationship between them than has often been acknowledged.

Religious practice and burial

Recent studies have underlined the importance of the religious landscape in the perception of a relationship between two settlements (e.g. Shepherd 2000: 55), but once again the difficulty is in interpreting particular activities in terms of their impact on that relationship: for example, does the establishment of an oikist cult in a colony signify proximity to or independence from the metropolis? (Malkin 1987: 189). The religious landscapes of Syracuse and Corinth are, perhaps unsurprisingly, complex. While most of the divinities worshipped at Corinth (excluding its hero cults) can be found also worshipped in Syracuse, there are two notable exceptions: Hera and Aphrodite (Reichert-Südbeck 2000: 180 (hero cults), 297 (Hera and Aphrodite)). Neither of these goddesses, from the surviving evidence, was heavily worshipped in Syracuse in comparison to their growing importance in Corinth, attested by the Heraion at Perachora and the well-known Aphrodite sanctuaries in Corinth and on Acrocorinth (cf. Figure 4.2; Will 1955a: 223). This is particularly revealing, given that in Syracuse's own colonies the worship of Aphrodite is well attested, and suggests that the religious landscape of Syracuse was different not only from its own metropolis but also from that of its dependents in the surrounding area (Reichert-Südbeck 2000: 33–56). At the same time, certain deities received heavier emphasis in one city (e.g. Poseidon was more heavily emphasised at Corinth), and other divinities underwent subtle shifts in the form of their worship, particularly through processes of acculturation with local deities (e.g. at Syracuse, Demeter and Artemis take on attributes of local river and spring gods).

An even wider gap in the religious interaction between Syracuse and Corinth appears when one considers the active participation of these two cities in each other's sanctuaries. Kilian-Dirlmeier's analysis (Kilian-Dirlmeier

1985) of dedications at the sanctuaries of Olympia, Perachora, Pherai and Heraion on Samos for the eighth and seventh centuries BC, while not allowing specific reference to Syracuse, does offer a picture of 'Italian' interest in these sanctuaries. At Perachora near Corinth (Figure 4.2), the percentage of Italian finds is low (2.5 per cent), slightly lower than that of Thessalian Pherai (2.6 per cent) and not significantly higher than that of the Heraion on Samos (1.7 per cent), and the goods are restricted to a narrow range of items (mostly fibulae). Most scholars have interpreted this lack of Italian presence as symbolising the absence of active effort particularly by Syracuse to form a strong relationship with its metropolis, and as evidence for a sluggish trading relationship between the two cities, since a more active engagement between the two would have resulted in more dedications by visiting traders at Perachora.

The stark contrast is with Olympia, where 8.9 per cent of goods from this period are 'Italian'. In addition, their range is much wider: armour, jewellery and other metal artefacts, all of which can be paralleled in west Greek sanctuaries or graves (cf. Shepherd 1995: 74; 2000: 67). Indeed, Syracuse, along with many other west Greek cities, will continue to have a very high profile at Olympia, and a comparatively high profile at Delphi, throughout the Archaic and Classical Periods. The vast proportion of treasuries built at Olympia (including one by Syracuse) come from colonial cities (cf. Shepherd 2000: 68; Scott 2010: 163). The presence of Italian Greek athletes at Olympic and Pythian contests is attested from their appearance on the Olympic victory lists from an early date (e.g. 648 BC Lygdamis of Syracuse, 572–558 BC, Tisander of Sicilian Naxos, who won the boxing four times at Olympia and four times at Delphi). Corinth of course was active at Delphi and Olympia too, particularly under the tyrants Cypselus and his son Periander; indeed, there will be a marked shift in Corinthian interest from Delphi to Olympia following the First 'Sacred War' (cf. Snodgrass 2001; Scott 2010: 44, 52, 152). Thus we should not understand the Syracusans' presence at Olympia as a case of avoiding Corinth, but rather as an active choice to present themselves on a platform which gave them the potential for equal billing. As Shepherd puts it, this is evidence of 'self-assertion, not nostalgia' (Shepherd 1995: 75).

Shepherd's work has also been invaluable in illuminating the burial practices at Syracuse. Her original PhD dissertation, using material from the north cemetery at Syracuse, makes clear the different burial practices and grave offerings attested in Syracuse and Corinth from the centuries immediately after Syracuse's foundation (Shepherd 1993: 62–72, 105–110, 150). This material was recapped in her 1995 article, which underlines 'a very pronounced deviation from the standard set by Corinth' (Shepherd 1995: 54). Such deviations include the Syracusan tendency to place bodies in the grave in the extended position (in contrast to Corinthian contracted-body practice), the occurrence of multiple burials in the same tomb at Syracuse (again, unheard of in Corinth), and the much higher percentage of metal goods in Syracusan graves compared to those in Corinth. A reverse difference is the construction of tombs with space for multiple generations at Corinth, but not at Syracuse. These differences underline Syracuse's position in the local landscape: many of its burial practices were adopted from local tradition (cf. Shepherd 1999). For Shepherd, this evidence does 'not show tight connections with the mother-city, but ... a sharp distinction and assertion of cultural independence' (Shepherd 1995: 73). More recently, she has argued that the coherent nature of burial practice at Syracuse in turn also makes it impossible to tell whether it is indigenous people, Syracusans, Corinthians or indeed Greeks from other parts of the Greek world who are being buried there. Such coherence may be the result of an active desire for a unique, independent identity not attributable to any one particular heritage (Shepherd 2005a: 132). Overall, once again, the religious and burial record suggests perceptible wide divergence in the nature and experience of the physical spaces of these two settlements, which in turn contributed to the active articulation of distance between Corinth and Syracuse that is also noticeable particularly in their religious interaction at different key sanctuaries.

The relationship of Syracuse and Corinth in context

To sum up so far: the relationship between Syracuse and Corinth during the Archaic Period is, without doubt, complex and hard to interpret, given that we are reliant almost exclusively on the archaeological and occasional epigraphic evidence. Yet a picture is emerging, particularly through the architecture, art, religious and burial practices at Syracuse and Corinth, of a much more subtle and complex mixture of similarity and difference between these two spaces. This includes several active attempts, particularly on the part of Syracuse, to distinguish itself from its metropolis and at the same time to engage with Corinth on an equal footing. Those attempts, especially on the international stage at Delphi and Olympia, would have been perceived by a wide audience. They run counter to the traditional picture of a colony as a 'possession' of its metropolis.

How can an examination of the wider context of other Greek colonial spaces and relationships in this period help us understand better the particular nature of the Syracuse–Corinth relationship? We have already seen differences in the religious landscape between Syracuse and some of its own colonial foundations. A similar difference emerges in burial practice. The Syracusan settlement of Acrae, for example, shows evidence for only typical mainland Greek burial practice, as well as little native Sicel pottery or artefacts (Sjöqvist 1973: 37–8). So whereas Syracuse may have sought a coherent blend of Greek and local practice which became distinctively 'Syracusan', one of its own foundations appears content with traditional Greek mainland practices. Syracuse also shows distinct differences from other colonial foundations in the burial record. Megara Hyblaia in particular offers an inverse burial picture to that of Syracuse: multiple burials in the same grave stop at Syracuse soon after they had begun at Megara, a sign perhaps of the two cities striving for differentiation given their physical proximity (cf. Shepherd 1993: 108; Antonaccio 1999: 119–20; Hodos 2006: 115).

We can also begin to see differences in the way different Corinthian colonies related to their metropolis, particularly in the way they structured their administration. Corcyra, for instance, often compared with Syracuse because of their very close foundation dates, may well have had the same calendar as Corinth (Hadzis 1995), and certainly used the Corinthian alphabet in public inscriptions. While the evidence is too fragmentary for us to know whether Syracuse used Corinth's calendar, we do know that it did not use the Corinthian alphabet but its own Syracusan one in public inscriptions (Meiggs and Lewis 1988: No. 3; Arena 1998: 112–13).

The picture thus emerges in the Archaic Period of Syracuse not only absorbing influences from different parts of the Mediterranean but also actively constructing a significant sense of distance between itself and its metropolis, which was perceptible both in the characterisation of the space and practices of its own city and in its interactions with Corinth in Corinthian sanctuaries and on the international stage. It was a distance that in turn distinguished it not only from other Corinthian colonies and from its competitors in Sicily, but even from the way in which its own colonial foundations went about their business.

SYRACUSE AND CORINTH IN THE FIFTH CENTURY BC

Syracuse and Corinth in the material and epigraphic sources

The sense of both physical and perceptual similarity and difference between the spaces of Syracuse and mainland Greece was perpetuated within the space of Syracuse itself during the fifth century BC, particularly through architecture. The development of an identifiably Western Greek style continued in Syracuse as elsewhere in Sicily. The expansion of internal temple space continued to be a feature of architecture not just in Syracuse but also across many Sicilian Greek cities, which in turn necessitated new roofing systems and led perhaps to the developing use of the roof space itself (as witnessed by the construction of occasional staircases allowing access to the roof). At the same time, however, Syracuse differed from its Sicilian neighbours in adopting a very mainland Greek style of theatre construction in contrast to the multi-storey stages developed at both non-Greek settlements such as Segesta and Greek ones such as Tyndaris (Polacco et al. 1981; Mertens 1990: 382; Cerchiai et al. 2004: 210).

Syracuse further distinguished itself from its colonial neighbours, down to the time of the Athenians' Sicilian expedition, through its close relationship, particularly in the field of the art and architecture, not with its metropolis, but with Athens. Along with Syracuse's mainland-style theatre came an eagerness for Athenian tragedy. Aeschylus' *Aetnaeae* and *Persae* were performed in Syracuse during the fifth century BC (cf. Dearden 1990: 231–2). Important lyric poets who had congregated in Athens, including Pindar, Simonides and Bacchylides, all also spent time in Syracuse. We learn from multiple sources that important Syracusan individuals, such as the arms-manufacturer Cephalus (father of Lysias) and the rhetorician Tisias, were invited to live and work in Athens, and grave stones for Syracusans who married Athenians have also been found in Athens (e.g. *IG* I^3 1371). As Loicq-Berger puts it, 'entre Syracuse et Athènes, l'art était donc une monnaie qui avait cours' (Loicq-Berger 1967: 125). All this would have contributed to the nature and experience of the physical space of Syracuse as well as towards the construction of the perceived proximity of its relationship with Athens and distance from Corinth.

The takeover of Syracuse by Gelon had significant implications both for Syracuse (he imposed on it several thousand of his own mercenaries and citizens from neighbouring Gela (cf. Shepherd 2000: 58)) and for Syracuse's relationship with mainland Greece. After the Greek victory in the Persian wars, Gelon (despite his ambiguous stance during the conflict), and subsequently Hieron, actively sought closer ties with Greece, and particularly attempted to make their own victories against the Carthaginians at Himera and against the Etruscans at Cumae equal to the victories at Salamis and Plataea against the Persians. This ambition was clearly visible at the sanctuaries of Olympia and Delphi. Both Gelon and Hieron offered monumental dedications at Delphi, which mimicked the design and placement of the Plataean serpent column on the temple terrace (Scott 2010: 88). Hieron would continue to offer several more dedications at Delphi, including a statue of himself (Scott 2010: 89–90). At Olympia, as was the normal practice, inscribed helmets from the battles of Cumae and Himera were also dedicated (as the Athenians had also done after Marathon). Yet the dedicatory inscriptions which survive from these offerings once again mark Syracusan independence and presumed equality with the other cities of Greece: they are resolutely inscribed in the Syracusan alphabet (Meiggs and Lewis 1988: Nos. 28, 29; Dubois 1989: Nos. 93, 94; Arena 1998: Nos. 67a, 67b; Scott 2010: 171).

Thus the relationship of Syracuse and Corinth, seen through the available material and epigraphic evidence, once again demonstrates a complex sense of similarity and difference. Syracuse, in its art and architecture, was perhaps more visibly related to mainland Greece than some of its neighbouring colonial foundations in Sicily, but those links placed it, if anything, closer to Athens than to Corinth. Gelon built both a temple to Athena and a new sanctuary to Demeter and Core on Ortygia at Syracuse after 480 BC (Figure 4.1), perhaps reflecting the prominence of these deities in Athens and Corinth respectively (although Demeter and Core were also prominent in Attica). Equally Syracuse continued, especially under its tyrant rulers, to use the sanctuaries of Delphi and Olympia as spaces in which to broadcast both their independence and their important role as part of (and defenders of) Greece. Such a position, however, did not create any specific links with their metropolis, nor did it prevent them from celebrating their success over other Sicilian Greek and native communities during the course of the fifth century at Delphi and Olympia (cf. Dubois 1989: No. 95; Jacquemin 1991). Nor did it stop them from representing at Delphi the souring of their relationship with Athens after the Sicilian expedition, in the form of a Syracusan victory dedication, which may well have been specifically located so as to confront earlier Athenian offerings (Scott 2010: 105). Once again, therefore, the message from the material and epigraphic evidence is of strong independence for Syracuse, engaging with other cities as and when it saw fit, creating a wider network of relationships, the proximity and distance of each of which ebbed and flowed in accordance with wider Mediterranean history.

Syracuse and Corinth in the literary sources

During the fifth century BC, we have plentiful literary sources that treat both of the perception of Syracuse as a space within the wider Mediterranean and of the proximity and distance of the relationship between Syracuse and Corinth (as well as Syracuse's growing spatial links with other cities and sanctuaries in Greece). Pindar's *Pythian* 1, written for Hieron (470 BC), specifically portrays Sicily as part of the space of *Hellas* (cf. Finley 1979: 54). Yet the ode also underlines Syracuse's increasingly dominant role within Sicily through its emphasis on Syracuse's own colonial foundations (echoed also in Aesch. *Aetnaeae*). Pindar's *Olympian 6*, written for Hagesias of Syracuse (472– 468 BC), links Syracuse in a more particular spatial direction when it describes Hagesias as '*sunoikistēr*' of Syracuse (*Ol.* 6.6–8). The Scholia Vetera later explains this by suggesting that one or more of the Iamidai prophetic family resident at Olympia (who were Hagesias' ancestors) had participated in Syracuse's original founding and that the title '*sunoikistēr*' was thus a hereditary one (cf. Malkin 1987: 93). If this was Pindar's intention, then he was linking Syracuse's origins not solely to a specific city, but to the space of a central Hellenic sanctuary, in which, in the form of dedications and athletic competitors, we have already seen a significant Syracusan presence.

Such attempts to strengthen the spatial relationship between Syracuse and Greece can be found not only in Pindar. In the late-fifth century, Herodotus (4.23.4–5) specifically located the tenth labour of Heracles, the panhellenic Greek hero par excellence (whose labours adorned the temple of Zeus at Olympia constructed by the middle of the fifth century BC), in the space 'where today Syracuse is located' (cf. Sjöqvist 1973: 3–5). Both Pindar and Herodotus thus resolutely claimed the very space of Syracuse as a space indissolubly bound up with Greece.

Herodotus also recounts more specific military and political events during the fifth century BC, in which the proximity and distance between Syracuse and Greece, and particularly between Syracuse and Corinth, were put under the spotlight. The resulting picture is mixed. On the one hand, Herodotus recounts (7.154.3) how Corinth (along with Corcyra) intervened directly in Syracusan space on Syracuse's behalf in 492 BC following its defeat by Gela, acting in a mediating role. Herodotus also relates how later Syracuse chose Corinth as the space in which to exile the troublesome Sicel king Ducetius (7.8), from where he promptly escaped. Equally, Herodotus (7.157–63) reports how the Greeks specifically asked Syracuse, or rather Gelon, for help against Xerxes' invasion, on the grounds of panhellenic Greek and colonial solidarity, that is to say, on grounds specifically alluding to the close proximity and spatial inclusivity of their relationship. Yet, at the same time as such events underlined the spatial proximity of Syracuse and Corinth (or at least appeals to such), the distance between them was equally highlighted. Gelon, for example, responded to the Greek allies' request by offering impossible terms in return for his aid, and even sent gifts to Delphi in anticipation of Xerxes' victory (cf. Sjöqvist 1973: 49). The proximity and distance between Syracuse and Corinth were also impacted by the continually oscillating internal political affairs of Syracuse during the fifth century, which saw an oligarchy replaced by a democracy, the imposition of a tyranny, the reimposition of democracy and several further changes to its democratic make-up. Some of these events are known to us through contemporary sources such as Herodotus and Thucydides, but the vast majority of them are recounted for us only by Diodorus Siculus in the first century BC (see the later sections of this chapter; Berger 1992).

It is in Thucydides, however, that we are given the most complex portrait of the dynamic relationship of proximity and distance between colonies and their metropoleis, as well as particularly between Syracuse and Corinth, during the fifth century BC. In a well-known passage, Thucydides' Corinthians complained specifically about the behaviour of their colony, Corcyra. The Corcyraeans 'were not reserving the first portions of sacrifice for Corinthians as did the other colonies' (1.25.4). At 1.38.2, the Corinthians continued to complain:

…neither did we colonise them to be insulted by them, but to be their leaders and receive from them all due reverence. The rest of our colonies, at any rate, honour us and by our colonists we are more beloved than is any other metropolis.[1]

This fifth-century, Thucydidean, attitude towards how colony–metropolis relationships were supposed to work (and Corinth's assertion that the rest of its colonies fitted that model) is supported by some examples of Corinth's close proximity to, and direct involvement in, the spaces of its other colonies. At Potidaea, for example, Corinth was actively involved in their political constitution, particularly with the annual appointment of *epidemiourgoi* (Thuc. 1.56.2). Equally, involvement in the founding of a particular colonial space is shown to be enough to warrant military intervention: at 1.25–6, Thucydides says that Epidamnus successfully secured Corinthian intervention in 435 BC on the claim that Corinth had founded the city (even though it had actually been founded predominantly by Corcyra: Thuc. 1.24). Yet the notion of the continuing power of the memory of spatial involvement at the time of foundation is also contradicted (or at least shown to be only one way of understanding the duties of metropolis–colony relationship) by Thucydides' own account of how, in 431 BC, the Spartans, supported by Corinth, asked for Syracusan military aid but received no reply (Thuc. 2.7.2).

By the time of the Sicilian expedition, however, as Thucydides relates, the perceptual proximity between Syracuse and Corinth had understandably increased significantly. Syracuse made a request to Corinth for help (Thuc. 6.88.7), which Corinth offered, sending 14 ships and 500 hoplites

---

[1] Translation: C. Foster Smith (1919) Thucydides *History of the Peloponnesian War* vol. I Loeb Classical Library.

(Thuc. 6.104.1, 7.16.2). The terms of that request are revealing (cf. Patterson 2010: 53). Syracuse specifically cites the '*suggeneia*' (the 'kinship') between Syracuse and Corinth as the justification for their demands and Corinth's duty to honour them, which Thucydides emphasises that they fulfil zealously ('*pasei prothumiai*', 'with all eagerness'). The citing of *suggeneia* as justification may not, however, refer solely to the spatial proximity of the colony–metropolis relationship between Syracuse and Corinth, but more widely to the way in which the Peloponnesian War split the Sicilian colonies back into their ethnic groupings of Ionians v. Dorians, with Dorians supporting Sparta and Ionians Athens (Thuc. 3.86, 4.61.3; cf. Antonaccio 2001: 113).

Yet at the same time as Thucydides portrays a much more specific and close kinship and spatial relationship between Syracuse and Corinth (or perhaps rather between Ionians and Dorians), it is noticeable how Thucydides presents the Athenians as countering the Herodotean and Pindaric impression of Sicily as part of Greece. As Hall has pointed out (2002: 123), in all the speeches regarding Sicily in Thucydides, there is only one reference to Sicilian Greeks as *Hellenes* (Thuc. 6.30.2), and even that mention is rebutted, labelling them as *Sikeliotai* instead of *Hellenes*. Alcibiades, in attempting to whip up Athenian support for non-Greek Segesta and play down the much more Greek Selinous, cunningly describes Sicily (Thuc. 6.17.2–4) as a mob in which 'no one really feels he has a hometown of his own', in contrast to mainland Greece. As such, the Athenians in Thucydides are convinced to believe that Sicily is resolutely not part of the space of Greece, and, as a consequence, that there was nothing odd in going to war in Sicily on behalf of a non-Greek city against a Greek one.

It is in the context of this discourse about the place of Sicily in Greek space, and the normal balance of proximity and distance in the relationship between colony and metropolis that Thucydides relates how Syracuse was founded by the oikist Archias, one of the Heracleidae from Corinth (6.3.2). The story of Syracuse's historical foundation by Corinth thus comes into play as part of a wider political (and literary) framework, in which Sicily and Syracuse are both being detached from the space of Greece, and reattached, more closely than ever before, to their ethnic ancestry and particularly to the space of their founding city, as the Greek world fragmented into its respective power blocs during the Peloponnesian War. The moment of colonisation, and the continuing spatial proximity between colony and metropolis formed as a result, become important because of the current military struggle. At the same time, that military struggle defines the way in which the act of colonisation was figured to have occurred (cf. Wilson 2006: 51; Figueira 2008). Archias founded the city, having 'expelled the Sicels from the island' (Thuc. 6.3.2), and, more generally, Thucydides portrays the founding of colonies as identical to the act of going to war, in which they must, on the first day, secure the land (Thuc. 6.23). The proximity of the colonial spatial relationship is thus conceived exclusively as the physical occupation of the space of the settlement.

The fifth century BC thus sees a dramatic spectrum of change in the characterisation of the spaces of Sicily and mainland Greece, including specifically that of Syracuse and Corinth, in addition to a change in the perceptual space between them, as presented by both the material and the literary sources. In the first half of the fifth century BC, the space of Syracuse remained, at least architecturally, perceptibly different from its metropolis, and Syracusans constructed a proximity with, and roles in, the space of the city of Athens. At the same time, through the writings of Herodotus and Pindar, as well as through the active efforts of the Syracusan tyrants, Syracuse and Sicily were represented as distant from their colonial links and yet fully part of the wider space of Greece. That relationship was turned on its head through the polemical attitudes and outright warfare of the second half of the fifth century BC. Thucydides' narrative portrays how both Syracuse and Athens abandon the notion of a wider Greek space and identity, resorting instead to portraying, demanding and acting on closer ties between individual city spaces, particularly focused on colonial foundations, which are themselves configured as military spatial conquests. The Athenian expedition to capture the physical space of Syracuse may have been a disaster, but the overall outcome of the fifth century BC was that Syracuse, at least within the literary sources, was perceived as being firmly linked into a much closer spatial relationship with its metropolis as part of a wider rearticulation of the proximity and distance within the networks of relationship that made up the Greek world.

SYRACUSE AND CORINTH IN THE FOURTH CENTURY BC

The rise to power of Dionysius I in Syracuse in 405 BC marked an important shift in Syracuse's oscillating proximity and distance, not with its metropolis but with Athens. The growing strength of that relationship is fully attested through surviving inscriptions. Early in 393 BC, Athens honoured Dionysius (Rhodes and Osborne 2003: No. 10). The text called him the 'archon of Sicily' (line 7), to an extent recharacterising Sicily as part of the space of the Greek world through its application of Greek political and civic terminology (though this time applied to an autocrat rather than a civic official and to a whole island rather than a polis). The proximity between the mainland and

Syracuse and Corinth in the fourth century BC

Sicily was further reinforced by the relief accompanying the inscription that depicted Athena giving her hand to the personification of Sicily portrayed as a woman holding a sceptre/torch.

In 369–68 BC, Athens extended further honours to Dionysius (Rhodes and Osborne 2003: No. 33), making him and his descendants citizens of Athens (line 16), giving them priority access to the Athenian *boule* and the demos after the completion of the sacred business (line 36). The inscription also notes that Dionysius was sending envoys to the Delphian peace congress happening at the time (line 5). Not only was Dionysius firmly linked here to Athenian space and civic institutions, but clearly too he was fully participating in affairs important to the wider space of Greece. Just the following year, Athens went one stage further and agreed a formal defensive alliance with Dionysius, thereby linking the spaces of Syracuse and Athens, in which they each promised to help one another and not attack each other (Rhodes and Osborne 2003: No. 34). Yet this blossoming relationship was brought to a swift halt by Dionysius' death.

There are two key points to note about this increasing proximity between Athens and Dionysius in the first half of the fourth century BC. The first is that it was very much a relationship between Athens and Dionysius, not Athens and Syracuse. All three texts speak specifically of the agreement being with Dionysius, although the oaths of the final alliance were also to be sworn by an unknown body of Syracusan officials (Rhodes and Osborne 2003: No. 34, lines 36–7). The second is that this close relationship with Athens underlines the lack of relationship with Corinth in this period (despite a short alliance against Sparta 395–386 BC). Indeed, Diodorus (14.63.4) will later say that Dionysius received from (and gave to) Sparta more help than he did vis-à-vis Corinth. Diodorus (15.74) also supplements the evidence provided by inscriptions on the activities of Dionysius I in Athens: he won at the Lenaia festival in 367 BC with his own composition (the *Ransom of Hector*). Yet it was not only Dionysius who was bringing theatrical creations from Sicily to Athens. Xenophon's *Symposium* (2.3.7) also recounts a performance of mime, a form of theatre native to Sicily, in the house of Callias in Athens. Equally, a famous writer of Sicilian mime, Sophron, had his work introduced to Athens, according to the Suda (s.v. Sophron) and Diogenes Laertius (3.18), by Plato (Dearden 1990: 238). Thus, the first half of the fourth century BC, as part of the much wider series of changes in the political framework of the Greek world, saw a definite distancing between Syracuse and Corinth and several deliberate attempts to narrow the distance between Syracuse and Athens, in terms of politics, military alliance and the arts within both Syracusan and Athenian space.

The succession of Dionysius II, however, widened the distance in the relationship between Syracuse and Athens, as well as with the rest of Greece. Writers such as Plato (themselves fully involved with the political machinations of power brokers at Syracuse), now emphasised Syracuse's burgeoning reputation for luxury (e.g. Pl. *Resp.* 404d). This distancing of luxurious Syracuse from Greece is echoed also in a pseudo-Platonic letter (VIII), which underlines the loss of Greek language in Sicily and more generally of Hellenic culture (cf. Sjöqvist 1973: 59). Syracuse's place within the space of Greece was once again in jeopardy.

While most of what we know about the political events during the reigns of Dionysius II and Dion in Syracuse comes from the later authors Diodorus and Plutarch, we do have more contemporary evidence for the Corinthian Timoleon's impact on Syracuse and the way in which his influence once again closed the distance particularly between Syracuse and its metropolis, as well as between Sicily and Greece (cf. Talbert 1974). Timoleon's military activities in Sicily against the Carthaginians, who had moved to threaten Syracuse itself, are attested through a surviving inscribed base from Delphi, which indicates that Timoleon dedicated in the sanctuary one of the two hundred chariots captured in his battles against the Carthaginians (Pomtow 1895). At the same time as Timoleon's dedication at Delphi, three Syracusans (who indeed may have been responsible for bringing that dedication to Delphi) were also recorded in the sanctuary's accounts as contributing money to the rebuilding of the temple of Apollo, and they did so with Corinthian coinage, perhaps because it was more acceptable than the Syracusan in Delphi (Bousquet 1938). In the space where, in the sixth and fifth centuries, the distance between Syracuse and Corinth had been so noticeable, now the proximity and overlap between these two were on public display.

Timoleon's victories in Sicily on behalf of Syracuse were also echoed in the space of Corinth. A monument consisting of an inscribed base and statue (probably of Poseidon) was erected, either on the triglyph wall near the city's sanctuary of Poseidon or in the city's agora (cf. Figure 4.2), commemorating the Corinthians, Syracusans, Sicels, Corcyraeans, Apollonians and Leucadians (line 1) who, in conjunction with Timoleon, were victorious in 341 BC against Carthage. The inscription, though surviving only in fragments, specifically mentions '*ktistera korinthon*' ('the Corinthian founder') in line 3 (Kent 1952), once again articulating a close spatial proximity between Syracuse and Corinth. The monument appears to have been seen by Plutarch's source Timaeus, himself a Sicilian, as Plutarch mentions the existence of this monument in his biography of Timoleon (Plut. *Vit. Tim* 29.6).

Those same victories against the Carthaginians were also highlighted in Syracuse itself through the minting of a new coinage. Timoleon revised the Syracusan monetary system and based it on the Corinthian stater, to which the Syracusans added their own ethnic (Karlsson 1995: 164). The ubiquity (and perhaps popularity) of this new coinage is demonstrated by the fact that the vast majority of coins found within the space of, and around, Syracuse, both in this period and throughout the fourth century BC, have been of this type (Salmon 1984: 174). Yet there appear to have also been special coin issues at Syracuse to celebrate recent events. Karlsson (1995: 165–9) has argued that a series of coins with images of Zeus Eleutherius, and others with that of a wild horse, should be ascribed to the period of Timoleon's control, specifically in celebration of democracy and victory over the Carthaginians (not least because Diodorus (11.72.2) comments that Timoleon reinstituted an old annual festival in honour of Zeus Eleutherius at this time). Timoleon also celebrated the full offensive and defensive *summachia* ('alliance') he created between Greeks and Sicels in Sicily in the war against Carthage, by minting a coin showing a personified *Sicelia* on the obverse and the title '*summachikon*' ('alliance') on the reverse (Antonaccio 2001: 138). As a result of these different actions, the proximity of the relationship between Syracuse and Corinth (and the similarity of the experience of their respective physical spaces), as well as of that between the Greek and Sicel parts of Sicily, was heavily re-emphasised.

Plutarch and Diodorus provide many more details of the political and military events in this period, and their evidence will be considered more fully in the next section. For now, what the contemporary literary, archaeological, inscriptional and numismatic evidence shows us is the dynamic way in which, during the fourth century BC, the spaces of Sicily and Syracuse were conceptualised from the Greek mainland, first as part of the wider space of Greece, subsequently as distinct from Greece, and then, eventually, under Timoleon, part of Greece space. Moreover, Syracuse under Timoleon was closely linked to and embedded within its founding metropolis, as well as placed in alliance with the different populations of Sicily as part of a wider Sicilian identity. Within that oscillating relationship of proximity and distance, Athens actively sought to minimise the distance between itself and Dionysius I, and maximise it under his successor, whereas Corinth had little to do with Syracuse until the period of Timoleon, at which point the two cities not only began to use the same coinage system but were also linked through victory dedications placed in the heart of the city of Corinth and at Delphi as well as through celebrations of that victory on Syracusan coinage, all of which demonstrated a degree of closeness in their spatial relationships (and perceptible similarity in the nature and experience of their physical spaces) never before witnessed (at least in the surviving evidence).

SYRACUSE AND CORINTH FROM THE THIRD CENTURY BC ONWARDS

There were long-term effects of Timoleon's actions and reforms. We learn from later literary sources that he issued a call for new settlers to come to Syracuse from Corinth, the rest of Greece, Italy and from around the Mediterranean (cf. Plut. *Vit. Tim.* 38.4). The effect of that resettlement was to create new relationships between the space of Syracuse, its surrounding area and particularly its own colonial foundations, and especially in the eastern Mediterranean. In the mid-third century BC, surviving documents from the Asclepieion on Cos attest to Cos' position as a 'co-founder' of the settlement of Camarina, which was one of Syracuse's own colonies that Syracuse had in turn destroyed following its rebellion in 553 BC (Thuc. 6.5.3), but which was functioning again by 414 BC, in addition to Cos being the co-founder of Gela (Herzog and Klaffenbach 1952: Nos. 12–13). This construction of a stake in the spatial territory around Syracuse for a city in the eastern Mediterranean, perhaps as part of a second 'founding', is further illuminated by the changing religious landscape of Syracuse itself in this period. The cult of the Great Mother of the Gods, always popular in Asia Minor, flourished in Syracuse under Hieron II, her worship being attested all over the city (Holloway 1991: 162; Lehmler 2005). In addition, in one of the few surviving epigraphic documents from the third century BC to mention Syracuse, Syracuse specifically recognises the competitions and right of *asylia* ('asylum') of the sanctuary of Artemis Leucophryene at Magnesia on the Meander on the Asia Minor coast (Dubois 1989: No. 97, 207/6 BC). The inscription not only was put up in a prominent place on the wall of the west stoa of the sanctuary, but also specifically speaks of Magnesia's '*suggeneia*' ('kinship') with Syracuse and specifically with the '*synkletos*' of Syracuse, part of the city's official administration (Curty 1995: No. 46.i).

In contrast to this burgeoning closeness in the relationship between Syracuse and Asia Minor, from 290 BC, the perceptual proximity of Syracuse's relationship with mainland Greece, and specifically with Corinth, appears to have dramatically declined. Corinthian coinage, which had been omnipresent at Syracuse since the revisions introduced by Timoleon, disappeared altogether (Salmon 1984: 174). Syracuse's involvement with Pyrrhus of Epirus and subsequently Hieron II in the first half of the third century BC, during which time Pyrrhus became king of Sicily (and Hieron subsequently

Syracuse and Corinth from the third century BC onwards   131

king of Syracuse), opened up a new chapter in Syracuse's international relations, in which Corinth had little or no place (cf. Lehmler 2005; Zambon 2008; Engels et al. 2010). Although Hieron II did keep some links with the space of Greece, particularly through dedications at Olympia, the real focus for both Pyrrhus and Hieron was Sicily's position as between Carthage and Rome. The alliance which Hieron II made with Rome after 263 BC secured Syracuse's survival through the First Punic War (264–241 BC), and underlined Syracuse's new relationship with Rome within this changing Mediterranean world. In 216 BC, for example, a convoy was said to have arrived at Ostia from Syracuse containing not only 300,000 *modii* of wheat and 200,000 of barley, but also a gold statue of Victory which was placed in the temple of Jupiter Optimus Maximus on the Capitol (Finley 1979: 117). The Second Punic War greatly harmed Syracuse, and after Hieron's death in 215 BC his successor chose to ally with Carthage. As a result, repeated Roman attacks on the city were made until it fell to Marcellus and to Roman control in 212 BC, a fate which would also befall its metropolis in 146 BC. At which time, appropriately, Timoleon's victory monument, linking the spaces of Syracuse and Corinth in their victories over Carthage back in 341 BC, was destroyed and its stone blocks reused in other buildings (Kent 1952).

The characterisation of Syracuse as a space within the Mediterranean world, and of its proximity to and distance from its metropolis amongst the writers of the Roman period, is complex. Sicily's lack of loyalty to Rome had been a cause for concern throughout the second century BC, following a host of revolts, particularly by slaves (Finley 1979: 140–6). Yet, in the first century BC, writers such as Cicero underlined both the beauty and the magnificence of the city of Syracuse as well as its Greek heritage (e.g. Cic. *Verr.* Part 2 11.1.2–3; 2.3). The (continuing) 'Greekness' of Syracuse, and thus its inclusion within the space of Greece, was a theme taken up by several other authors over the course of the first centuries BC and AD. Livy argued that the taking of Syracuse by the Romans in 212 BC was the moment when Rome first acquired its admiration for Greek art (Livy 25.40.2). Diodorus, himself from the island, was at pains to point out that he could, unusually, speak Latin as well as Greek (Diod. Sic. 1.4.4); in this he was reacting perhaps against the general perception that Sicily was exclusively a Greek-speaking space. In that vein, Diodorus also highlights (14.78) the fact that, back in 345 BC, Syracuse had signed a treaty with a collection of Sicilian cities under the umbrella title of the '*poleis Hellenides*' ('the Hellenic cities'), a phrase emphasising their inclusion within and proximity to the space of the Greek world. Equally, Strabo, himself from Asia Minor (*Geography* 6.1.2), places Sicily and South Italy in the space of his *'megale Hellas'* ('Great Greece'), even though he underlines the Sicilian reputation for luxury in comparison to mainland Greece (see Chapter 5).

Other 'Greek' sanctuaries were also keen to incorporate Syracuse into their historical story and physical space in this period. The 'inventory list' from the sanctuary of Athena Lindia on Rhodes, for example, created following a fire (*c*.99 BC) which destroyed all the sanctuary's dedications, specifically wove important individuals associated with Syracuse into its 'myth-historical' narrative of dedicators coming to the site: Hieron II, Pyrrhus, the uncle of Hippocrates and Deinomenes, the father of Gelon and Hieron, were all said to have made dedications there (Shepherd 2000: 60; Higbie 2003: sections XLI, XL, XXXI, XXVIII; Scott 2011).

It is within this complex environment – where Syracuse, under Roman control, has little physical proximity with the space of mainland Greece, and yet, at the same time, the literary and inscriptional sources are keen to highlight its perceptual proximity and Greekness – that Diodorus and later Plutarch give us a much more detailed account of the close relationship between Syracuse and Corinth and their mutual involvement over the course of the fourth century BC.

Diodorus (14.62.1) indicates that Dionysius I appealed specifically to Corinth for help in 396 BC and that Dion (16.6.5) also subsequently appealed to Corinth for help in overthrowing Dionysius II (after Dion had spent time in Corinth (Plut. *Dion* 53.2) and left on his mission to Syracuse from Corinth (Diod. Sic. 16.6.5)). Plutarch says that Corinth responded to Dion's request by sending *sumbouloi* and *sunarchontes* (Plut. *Vit. Dion* 53.2–3).

Both Diodorus and Plutarch indicate that it was aristocratic exiles from Syracuse who made the appeal for help to Corinth following the murder of Dion, to which Corinth responded by sending Timoleon (Plut. *Vit. Tim.* 2.1, 3.1; Diod. Sic. 16.66–9). His successes led to Corinth's sending further troops (Plut. *Vit. Tim.* 16.3). Diodorus states that Timoleon even asked for a legislative committee from Corinth to help revise Syracusan laws (Diod. Sic. 13.35.3). Plutarch tells us that Timoleon asked Corinth to send new settlers for Syracuse (Plut. *Vit. Tim.* 23.1), and that Corinth actively advertised Corinthian success at Syracuse, and made the appeal for new settlers at all the Greek festivals (*Vit. Tim.* 23.2). In return, Plutarch says, the Syracusans agreed always to appoint a Corinthian general in any of their wars against foreign enemies (*Vit. Tim.* 38.4). Both Plutarch and Diodorus indicate that a heroön for Timoleon was established in the agora of the city of Syracuse (Plut. *Vit. Tim.* 39; Diod. Sic. 16.90.1). Indeed, Polybius (12.23), back in the second century BC, had already hinted at Timoleon's possible divinisation (cf. Mari 2010: 97).

The heroön for Timoleon was allegedly placed near that of the city's original founder (Cerchiai et al. 2004: 202). This 'saviour' of Syracuse was thus, through the worship given to him and the spatial proximity of his tomb to that of Archias, recast as a second founder of the city. Equally, Diodorus (Diod. Sic. 11.26.2, 11.38.5, 14.66.2–3) also cast Gelon as a 'refounder' of Syracuse, saying that he was accorded *timai heroïkai*, akin to that of an oikist (cf. Malkin 1987: 96) The history of Syracuse was thus reframed in the literary sources as a series of colonial (re)foundation 'moments', linked back through time to its original foundation (cf. Pindar's earlier fifth-century representation of Hagesias as a descendant of the Olympian co-founders of Syracuse).

The representation of Syracuse in the sources of the first centuries BC and AD, and particularly those that focus on the relationship of Syracuse and Corinth, thus fundamentally alter our picture of these spaces and the bond between them: they increase the importance of Syracuse in the story of Greek history and space of the Greek world; they recast Syracuse's story as one in which there had been continued and meaningful Greek interaction and close relationship; they underline Syracuse's – and Sicily's – continued active desire to be part of the space of the Greek world, and, particularly in relation to the interactions of Dion and Timoleon, they link Syracuse and Corinth tightly together in military and political terms, but also in terms of their physical spaces, since monuments are set up for (and by) Timoleon in central locations in both cities.

It is within this recasting of the spaces of Syracuse and Corinth, and in the minimalising of the distance between them, that we see also the emergence in Plutarch of a more complex foundation story (Plut. *Moralia* 772e–773b). In contrast to Thucydides, who narrated the story of the foundation as one of warlike invasion and occupation, Plutarch tells us that internal strife at Corinth, involving the death of handsome Actaeon because of drunken struggles between his family and his admirer, Archias, went unresolved by the Corinthian people and so engendered the wrath of the gods. Corinth suffered drought and pestilence, which, according to the Delphic oracle, could be cured only through the expulsion of those responsible. As a result, Archias willingly volunteered to leave Corinth, sailed for Sicily and founded Syracuse (where he too would be murdered).

Thucydides' bloodshed in the colony is doubled in Plutarch by bloodshed in the metropolis. The solution to the metropolis' misfortune is found in the colony (cf. Dougherty 1993a; 1993b: 31), mediated and sanctioned by the weight of the sanctuary and oracle at Delphi (for other evidence of the strengthening early relationship between Delphi and Corinth, see Salmon 1984: 72–3, 84–9; more generally for the relationship between Delphi and colonists, see Londey 1990). Plutarch's tale creates a complex and close, reciprocal, bond between the spaces of Syracuse and Corinth, which goes above and beyond both previous literary accounts of that relationship and any physical evidence for their closeness from the point of their foundation onwards. The spaces of Syracuse and Corinth are tied together as necessarily needing each other. Strabo realigns that story (8.6.22) by indicating that, though Archias was from Corinth, most of the colonists came from Tenea, where there was a local temple of Apollo (Malkin 1984: 53–4; 1994a: 3). Tenea, according to Strabo, prospered hugely from the venture, and later revolted from Corinth and sided with Rome. At the same time, earlier in his narrative, Strabo in addition recounts (6.2.4) that Archias and the Teneans also picked up at Zephyrion in Italy other Greeks (whom he labels 'Dorians'), who had parted company with the founders of Megara. For Strabo, Syracuse is tied, on the one hand, not only with the space of Corinth but also with an even more specific region (indeed religious centre) in the area, which had a close enough relationship with Syracuse to benefit subsequently from participating in the founding, and, on the other hand, with Greeks from other 'Dorian' parts of Greece. Syracuse is, at one and the same time, tied in tighter to the space of Corinth and to the space of Greece as a whole.

That spatial proximity, and the role of Delphi in sanctioning, indeed commanding, the colonisation, are emphasised further in later writers. Pausanias (5.7.3) tells that Archias of Corinth was specifically despatched by Delphi to found Syracuse. But the location was given in a traditional Delphic riddle: 'a certain Ortygia lies in the misty sea... where the mouth of the Alpheus erupts, having mingled with the streams of the fair-flowing Arethusa'. The river Alpheus, which rose in Arcadia, was thought to pass under the surface of the sea and mix with the Syracusan spring. Pausanias uses a metaphor for sexual intercourse, '*misgomenon*', to describe the mixing of the streams. Dougherty interpreted this as Pausanias inferring that Greek and indigenous populations had intermarried at Syracuse (Dougherty 1993b: 69). Yet I would argue that the metaphor does not need to be carried so far as to include populations, but should be considered in spatial terms. In Pausanias, the colony and its Corinthian metropolis are tied together even more tightly because of the fact that the spaces of Syracuse and Greece are physically, sexually, connected, through the blending of the same water. As Dougherty also rightly points out (1993b: 4, 8), the description of a foreign landscape using the Greek vocabulary of a Delphic riddle helps further to 'hellenise' that space and strengthen the proximity between the two.

Several scholars have commented on the tendency for these later authors, especially Plutarch, to represent the relationship between Syracuse and

Corinth as a particularly close and benevolent one (e.g. Graham 1983: 144; Talbert 1974: 52). In his *Life of Alcibiades* 18.3–4, Plutarch even goes so far as to claim that the Corinthians were responsible for defacing the herms in Athens, 'since Syracuse was a colony of theirs, and they hoped that such signs would encourage Athens to pause or halt the war'. Corinth, according to Plutarch, would commit a sacrilegious act and risk war with Athens in order to protect their colony. The irony is that this literary desire to represent these two spaces as joined came at a time in the wider Mediterranean world when Syracuse and Corinth could not have been more physically or perceptually separate, and when there is little non-literary evidence to link them apart from the fact that they both suffered destruction under Rome and both were active Roman settlements; indeed, Syracuse received one of the three Augustan theatres to be built in Sicily (cf. Wilson 1990).

This tendency of the Greek historians of the Roman period to recast so strongly the spatial proximity between Syracuse and Corinth, indeed to make that relationship stronger than it ever appears to have been in reality, is symptomatic of continued attempts by particular emperors to envisage a united Greece. The most active example of this was Hadrian's *Panhellenion* in the first quarter of the second century AD, which was intended to create an Achaia composed of Hellenic metropoleis and colonies, whose collective history and culture not only demonstrated Greek unity but also could be made to act as a counterweight to the contemporary economic and political weight of the East (Spawforth and Walker 1985; 1986).

CONCLUSION

Over the last three decades, the study of Greek interaction not only with the West but with cultures in all directions of the compass has changed dramatically, to allow for a much more gradual, two-way process of interaction and acculturation. At the same time, scholarship is becoming more and more sensitive to the different forms, trajectories and outcomes taken by that process not only between settlements in different parts of the Mediterranean world including the Black Sea, Asia Minor, Libya, Sicily and South Italy, but also between settlements geographically close to one another, and between settlements 'founded' by the same city.

This chapter has argued that, within this new framework, we should not abandon the investigation of the relationship between metropolis and colony. Past approaches have tended to understand that relationship only in terms of the degree to which the colony was a military or political 'possession' of the metropolis. This chapter has, by taking a spatial approach, argued for a much more subtle and complex way of thinking about how that relationship might have been constructed and perceived over time. Focusing on Syracuse and Corinth, it has examined how the physical spaces of the two settlements developed, and a number of the ways in which their similarities and differences might have been perceived, both at home and on the international stage. In turn, it has also sought to harness the contemporary archaeological and epigraphical evidence to aid thinking about how these two cultures actively attempted to reduce or expand the distance between them. Finally, it has examined how the literary and historical sources of different periods sought to reframe the nature of that relationship and, in particular, their spatial proximity or distance.

As a result, this chapter has argued that the relationship between Syracuse and Corinth was part of a complex and changing discourse operating simultaneously on numerous levels, of which the nature of the 'moment' of colonisation was only one. What is striking is the dynamic nature of that discourse. Syracuse in the sixth and fifth centuries BC often conducted independent religious, burial, architectural and artistic practices at home, as well as actively making the case for its independence and equality within panhellenic sanctuaries such as Delphi and Olympia. At the same time, certain authors linked Syracuse to Greece, and others not to Greece, but specifically to Corinth, in part through highlighting (indeed, creating) a particular version of the colonisation 'moment'. In turn, during the fourth century BC, the active creation and adoption of a series of monuments, inscriptions and kinds of material culture such as coinage within their physical landscapes not only demonstrated Syracuse's proximity with more far-flung parts of an expanding world, but also drew the spaces of Syracuse and Corinth perceptibly closer together, reflecting their increasing political and military interaction.

But it was only as the relationship between Syracuse and Corinth became more and more distant, as they became linked by little more than their status as parts of the Roman imperial landscape, that the literary sources reframed this colony and metropolis relationship as closer than it had ever in reality been, particularly through the recasting of the 'moment' of colonial foundation and its use as a metaphor for telling the story of Syracuse's history. In this recasting of their spatial relationship, not only did the colony and metropolis share a linked physical landscape from their very inception, but also the space of the colony provided a method of divine salvation for the population and landscape of its metropolis; because of that, the metropolis was even willing, in time, to risk the wrath of the gods and war to protect it.

CHAPTER 5

The place of Greece in the oikoumene of Strabo's Geography

INTRODUCTION

Lefebvre argued in his influential book *The Production of Space* (1991 (1974): 15) that 'any search for space in literary texts will find it everywhere and in every guise: enclosed, described, projected, dreamt of, speculated about'. Since the original publication of Lefebvre's work, there has been, as noted in the introduction, a vast growth in interest in space and spatiality across a wide variety of literary genres in both Greek and Roman scholarship. This final case-study seeks to utilise these recent advances in the understanding of space and text in the analysis of a work particularly concerned with space: Strabo's *Geography*.

The first section aims to set up the context for, and demonstrate the importance of, that analysis, first by examining recent approaches to the genre of geographical and universal history-writing and second by looking at how past scholarship has investigated and characterised Strabo and his *Geography*. In particular, it will focus on showing how past scholarship has been insufficiently interested in Strabo's treatment of the world at a regional level (i.e. that of 'Italy', or 'Greece'). This chapter will then take as its focus Strabo's portrayal of Greece within the *Geography*, investigating the meaning and value of Greece as a space within the *oikoumene* of Strabo (cf. Figure 5.1), and the ways in which that spatial meaning has been constructed. The analysis will be divided into three sections: first, an examination of how Strabo conceptualises geographical knowledge and frames his project; second, an investigation of how Greece is constructed as a space within Strabo's narratives of other parts of the *oikoumene;* and third, Strabo's narrative construction of the space of Greece itself. In so doing, I hope to show how a spatial approach can contribute also to our understanding of the wider context of Strabo's writing, his audience, the transitional world of Augustan and Tiberian Rome, and Strabo's place within it.

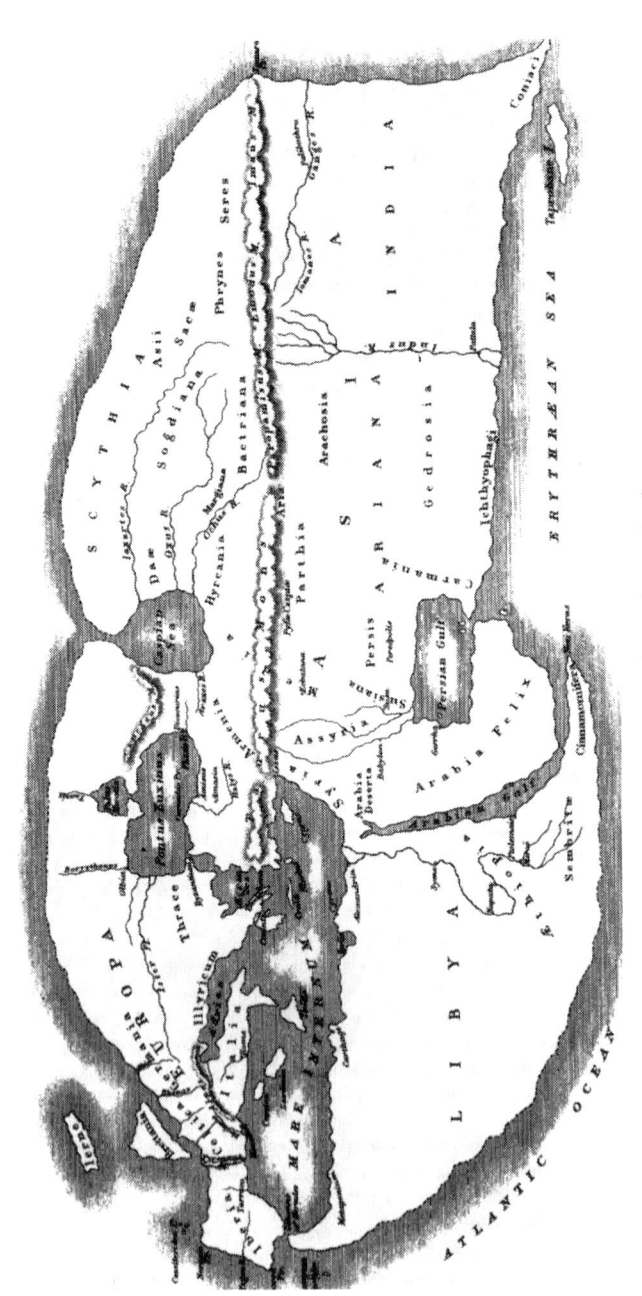

Figure 5.1 The world according to Strabo

APPROACHING SPACE AND STRABO

Much work has been done on the developing concept of cartography and geography in the ancient world (e.g. Harley and Woodward 1987; Jacob 1991; Romm 1992; di Donato 2001; Geus 2003; Talbert and Brodersen 2004; Harrison 2007; Raaflaub and Talbert 2010). There has been equal interest in the development of the connected genre of universal history, which some see as developing out of the intellectual engagement with the wider and more integrated ancient world following the conquests of Alexander the Great (e.g. Marincola 2007a), and which others trace back to earlier writers such as Herodotus and even Hesiod (e.g. Momigliano 1982; Alonso-Núñez 1987; Pigon 2008; Cole 2010). Such universalising histories (and indeed equally the developing Hellenistic trend of local histories: Harding 2007; Sprawski 2008) inevitably cross over in their scope and aim with works of geography, and much discussion has been given to whether or not these two disciplines were ever considered in antiquity to be separate and whether such distinctions are useful for study of them now (Chevallier 1974; Langton 1988; Clarke 1999a; 1999b; Engels 2007; 2008; Liddel and Fear 2010).

Two facts seem to be generally agreed. The first is that whatever one calls them and whatever their claims to universalism and geographical coverage, these texts always make choices about what to include and what not to include; they offer not so much universality but, as it has been termed, 'focalised universality' (Engels 2010: 74). Second, given that writing geographical and universal history texts inevitably constructed a particular kind of world, that world both reflected and constructed the cultural *mores* of the time (cf. Pelling 2007). Such texts are thus particularly suitable for provoking reflection in spatial terms; they are constructions of worlds in which geography and history overlap and interlock to create a particular view both of the wider inhabited world (the *oikoumene*) and of its constituent parts. In so doing, these texts offer us a chance to bring the micro, regional and macro scales of textual space together, and relate them all to the cultural world in which the work was produced.

Of the plethora of universalising historians/geographers surviving from the ancient world, Strabo has sometimes been curiously neglected (even totally, as in the survey of Chevallier 1974). More recently, however, there has been a reappreciation of the aims and methods of Strabo in conceptualising and constructing his *Geography*. This more recent work has focused primarily on Strabo's vision of the inhabited world (the *oikoumene*) which Clarke argues to have been constructed on a centre-and-periphery model that wove together time, local space and universal space (Clarke 1999a: 193,

300–35). In conjunction with this there has been recent reanalysis of Strabo's terminology for his work, particularly focusing on his labelling of the *Geography* as both a '*chorographia*' (Dueck 2000: 154; Engels 2008: 158; 2010: 80) and a '*kolossourgia*' (Clarke 1999a: 295; Pothecary 2005a), terminology which underlines how uncartographic Strabo's intentions were. The concept of *kolossourgia* needs to be understood as a cultural vision in which the provision of detail is not necessary unless motivated by its function in service of the wider narrative (cf. 1.1.23).[1] At the same time, Strabo's review of the *oikoumene* specifically set out to offer a world-view different from that of all his predecessors: a *chorographia* which maintained particular places as its primary focus in contrast to the unfocused *periplus/ periegesis*. Strabo's *Geography* is a work thus intimately involved with the notion of making particular places and spaces work not only to express what they contain but also to signify the larger themes and goals of his project to describe the inhabited world.

It is therefore somewhat surprising that, while the recent work investigating the overarching framework of Strabo's world has been conducted often in tandem with continuing thematic studies of the *Geography* (for example, his use of poetry (Dueck 2005), the naming of famous men (Engels 2005), his ethnographic descriptions (Almagor 2005; Dench 2007; Woolf 2011: 24–7, 75–9) and his view of colonies (Trotta 2005)), the study of that world as a series of spaces, particularly the different geographical regions within the *oikoumene*, has not advanced in quite the same way. Since the original 'regional-themed' publications by the University of Perugia, studies of the region of Asia Minor have continued (Syme 1995; Lindsay 2005; Panichi 2005), as well as of Italy (e.g. Morcillo 2010) and of regions not covered by the Perugia school (for example Northern Europe: Pothecary 2005b). Greece, however, lags behind. It was not a focus for the recent major monographical investigations by Clarke (1999a) or Dueck (2000), which have both been concerned with Strabo's wider historiographical goals. Indeed, since the work on the micro-regions of Greece (Boeotia: Wallace 1979; Peloponnese: Baladié 1980; Macedon: Georgiades 1993) and the edited volume by the Perugia school on Greece (Biraschi 1994b), the only new piece to focus exclusively on Strabo's conception of Greece has been Pretzler (2005), who sought to contrast Strabo's approach to Greece with that of Pausanias. It seems not to have been an understatement of Baladié in 1980 that 'books 8 and 9 [which contain Strabo's

---

[1] All textual references in this chapter are to Strabo's *Geography* unless otherwise stated.

description of Greece] have been thought to be the least interesting in the *Geography*' (1980: 339).

What of Greece, then, as represented in Strabo's *oikoumene*? The edited volume by Biraschi in 1994 concentrated mainly on micro-regional issues (e.g. natural phenomena in Chalcidice: Amiotti 1994), accompanied by thematic pieces looking at Homer's influence on Strabo, or at Strabo's division of Greece into peninsulas. Pretzler (2005) attempted to resuscitate Strabo's description of Greece, which has often been dismissed as inaccurate and superficial (in comparison to Pausanias), by underlining the important point that his Greece was part of a wider project. She pointed to its importance as a hub of myth, a space whose geography could be fully described only through history, by a man whose own focus, however, was his homeland of Asia Minor, within a wider world now held together and ruled by Rome. Yet what I want to argue in the following sections is that by focusing, first, on the ways in which Strabo frames his narrative and project, second, on how he constructs and expresses Greece's place through other spaces within the *oikoumene*, and, finally, on how he formulates the space of Greece itself, what emerges into view is a Greece with a far more interesting, multi-faceted and important part to play in Strabo's world than previous scholarship has allowed for.

GREECE AND THE FRAMEWORK OF STRABO'S PROJECT

Strabo's starting point, as has often been pointed out, is Homer (cf. 1.1.2–11), the 'founder of the science of Geography', who is posited as sitting at the beginning of a long line of Greek geographers culminating with Strabo (cf. Dueck 2010: 237). Indeed, the first two books of the *Geography* are explicitly preoccupied with setting out Strabo's almost universal agreement with, or slavish following of, Homer, as well as his points of agreement and disagreement with each of the subsequent geographers he engages with. What is key here is that the literary tradition in which Strabo is working is a Greek (as opposed to Roman) one, and what his work offers is therefore predominantly a Greek conception of the known world (into which Strabo will weave the story of current Roman power (cf. Maas 2007: 71)).

Such a predominance and superiority of the Greek geographical literary tradition, and the resultant Greek world-view, is underlined even further by the way in which Strabo actively denounces what Roman writers have added to this corpus of knowledge (cf. Engels 2007: 551):

Although the Roman historians are imitators of the Greeks, they do not carry their imitations very far (*all' ouk epi polu*); for what they relate they merely translate from the Greeks, while the fondness for knowledge that they of themselves bring to their histories is inconsiderable (*ou polu*); hence, whenever the Greeks leave gaps, all the filling in that is done by the other set of writers is inconsiderable (*ouk esti polu*) – especially since most of the famous names are Greeks. (3.4.19)[2]

At this moment, Strabo is actually discussing Iberia (book 3), which makes his denunciation of the Roman contribution (stressed in the Greek through the repetition of his description of that contribution as '*ou polu*') all the more striking, not only because Greek interest in the region was usually restricted to the eastern coastline in contrast to the much more in-depth Roman military involvement, but also because Strabo's own description of Iberia will focus so heavily on the current Roman presence (see the next section of this chapter). Even here, Strabo seems to argue, in a place where the Greeks never much travelled and the Romans are now so prevalent, it is the Greeks who have provided the vast majority of our knowledge.

Strabo adds to this picture of Greek-led geographical knowledge by arguing also that the discovery not just of Iberia but of the entire *oikoumene* has been delivered principally through four different historical entities (Figure 5.1). Alexander the Great 'opened up for us geographers a great part of Asia and all the northern part of Europe' (1.2.1), western Europe was made known by Rome, the area from Tyras to Colchis by Mithridates, and that of Hyrcania and Bactria by the Parthians.

For Strabo, however, it is not just the space of the *oikoumene* that has been discovered and described in large part by Greeks. Greek mythohistorical figures and events are also fundamental to the way Strabo structures his temporal narrative. Strabo organises his *Geography* around three key temporal 'moments': the Trojan War, the Return of the Heraclidae to the Peloponnese and the battle of Actium (cf. Clarke 1999a: 252; Pretzler 2005: 150). Such events not only underline Greece's historical longevity and importance, but also implicate Greece further in the different spaces of the *oikoumene* by tying their landscapes to temporal events, two of which are based in the Greek mythical past and one of which took place in the physical space of Greece itself. Moreover, scholars (e.g. Dueck 2000: 105) have noted Strabo's reluctance to associate the battle of Actium with Italian space at all (references to it are nearly always located outside Italy, e.g. 7.7.6, 8.4.3, 17.1.9–11); this is perhaps because the implications and memories touched on still too raw a Roman nerve. The result of this narrative decision is an even stronger emphasis on the fact that this was an event that took place in

---

[2] All translations are taken from the Loeb edition of Strabo in eight volumes (Jones 1949, 3rd edn).

Greece and the framework of Strabo's project

Greek space, thus only adding to the importance of the role Greece continues to play in the *oikoumene*.

As a result of Greek responsibility for discovering parts of the world, as well as narrating its time clock, Strabo does not only take for granted how well Greece will be known to his (Greek and Roman) readers (cf. 9.1.16; Pretzler 2005: 147); but, more importantly, especially in his disagreements with other geographers over the boundaries of the *oikoumene*, he will also often refer to Greek figures as a means of proving his case (so, for example, in the East, his case in point is Alexander the Great, e.g. 2.1.6). In addition, Strabo also uses areas of the Greek world when giving particular examples of geographical curiosities. The island of Euboea, as Aujac (1994) notes, is not treated in detail by Strabo until book 10, and yet it is singled out in the prolegomena of books 1 and 2 as key to explaining a series of geological and hydrological hypotheses about how the world developed (e.g. seismic activity 1.3.10, 1.3.16, 1.3.20; sea currents 1.2.10), as well as being employed to help explain the geography of other islands around the Mediterranean (e.g. Pithecusae and Sicily: 1.3.12, 1.3.19, 5.4.9, 6.1.6) and even that of areas of mainland Italy (e.g. Lucania 6.1.13). Thus not only is Greece the guiding framework for 'doing' geography, not only are its historical figures responsible for discovering large parts of the space of the *oikoumene*, not only is its history deemed responsible for setting the time clock of the *oikoumene*, but parts of its physical space are often considered the best way of explaining that wider world.

Within this Greek tradition and Greek world-view, Strabo also has a very precise way of splitting up the world inside his narrative. His analogy is surgery (2.1.30), in which amputation occurs at joints, producing pieces 'which have a natural configuration' and are 'significant and well-defined'. Greece is one of those well-defined areas, but it is significant that Strabo, in the way he situates Greece, specifically underlines its ambiguous place at the boundary of Europe. Strabo's *periplus* narrative structure takes him from the Pillars of Hercules across Europe to Italy, before moving on to the remaining 'eastern' countries of Europe. As he says: 'and it leaves on the right the whole of Thrace, Illyria, and lastly (*loipên*), finally (*de kai teleutaian*), Greece' (2.5.30; cf. Figure 5.1). Greece is marginalised, distanced, from the rest of Europe through the direction of Strabo's narrative journey, and that marginalisation is underlined by his sentence structure, in which even the word Greece is cut off and separated away at the end of his sentence by the descriptors of its marginal position. Moreover, that sense of Greece's position at the very end of Europe is shown to be an active choice of Strabo's in book 7, since Strabo chooses first to describe the seaboard all the way to Byzantium (7.6.2), before returning to describe the limb of Greece left below (7.7.1, reinforced again at 8.1; cf. Figure 5.1).

Yet there are several levels of irony and ambiguity in Strabo's description, which complicate how we should read the place of Greece within his narrative frame. First, Strabo's tendency to hug the shoreline throughout his narrative, which encourages him to go on Byzantium first before returning to describe Greece, thus ensuring its position at the edge of Europe, is a very Roman geographical trait (cf. Salway 2004: 96), undercutting Strabo's stance as a geographer positioned squarely within the Greek tradition. At the same time, however, the rhetorical strategy employed to separate out Greece at the end of his sentence quoted above could be interpreted not as marginalising Greece, but rather as a use of the rhetorical trope of saving the best till last. Depending on the reader's cultural background and education, the place of Greece in Strabo's narrative frame is thus mobile. But perhaps the most important point is this: thanks to the placement of his description of Greece at the very boundaries of Europe, Greece becomes the mid-point of his journey around the entire *oikoumene* (cf. Prandi 1994: 11). Across the seventeen books of the *Geography*, the mid-point is halfway through book 9, when Strabo is in Boeotia (appropriately enough not far from discussing Delphi's claim to be centre of the world (9.3.6)). Strabo thus situates himself in line with previous philosophers and geographers, including Plato, Aristotle and Ephorus, who had supposed Greece to be the centre of the known world (cf. Geus 2003: 234; Romm 2010: 224).

The place of Greece in Strabo's project is thus already complex. Strabo writes within a Greek literary tradition and Greek world-view about a world which was discovered by Greeks, is infused with Greek history and people and often exemplified through Greek physical space. At the same time, Greece is ambiguously positioned within a framework that betrays the influence of Roman conceptions of space on Strabo's narrative and treated as a place that is simultaneously geographically remote and textually central, over which the power of Rome (if not its literary folk) is now dominant and expanding. To that curious mixture of importance and impotence, I want now to add by focusing more closely on how Greece is represented within the stories of other parts of the world, and then, finally, commenting on how this prepares us for Strabo's description of Greece proper in books 8–10.

THE PLACE OF GREECE IN OTHER SPACES OF THE *OIKOUMENE*

Strabo's description of Iberia in book 3, despite the fact that it is the location for Strabo's claim that the Romans have added little to Greek historical and

The place of Greece in other spaces of the oikoumene

geographical knowledge, leaves scant space for Greece or Greek influence in Strabo's day. The focus is predominantly on the Romans' current presence, their cultural influence and their system of administration (e.g. 3.4.19–20). The aim of the description is to offer strategic and military information (3.3.6; cf. Strabo's general aims 1.1.16, 1.1.19). In both this book and in book 4, which focuses on Gaul and the northernmost reaches of the *oikoumene*, a comparison is established between the local 'barbarians' and the Roman way of life (cf. Dueck 2000: 170; Woolf 2011: 24–7). Both these books are intently focused on the present rather than the past, setting up a direct comparison especially between Iberia (the westernmost part of Europe: 3.1.4) and Greece (the easternmost part of Europe: 7.7.1), which is characterised, in contrast to Iberia, as a place of the past.

The relationship between Greece and Italy, however, is far more complex. Books 5–6, focusing on Italy and Sicily, move the temporal focus of Strabo's work strongly to the past, particularly by highlighting the foundation stories of many (now) Roman cities. Strabo begins (6.1.2) by calling the area of southern Italy and Sicily '*megale Hellas*', 'great Greece' (cf. Biffi 1988: xxviii; Musti 1994: 61–94). As Strabo makes clear, many of the cities in this region were originally Greek foundations, e.g. Cosa (5.2.8), Elea (6.1.1), Pisa (5.2.5) and Lipara (6.2.10). Most importantly, Strabo even stresses the parallel stories of Rome's foundation, either by the locals Romulus and Remus (5.3.2), or alternatively as an Arcadian Greek colony (5.3.3). This latter story, while 'older and more fabulous' (*protera kai muthodês*), is shown to be believed by at least one Roman historian (Coelius Antipater) on the grounds that, down to the present, Rome's sacrifices to Heracles have been conducted in the Greek manner (cf. Clarke 1999a: 265). Such a decision to focus on the importance of Greece in Italy and Sicily's past, indeed to give it as a possible explanation for the foundation of Rome, now the most preeminent city in Strabo's world, is complemented by his structuring of time. He deploys a tripartite division of time (*proteron . . . husteron . . . nun*) in the Italy and Sicily books roughly three times as often as in those focusing on Iberia and Gaul (Massaro 1986). Greek involvement in Italian space (the '*proteron*' moment) places Greece, and Greeks, at the fount of Italian development, just as Homer stands at the fount of the geographical tradition and world-view that Rome now dominates.

Yet almost immediately Strabo contrasts this picture of the past with that of the present (the '*nun*' moment): 'now, all parts of it, except Taras, Rhegium and Neapolis, have become completely barbarised' (6.1.2). Strabo continues to emphasise the current decay of much of Greek civilization in Sicily (cf. Dueck 2000: 173; Morcillo 2010: 90–3), the moral extravagance (*truphê*) of Greek poleis such as Tarentum (6.3.4), and the evolution of Sicily from *megale Hellas* to Rome's granary (6.2.7). This is part of his wider construction of Rome as the central force, being served by a series of Greek towns that act as gateway communities to the centre (e.g. Brundisium), although he will also praise Cumae for maintaining its historic traditions (its '*kosmos*') in spite of current Roman control (5.4.4.).

As a result, Greece is once again placed in a position of both importance and impotence. The spaces of Italy and Sicily are intricately interwoven with the space of Greece (indeed, their landscape used to be known as part of the Greek world), both through the past connection between colony and metropolis, and also through the continuing (or not) presence of Greek culture and political order. Most scholars have acknowledged that Greece features heavily in the past space of Italy and Sicily. Yet I would argue that, for Strabo, such past importance actually needs to be interpreted as an important feature also of the Roman present. As Strabo himself argues in book 2, when talking about how geography should be written:

... and [of the things resulting from human design] he [the geographer] should indicate those such as can persist for a long time, or else such as can persist not for long and yet somehow possess a certain distinction (*epiphaneian*) and fame (*doxan*), which, by enduring to later times, make a work of man, even when it no longer exists, a kind of natural attribute of a place (*tropon tina sumphuê tois topois poiei*); hence it is clear that these later attributes must also be mentioned ... (2.5.17)

For Strabo, past activities, if they are important enough, can become natural features of a landscape; action can become a permanent feature of space, part of the stratigraphy and shape of a place. Whatever the present condition of Italy and Sicily as part of the Roman world, Strabo, I argue, thinks it impossible to understand the landscape of that world without reference to the important place of Greece as a 'natural feature' of its landscape. Just as Rome's present physical landscape is bound up with Greece because, as Strabo will later point out, so much of the city is built out of variegated marble from the Greek island of Skyros (9.5.16), so too must we understand that Rome's present landscape is also littered with Greek features originally created in its distant past.

Italy and Sicily, however, are not the only places in which Greece is constructed as a crucial player, both past and present. In the second half of the *Geography*, Strabo's narrative turns to Asia Minor, the Middle East and finally North Africa (on the difficulty of getting practical information about places east of the Peloponnese even in Roman times, see: Salway 2004: 96). In these books (11–17), there is a continued emphasis on major Greek myths, events and historical figures as key elements that shape the space, history and

The place of Greece in other spaces of the oikoumene

place of these countries within the *oikoumene*. In book 11, for example, the use of the myth of Jason, Medea and the Golden Fleece, as well as that of the Amazons is marked (e.g. 11.5.3, 11.14.14), as is the presence of Alexander the Great (e.g. 11.11.4). In book 13, focusing on the Troad, the Trojan war is, as one might expect, central (e.g. 13.1.7). In fact the book develops into a long discussion of the Homeric text (cf. Salmeri 2000: 572). In book 15, set in India, the description, as well as much of the evidence, is concentrated on, and derived from, the campaigns of Alexander the Great (e.g. 15.1.5; cf. Dueck 2000: 177). Indeed, Clarke has argued that the inclusion of India in the *oikoumene* is related almost exclusively to its being part of Alexander's world in the past rather than of that of the Roman present, perhaps acting in turn as a guide to future Roman aspirations (Clarke 1999a: 327–8). The dominance of Alexander the Great as the historical linchpin of this part of the *oikoumene* continues in Strabo's descriptions of Mesopotamia and Arabia in book 16 (e.g. 16.1.9) and into Egypt in book 17 (e.g. 17.1.43).

This dominance of Greek myth and history is matched only by two focuses on Roman activities and on one of Strabo's own: the relationship of Parthia and Rome in books 11 and 16, the intellectual milieu of Strabo's own homeland in book 14, and the recent historical events involving Caesar, Pompey, Antony and Augustus in Egypt in book 17 (Salmeri 2000: 578). Yet even in these thoroughly 'Roman' and 'Strabonic' spaces and events, the Greek world is always implicated. Augustus, for example, throughout the *Geography*, is often characterised by his similarity to Alexander the Great (e.g. 1.2.1, 2.1.6, 15.1.4, cf. Dueck 2000: 104).

We must, however, be careful not to overstate Greece's place in Strabo's world. Clarke has argued that Strabo's *Geography* puts Rome at the point where 'various lines of movement of goods, peoples and ideas met' (Clarke 1999a: 223), as part of an *oikoumene* composed on a centre-and-periphery model with Rome as its centre (Clarke 1999a: 210). Without doubt Strabo argues for current Roman dominance. His mini-summation at the end of book 6 underlines the present-day situation: 'while I have already mentioned many things which have caused the Romans at the present time to be exalted to so great a height ...' (6.4.1). This is followed by a description of Italy's natural advantages: 'it not only is well-suited to hegemony because it surpasses the countries that surround it both in the valour of its people and in size, but also can easily avail of their services' (6.4.1). After this comes a recap of the territories that Rome has subdued (which will be recapped again at the end of the work: 17.3.24).

Yet Clarke herself subsequently argues for a second focus to Strabo's world besides Rome, namely that of his homeland of Amasia in Asia Minor. Strabo puts heavy emphasis on the present-day intellectual scene in Asia Minor, as witnessed by his failure to list any 'men of high reputation' (*andres eudoxoi*) from the western parts of the Roman Empire, from north and central Italy and even from Rome, in comparison to the plethora listed from his homeland (Clarke 1999a: 239, 242–3; cf. Salmeri 2000: 580; Engels 2005: 130).

This short review of the ways in which Greek myth and history are encountered outside Greece itself, both as part of Strabo's intellectual conceptualisation of his work and as a way of understanding and perceiving particular physical spaces throughout the *Geography*, has shown that Greece, alongside Asia Minor and Rome, must also be considered as a key focus of Strabo's world. Strabo constructs Greek writers all the way back to Homer as the intellectual heritage for his genre of geographical writing and the development of a conception (and time clock) of the *oikoumene*, which Roman writers, he insists, have done little to add to. At the same time, while he situates Greece purposefully at the very end of Europe, such a marginalisation actively places Greece at the very centre of his *periplous* tour. In his discussion of other spaces within the *oikoumene*, Strabo describes Greece as the power that once (*proteron*) dominated much of the region of Italy and Sicily, and thus, as a result, is forever at the base of much of the civilization of Italy (perhaps even of the city of Rome itself) that now (*nun*) dominates the world (for a similar idea see Dion. Hal. 1.5.1, 1.89.2; Pelling 2007). Yet Strabo also underlines how the past dominance of Greece makes it a physical part of the present landscape – as unavoidable a presence as the Greek marble that makes up Roman buildings. In addition, it is through Greek myth, history and a powerful individual figure such as Alexander the Great that Strabo is able to make sense of the different countries in the eastern Empire and enunciate their physical, metaphorical and historical value. It is also through Greek myth and history that Strabo sizes up current Roman achievements, particularly those of Augustus, and characterises the potential future direction of Rome's Empire. Far from being just a marginalised space geographically, Greece is implicated as central to understanding most of Strabo's world.

GREECE AS A SPACE WITHIN THE *GEOGRAPHY*

Greece as a microcosm of the oikoumene

The route of Strabo's *periplous* journey around the *oikoumene* left Greece at the very edges of Europe, as a place geographically remote (although ambiguously thus the centre of his *Geography*, cf. Figure 5.1).

After travelling as far as Byzantium, Strabo turns back to discuss the Greek peninsula (7.7.1). Our first introduction to the country, however, is only very briefly based on its geographical layout. Instead, Strabo immediately introduces us, in Herodotean style, to the cyclical nature of civilisation as demonstrated through the example of Greece: the place was once inhabited by barbarians, once colonised by barbarians, and now, today, most of what is 'indisputably Greece' is held by barbarians (7.7.1; cf. van der Vliet 1984).

This first portrait of Greece is reflected again when, having spent the remainder of book 7 examining, amongst other places, Epirus, Illyria, Macedonia and Thrace, Strabo finally turns to describe the remainder of Greece at the beginning of book 8. Once again his attention turns almost immediately to the tribes of Greece (8.1.2) and their ethnographic and linguistic divisions, before returning to describe the geography of the country (8.1.3) as two large bodies of land divided by an isthmus. The Peloponnese is considered by Strabo to be a larger and more famous body of land, the 'acropolis of Greece' (8.1.3), a place whose topography naturally created the conditions for its hegemony. Strabo outlines a series of five peninsulas that radiate outwards from the Peloponnese across the rest of Greece as natural divisions for his narrative (cf. Prandi 1994). He chooses to begin his account of Greece with the Peloponnese (thus necessitating a geographical jump from where he began in northern Greece to Greece's most southern point, only to journey eventually to the north again at the end of book 9).

Strabo's description of Greece as a series of peninsulas radiating out from its Peloponnesian acropolis, its hegemonic centre, towards its wilder and more barbarian extremities replicates in miniature the world-view of the *oikoumene* he puts forward throughout his *Geography* (as a centre-and-periphery model with civilised Rome as its centre). Greece is thus set up simultaneously as somewhere geographically remote, but also representative of the wider world in both its power structure and the cyclical nature of its civilisation (cf. Dueck 2000: 154).

In addition, Strabo is repeatedly interested in the debate over the degree to which Greece can be said to be (and to have been) unified. That debate is recounted through a series of different forums in books 8–10. A first forum is constituted by the arguments of Greek writers, such as at 8.6.6, when Strabo explicitly turns to the debate about the terms *hellas, hellenes* and *panhellenes*. The debate is rehearsed through the arguments of Thucydides and Apollodorus, based on the evidence provided by Homer, Hesiod and Archilochus. The second forum for the Greek unity debate concerns Greek participation in common sanctuaries. At 9.3.2–9 Strabo turns to consider how Delphi acted as a sanctuary which once 'was held in exceedingly great honour' by people coming from all over Greece to the centre of the world (a notion supported by, as Strabo adds, a 'fabricated' story of Zeus' eagles meeting at Delphi: 9.3.6), but which is now neglected, such that much of its wealth missing. The third forum is constituted by Strabo's continuing interest in what defines Greece – both in the past and the present – as determined by linguistic, ethnic and geographical criteria (e.g. 7.7.3–8, 8.1.2–3 and 10.1.10). At 7.7.3, for example, Strabo underlines how in earlier times the space of Greece had clear boundaries, but now most of the country is depopulated, and such boundaries – based on people rather than geographical features – are impossible to draw. The final forum for argument about Hellenicity is Strabo's own narrative tendency towards amputation, cutting the world up into discrete chunks. Thus Strabo decides to count the eastern Aegean islands in his description of Asia rather than of Greece and Europe (10.5.6, 10.5.14), thereby offering a new take on what is and is not part of Greece.

These different contestations of the nature of Greek unity, far from negating the importance of Greece as a space within the wider world, seem to me to underline the way in which Greece once again acts as a space of reflection on the processes ongoing in the wider *oikoumene*, which is itself undergoing, as Strabo's *periplous* tour makes clear, an uneven (and indeed disputed) process of unification under Roman domination.

Greece as a space of Homer

Homer, since the very opening of the *Geography* (cf. 1.1.2), has been taken as the founder of the tradition in which Strabo is writing, an indisputable source of knowledge, and a continual guide for Strabo in writing the geography and history of the world (cf. Biraschi 1984). Perhaps nowhere in the *Geography* is Homer more prevalent than in Strabo's account of Greece. Indeed, as Strabo points out, it was Homer who first studied the geography of Greece (8.1.1), although he also subsequently notes the importance of tying Homer's picture of Greece as it was then to the current state of Greece.

Within his narrative of the space of Greece Strabo is happy not just to recount details of Homeric geography, but to allow for, and indulge, contestation, particularly over Homeric historical issues (e.g. the dispute between Strabo and Ephorus over the place of the Aetolians and Acarnanians in the Catalogue of Ships in book 2 of the *Iliad* (10.2.24–5)).

Greece as a space within the Geography

The most expansive discussion, however, is over the location of Pylus and the home of Nestor (8.3.7–29); here Strabo feels it is his job to act as arbiter because of the importance of the issue as part of his (and everyone's) past:

> Perhaps I would not be examining at such length things that are ancient...if there were not connected with these matters legends that have been taught to us from boyhood, and, since different men say different things, I must act as arbiter. In general, it is the most famous, the oldest, and the most experienced men who are believed ... (8.3.23)

Nor is Homer a subject of interest simply for those who wish to debate singularly knotty problems of ancient geography. Strabo's tour of Boeotia reveals a particularly close relationship between Homer and contemporary Greece (for discussion of the use of Homer in other micro-regions, such as the Peloponnese, see Biraschi 1994b). In Boeotia, Strabo will depart from a narrative based on geographical proximity, as he moves from one city to another almost entirely using Homer's Catalogue of Ships as his guide (9.2.21–35). Indeed, nowhere in his account of Greece does Strabo follow the Catalogue of Ships more rigidly than in Boeotia (cf. Wallace 1979: 2–3, 171). Homer here provides not just material for debate about ancient Greece, but a description of Greece in Strabo's day. Yet at 9.2.36 Strabo also adds to the list of places named in the Catalogue other places mentioned by the poet in different parts of the Homeric narrative (Wallace 1979: 143), as well as several places not cited by Homer, all of which are mentioned because of their historic or religious significance (9.2.37–40).

Pretzler has commented that 'much of book 8 and 9 seems scarcely more than an attempt to describe the Homeric landscape and to bring it up to date' (Pretzler 2005: 150). While many scholars have lamented the fact that Strabo didn't do a better job as a travel guide, dismissing his description of Greece *because* it is a recap of Homer misses the point. For Strabo, there is no more important source than Homer. Greece described by Homer is thus not an out-of-date guidebook, but a critical part of the interwoven layers of history and geography that make up both the literary tradition in which he writes and the *oikoumene* he is writing about. It is a layer of the past that defines how things are now. By prioritising Homeric Greece and making that Greece the Greece he describes in his *Geography* (with allowances for its current state of desolation, which we will come to later), Strabo not only offers up to his readers a Greece suspended in time (indeed, out of time and above reproach), but also echoes (and perhaps increases) Greece's cultural standing as a place of critical importance within the present-day wider world.

This is not to say that all his readers would have agreed with him. Indeed, we may want to understand Strabo's frequent apologies to his audience in books 8–10 for engaging so much in the history of a particular area of Greece (e.g. 8.4.11), or in a discourse of Greek theology (e.g. 10.3.23), or in relation to civic constitutions (e.g. 10.4.22), not as lax moments in Strabo's narrative drive, but as an acknowledgement that not everyone would see Greece as he saw it. Not everyone, perhaps, was as powerless as Strabo to resist telling Greece's stories (although at other times he does manage to hang back, as in his decision not to recount all the 'wonders' of Athens, perhaps in order to avoid the common Hellenistic trope in such things: 9.1.16). But Strabo was, after all, writing in a world that valued and envied Greek cultural achievement, a world in which many were readily prepared to accept the preferential treatment Strabo gives to Homer's Greece (cf. for example Plin. *Ep.* 8.24.1–4: 'Remember you have been sent to the province of Achaia, to the pure and genuine Greece, where civilization and literature, and agriculture too, are believed to have originated').

Greece as a space in Strabo's present-day world

Much has been made of Strabo's repeated assertions of the current desertion of Greece in comparison to its glorious past (e.g. 7.7.3, 7.7.9, 8.4.11, 8.8.1). Yet that does not mean that Greece is an irrelevant space for the present day; indeed, we have already seen the way in which Strabo offers Greece up as a sort of microcosm, and reflection of, the present-day developing *oikoumene*. But Strabo also manipulates Greece's place in the present-day wider world through specific reference to particular poleis. This is done, in part, in purely geographical terms. Certain poleis are not simply placed within their local geography, but specifically positioned within the wider world. Sparta, for instance, is specified as 3,000 stades away from Phycus in Cyrenaica, 4,600 stades from Pachynus in Sicily, and 670 stades from Malea to the south-east (8.5.1). Corinth for its part is described, not in specific distances, but in its ideal position as a trading port, connecting Italy and Asia (8.6.20). The choice to discuss the geographical situation of these particular places within the current wider world is almost certainly no accident. As scholars have discussed, Corinth is one of the places Strabo definitely visited, and Sparta, in Strabo's time, had particularly good relations with Rome (cf. 8.5.5, Weller 1906; Bowersock 1961; Wallace 1979: 170; Pretzler 2005: 145, 147). Yet in doing so, Strabo not only upholds his own goal to write a *chorographia* (in which particular places are key to articulating the wider world, echoing a way of understanding the world that dates back to

Eratosthenes (cf. Geus 2003: 243)), but also, by setting up these particular cities as cardinal points on the present-day world map, enhances the position of Greece as a space within that world.

These cities, along with several others in Greece, however, have another role to play in Strabo's narrative about the present-day world. Throughout his description of Greece, Strabo is interested in the question of hegemony, particularly the criteria which made it possible for certain communities to exert hegemonic control (cf. his description of Rome as being naturally suited to hegemony at the end of book 6). Several Greek cities and states serve as his examples. Thus Boeotia was:

> ...naturally well suited to hegemony, but those who were from time to time its leaders neglected careful training and education...and the cause of this was the fact that they belittled the value of learning and of intercourse with mankind, and cared for military virtues alone... (9.2.2)

The Spartans, in contrast, did not have natural resources that made it easy to live off (although happily their city was surrounded by mountains that made its territory difficult to invade 8.5.6), but they did have good government, which allowed them to surpass the rest to the extent that 'they alone of all the Greeks ruled over land and sea' (8.5.5). Corinth too 'was always great and wealthy, and it was well equipped with men skilled in the affairs of state ... the city had territory, however, that was not very fertile, but dissected and rough' (8.6.23). For Athens, although there is no explicit comment, the contrast is made between the city which 'is a rock situated on a plain and surrounded by dwellings' (9.1.16) and its illustrious political and hegemonic past, which is 'to this day free and held in honour among the Romans' (9.1.20), and which has left the city so full of important things, that 'if I once began to describe the multitude of things in this city that are lauded and proclaimed far and wide, I fear that I should go too far and that my work would depart from the purpose I have in view' (9.1.16). The most expansive example, however, is Crete. The forms of political government on Crete provoke a long digression from Strabo (10.4.20–22), along with an apology for its inclusion (10.4.22). Crete, he says in an earlier summary, 'had good laws, and rendered the best of the Greeks its emulators...but later it changed very much for the worst ... the Cretans degenerated into the business of piracy' (10.4.9).

Such comparisons involving the conditions necessary for hegemony and good government immediately echo Strabo's comment on Italy's own predisposition for hegemony at 6.4.1–2: its geographical place in the wider world, long coastline, harbours, balance of air and temperature, types of landscape, and plentiful supply of water, fuel and food, alongside the good government and fair rules constructed by Romans which made it 'a base of operations for universal hegemony.' Neither Greece nor any of its individual cities can compare with Rome's combination of natural and man-made advantages. Yet what the Greek examples point up is that there is no guaranteed correlation between good government, hegemony and good natural resources. The Spartans, Corinthians and Athenians had hegemony without good natural resources, the Boeotians lacked hegemony, despite their good resources, because of sloppy education. In the new present-day *oikoumene* dominated by Rome, Greece works as a space of reflection, both encapsulating Rome's past and reflecting its possible future: Rome's balance of both natural resources and good government has not been well kept in the recent past (cf. the degree to which mention of Actium and thus recent political and military strife is kept away from discussions of Italy in Strabo's narrative), though it is now better maintained under Augustus and his new golden age, but may not necessarily remain so in the future.

Greece acts as a space of reflection on Rome in another way as well: as a place with which Rome has been fully involved for some time, and thus which can be regarded as a benchmark for Roman behaviour, especially as it wrestles with the subjugation of the boundaries of the *oikoumene*. The resulting portrait is mixed. On the one hand, Roman success stories in Greece are emphasised. The city of Nikopolis, for example, was recently founded in Epirus by Augustus, following the battle of Actium. It was a city which saved the region from continual depopulation and which was now successfully increasing in numbers and growing into a rich and well-apportioned city (7.7.6). Equally, the Romans saved the old city of Patras (8.7.5) and halted depopulation in the north of Greece (cf. Baladié 1980: 312, 327). Strabo underlines positive Roman relations with cities like Sparta and Corinth in his narrative, as well as Roman benevolence towards many cities, which had in contrast suffered under Mithridates VI (e.g. Athens: 9.1.20; Delos 10.5.4).

Rome is even said to have been able to change the perception of the physical landscape of Greece for the better. Whereas the narrow pass of Thermopylae was historically regarded as the key to mastery of Greece (the 'fetters' or 'shackles' of Greece), Greece's 'subjection to a single power' meant that now 'everything is free from toll and open to all mankind' (9.4.16). The crucial change, thanks to Rome, was not so much to do with the physical landscape, but rather with the meaning of that landscape. The impact of Rome here at Thermopylae is underlined I think, interestingly, by the fact that the narrative is accompanied by one Strabo's very rare citations from something directly observed on the ground. At Thermopylae he quotes the monument to the 300 Spartans, perhaps in order to emphasise the long-running history of this place as the key to Greece and thus the fundamental nature of the change that Rome had managed to bring about.

Yet on the other side of the equation, Rome's 'performance' in Greece is not so glowingly reported. Strabo described the destruction of Corinth (as well as Carthage) as a key turning point in Roman history, since its destruction heralded the beginning of a Roman moral decline (cf. 8.6.23, 14.5.2; Dueck 2000: 120). That decline was in part due to the amount of wealth Rome acquired through its conquest. It has been noted before that the books on Greece contain more references to artworks, monuments and sanctuaries (as well as use of poetry) than any other part of the *Geography* (Dueck 2000: 81, 94; 2010: 243). This focus on the artistic productivity and the religious landscape of Greece serves two purposes: on the one hand, it emphasises the continuing importance of Greece (Athens 'as a possession of the gods, who seized it as a sanctuary for themselves' 9.1.16) and its current vitality (e.g. the description of the lively religious landscape of the Peloponnese 8.3.12–16); on the other hand, it also emphasises further the negative morality of the actions of Romans in taking so much of that material back to Rome. The bad morality of Rome is exposed in the 'mirror' provided by Greece, particularly in Strabo's discussion of Corinth, which was heavily plundered (cf. 8.6.23: 'the most and the best of the other dedicatory offerings at Rome came from here [Corinth]'). Although Caesar later returned some of these items to Corinth when he recolonised the city in 44 BC, all of the city's graves were subsequently ransacked and the goods sold in Rome (8.6.23). Rome's future, in Strabo's eyes, and through the lens of his vision of the space of Greece, does not look perhaps as morally justified, or as certain, as it had done when Strabo announced Rome's natural disposition to hegemony at the end of book 6.

CONCLUSION

In this chapter, my aim has been to highlight the potential of a spatial approach to a text, particularly one explicitly concerned with geography and history, as a useful way of thinking about how the value of a particular literary space is constructed and how its links with its wider frame are formulated and nuanced (or as Strabo puts it, how we discern the 'shape, colour, and size of an apple, and also its smell, feel and flavour, and from all this the mind forms the concept of apple' 2.5.11).

156   *The place of Greece in the* oikoumene *of Strabo's* Geography

Biraschi, in her edited volume on Strabo's Greece, urged readers to consider the effort Strabo went to in his description of Greece to present his audience with the picture of a place with lots going on (Biraschi 1994a: 1). Despite that call, Strabo's Greece is still perceived in modern scholarship as a place primarily of the past, which is eclipsed by the dominant new space of Rome and merely competes with Strabo's homeland in Asia Minor for second place in the order of this new *oikoumene*.

I have argued here that the way Strabo constructs Greece as a space in his *oikoumene* does not allow for such a clear hierarchy. The place and value of Greece as a space in the *oikoumene* is constructed within Strabo's *Geography* in five main ways: first, through the Greek literary tradition and *oikoumene* world-view in which Strabo is writing, which situates Greece, though physically remote, as textually central and as a *colossus* in and of itself; second, through the way in which Greek colonies, myths and historical figures infuse the descriptions of Italy, Sicily, as well as much of the east in Strabo's world with a sense of the importance of Greece, making Greece a natural feature of their past and present-day landscapes; third, through depicting present Greece as a microcosm of the power structures at work in the *oikoumene* and its cyclical civilisation; fourth, through privileging the description of the space of Greece itself as a land of Homer, thereby constructing a Greece in which everyone still has a stake, despite its present-day desertion; and fifth, by tying even the poor present-day condition of Greece into his wider narrative through locating its poleis as cardinal points within the wider world, and holding up the space of Greece as a mirror for Rome's hegemonic future and as marker of its moral quality. In sum, Greece for Strabo occupies a space and place of more importance and interest in the *Geography* than previous scholarship has allowed.

Some textual critics of the surviving Strabo manuscripts have argued that Strabo himself proclaimed Greece as, if not the most important space in the *oikoumene*, then certainly on a par with Rome. Following Strabo's description of the Peloponnese as the 'acropolis of Greece as a whole' in book 8 (8.1.3), scholars such as Groskurd, Kramer and Curtius have argued that Strabo went on to say 'and that Greece is the acropolis of Europe.'[3] I do not think we can, or should go that far. As has been made clear throughout this chapter, while we need to re-evaluate the importance Strabo attached to Greece, we must also recognise that Strabo maintains a certain ambiguity in

---

[3] Groskurd, Kramer and Curtius all subscribe to this view in their commentaries: Groskurd 1831–1834; Kramer 1844; Curtius 1851–2. Cf. Jones 1927–31: vol. IV, p. 11. For full discussion see Radt 2002: vol. II (392); vol. VI (382–3).

his representation of Greece: Greece is always both important and impotent in relation to Rome (and vice versa). Two examples show this perfectly: first, the Greek *colossus* statues (in Taras 6.3.1, Apollonia 7.6.1, Olympia 8.3.30, Argos 8.6.10, Samos 14.1.14, Rhodes 14.2.5) have been argued by Pothecary to be Greek cultural artefacts, which, 'in attracting Roman attention, reveal the strength of Greek cultural achievements and Roman dependency on Greek cultural heritage' (Pothecary 2005a: 25). Yet, in reality, even though Strabo describes many of the *colossi* in the context of their original location, he has to admit they have actually by his day been taken to Rome (e.g. at Apollonia 7.6.1). Greek achievements, great as they are, are now, so often, in the hands of Rome, even if their majesty still captures Roman admiration.

My second example is taken from book 10. Strabo is in the middle of his discussion of the Cyclades, having reached the small island of Gyaros, when he relates:

When we sailed away we took on board one of the fishermen, who had been chosen to go from there to Caesar as ambassador (Caesar was at Corinth on his way to celebrate the triumph after the victory at Actium)…he had been sent as ambassador to request a reduction in their tribute. (10.5.3)

This tale sums up nicely much of the way in which Greece is positioned as a place within the present-day *oikoumene*. It is subject to Caesar Augustus, to whom the Greeks must pay tribute. Yet Greece is a place that even the all-powerful Roman emperor is drawn to visit: he goes to Corinth on his way to Actium, the place of the victory that gave him that power, firmly located in Greek space, close enough for even a humble fisherman to travel to him.

There is another aspect, however, to this constant interplay of importance and impotence that needs to be considered: the way in which it unfolds. Literary constructs of space differ fundamentally from physical ones, since they unfold in a linear fashion as part of a narrative. Throughout this chapter, material has been gathered from different parts of Strabo's *Geography* in order to compile an overall picture of Strabo's construction of Greece as a space in the *oikoumene*. But that is not the way in which it would have been revealed to a reader of his text (ancient or modern). Instead, that reader is forced to discover parts of that construct as he travels along with Strabo in his *periplus* journey around the *oikoumene*. Learning is hodological; it is a process, a journey. Our perspective as readers alternates as Strabo moves in his own spatial perspectives from bird's-eye cartographical description, through mythological and historiographical landscape, to join us as he travels himself around (some of) these regions (as the boat story above indicates). He learns as he moves through space, just as we do, reflecting the deeply held belief in the connection between physical movement, mental thought and the acquisition of knowledge within Greek and Roman culture (cf. O'Sullivan 2011: 98). Thus until the very end of Strabo's world tour, the reader is left in a state of suspense about what direction Strabo's construction of the space of Greece might take (or indeed of anything or anywhere else but particularly I think of Greece because of the way it is infused into so many other spaces around the *oikoumene*). Only at the end of the tour can readers make their decision on how they perceive and react to Strabo's representation. The balance of importance and impotence struck by Strabo is thus heightened in its impact by the way that balance is represented and revealed as part of the linear narrative journey.

Such a way of understanding both how space is constructed and revealed within Strabo's narrative, and particularly how the space of Greece is characterised as both more important and more impotent than that of Rome, has two main repercussions for how we think about Strabo and the world in which he lived. First, for Strabo, denying his description of Greece as a place of present impotence alone, and stressing instead his offering of a more complex picture, place him much more on par than has been previously accepted with the literary agendas of other Greek writers within this new Roman world: particularly Polybius or Dionysius of Halicarnassus. He becomes, not a 'poor Pausanias', but an equally subtle and complex writer capturing the power balance of a world in flux. Yet the second important implication is this: highlighting the ambiguity with which Strabo casts the respective importance of Greece and Rome has the result that the surety of Rome's power – a feature so often underlined as the key message of Strabo – is undercut, and is instead replaced by a message of transience, uncertainty and expectation. It is that message, which may well have struck a chord with (at least) some of Strabo's readers in a post-Augustan world that was not always as secure as its leaders would have liked their subjects (or indeed us) to believe. It was also perhaps that message of uncertainty that made Strabo's *Geography* popular in future periods of transition, like that under Justinian, when several authors including Procopius took a good deal of interest in Strabo's work. It is perhaps also that uncertainty, which today resonates with the unusual uncertainty of our own world in the early twenty-first century, that has, as a result, encouraged many scholars to work on Strabo once again in the first decades of this new millennium.

Conclusion: space and society in the Greek and Roman worlds

INTRODUCTION

The case-studies examined over the previous chapters have sought to illustrate not just the variety of forms a spatial approach can take but also the kinds of advantages and insights such approaches can offer for the study of the ancient world. In Chapter 1, in response to spatial scholarship that has not recently been focused on agora-type civic space, and to scholarship on Cyrene that has focused on the city's turbulent political history so often constructed through sources from other places and times, I investigated the spatial development of particular structures within the city's agora. This chapter thus not only provided a way into understanding Cyrene's political development from a Cyrenean perspective but also offered a detailed window on the way that change was formulated, negotiated and perceived over time as well as the way in which, and the key moments during which, the agora space was developed and utilised in comparison to other types of space within the city (cf. Figures 1.1, 1.9).

The focus in Chapter 2 moved from civic space to sacred space and from individual structures to the relationships between spaces for the gods on Delos. In response to scholarship on Delos' wide pantheon that so often focused on the literary and epigraphical evidence, a spatial approach to how its multiple networks of polytheism developed on the ground over time was adopted in order to provide a crucial counter-vantage point from which to understand the changing experience of the sanctuary as well as its role in the wider world. That investigation highlighted not just the range of motivations behind spatial placement but also the range of types of relationships constructed between divinities as a result, as well as the way in which those relationships continued to change over time (cf. Figures 2.1, 2.2, 2.10). Crucially, it also underlined the reciprocal relationship between epigraphic, literary and archaeological evidence, by showing the ways in which the networks of polytheism presented by each could reinforce, contradict or complement one another.

Chapter 3 situated its investigation in funerary space, in particular the multiple tombs lining the roads emanating from and to Ostia, Pompeii and Rome, and sought to harness the recent advances in urban space scholarship, which have highlighted the multiplicity of ways in which the city was experienced and understood. In turn, it considered how different communities of tombs at different entrance roads to these cities created different impressions of the city they surrounded (cf. Figures 3.1, 3.4, 3.8). It argued that such varying impressions created a sense of both unity and alienation between cities within the Roman world, depending on who was viewing them (cf. Figure 3.10), and that the dynamics of tomb communities could, as a result, both support and undermine the model of centre and periphery which has been so dominant in the scholarly understanding of how the Roman world functioned.

Chapter 4 marked a shift in the consideration of space by widening its horizon of analysis to incorporate not just physical spaces but also the perceptual construct of the space (the proximity or distance) between spaces, as articulated through physical, literary and epigraphic sources over time. It did so by examining the changing relationship between metropolis and colony, and, as a result, sought to challenge the current scholarly consensus that the study of such relationships constitutes a dead end in colonisation scholarship. What the approach in this chapter offered was thus not only a new method of thinking about the complex and subtle ways in which these two spaces interacted and were perceived but also a means of highlighting the divergent pictures created through the material and literary evidence, to the extent that the literary sources created a sense of the metropolis and colony spaces as tightly joined at a time when physically they could not have been more different.

In the final chapter, the focus moved entirely to space as a literary rather than physical construct and to concepts of the place of particular spaces within the ancient *oikoumene*. In so doing, this chapter challenged current scholarly opinion on Strabo's conception of Greece as a place of the past and analysed the ways in which Greece was infused into the past and present of many different landscapes around Strabo's world. It argued for a much more complex and subtle appreciation of Strabo's world-view, as well as of the way in which readers understood his construction of space, which placed Rome's dominance within a context of uncertainty and transience. Such a message in turn, the chapter argued, demanded a reconsideration of

Strabo's place as a writer in comparison to other Graeco-Roman writers of the period and helped us perhaps understand why it was that his narrative retained its popularity, particularly in future periods of acute uncertainty.

As a result, what I hope this book has achieved is twofold: first, that it has connected spatial enquiry across a range of resolutions and genres of analysis, showing the ways in which space, both as a physical and as a conceptual construct as expressed through archaeological, epigraphic and literary evidence, can usefully and successfully add texture and depth to our historical understanding of particular places and events, cultural phenomena and societal interactions; second, as a result, that it has demonstrated the potential of spatial analysis as a useful tool in the armoury of historians for their analysis of the Greek and Roman worlds.

In the rest of this brief conclusion, I want to use the evidence provided by the case-studies, first, to think more broadly about how they can help us understand Classical, Hellenistic and Roman approaches to and conceptualisations of space, and, second, in particular, to think about how such an analysis can improve our understanding of the multiple ways in which the Roman world engaged with its Hellenistic and Classical predecessors in different places at different times. I shall end by returning to think again about how a spatial approach can deepen our historical understanding of the ancient world, and ask where next for the study of space.

CLASSICAL, HELLENISTIC AND ROMAN APPROACHES TO SPACE

Lefebvre once characterised the space of the Greek agora as one left physically open so as to allow for the gathering of the citizen body (Lefebvre 1991 (1974): 237). The case-study of the agora at Cyrene upholds to a large degree this general approach to civic space in the Classical Period: while constant building and rearticulation of the boundaries of the Cyrenean agora were undertaken, very little in the Classical Period was constructed in its centre (the exception being the 2-metre-tall circular shrine of local god Aristaeus which occupied the hitherto unelaborated centre of the agora in the first half of the fifth century BC: cf Figure 1.2). This Classical model of open, unelaborated space can be paralleled in other types of civic space, particularly areas of sporting competition and preparation; even the famous gymnasia of Athens were, for the most part, un-monumentalised park spaces for the majority of the Classical Period (cf. Scott, forthcoming). Yet equally it would be a mistake to see a preference for such open space as defining the Classical approach. Classical sacred space, as the case-study on

Delos showed, reveals a very different picture, as an increasing number of structures was added within the main Apollo sanctuary (indeed with several temples of Apollo being situated side by side rather than one replacing the other), as well as a plethora of smaller dedications occupying the central open space (cf. Figure 2.6).

More importantly, however, the case-studies also demonstrate how it would be a mistake to expect a slavish following of any general rule for the Classical Period. This is in part a function of the evidence, because of our uncertain and vastly incomplete archaeological knowledge of the Classical world, but also because that world was never a united construct, and was instead always made up of different groups, political systems and cultural *mores*, resulting in a wide spectrum of different attitudes to a whole host of issues, including how to conceptualise and engage with space. The case-study offered here in Chapter 4, the relationship between colony and metropolis, for example, emphasised how much we need to rethink our traditional portrayal of the similarity in the Classical Period between even these supposedly 'linked' spaces. But in addition, such a wide variety of responses to different kinds of space by different groups at different times is also due to the absence of any set of hard-and-fast rules even for the same kind of group. As has been emphasised for the polis in general, for example, no one physical characteristic or group of characteristics can currently be identified which were present in all Classical settlements known as poleis and absent from those which were not (Morgan and Coulton 1997: 88).

The Classical approach to space, therefore, is, for the moment at least, to be characterised by its indeterminacy, despite the occasional desire for something more determined: e.g. Aristotle, in his *Politics* (7.11.1), argued that sacred spaces in a polis should be grouped together in one suitable part of the city rather than spread out randomly. Conversely, it was that indeterminacy, that fluidity of forms in which space could be arranged, engaged with and conceptualised, that made space such an important part of the way in which communities presented themselves and engaged with one another. As I have argued elsewhere, for example, in relation to athletic space, the kinds of athletic spaces each city chose to construct reflected not just a city's ability to construct such structures but also its particular sporting interests and cultural priorities (Scott, forthcoming). Vlassopoulos (2007) has argued for the importance of what he terms 'free space' in allowing for the blurring of identities within the mixed community of Athens. Equally, as we saw in the case-study of Delos, such indeterminacy not only facilitated the creation and maintenance of spaces in which different communities could interact (e.g. the 'international' sanctuaries), but also, because of their flexibility, encouraged a high degree of cultural interaction between those people who engaged with the space around them.

How do Hellenistic approaches to space compare? Most obviously, as the case-study of Cyrene showed, Hellenistic monarchs had a tendency to fill open civic spaces with a series of structures that reflected and honoured them personally as autocratic rulers. Equally, more structures were built that served the new hierarchical power system (palaces, etc.). There was also more elaboration and incorporation of previously open and unarticulated civic spaces (such as those for sporting competition and practice). The argument has even been made that the entire polis was an evolutionary dead end, thanks to the power politics of the Hellenistic and Roman periods (cf. Runciman 1990). In spatial terms, at least, I would argue that the case-study of Cyrene shows that we need to reconceptualise that dead end. Poleis, and particularly their agora spaces, continued as useful spatial resources through which Hellenistic rulers could display their power. The space was not defunct or dead, but rather altered in its meaning and use.

In their attitudes to sacred space, the rulers of the Hellenistic kingdoms, as well as rich individuals within the hierarchical power structures of the Hellenistic world, departed less radically (or rather would have been perceived as departing less radically) from their Classical predecessors. Sacred spaces continued to be filled with dedications, though now they honoured individuals more often than poleis. Equally, Hellenistic monarchs continued to put huge emphasis on the articulation of sacred spaces through the construction and dedication of stoa-like structures at their boundaries, which, unlike specific cult buildings, could be singularly devoted to their own honour (cf. Figures 2.6, 2.7). Hellenistic monarchs were equally interested in the monumentalisation of entrance pathways (cf. the monumental entrance pathway to the sanctuary of Apollo at Delos), which again served as excellent spaces for self-glorification. Little thus seems to have changed from the Classical Period in the way those in power interacted with sacred space, except that the size and elaboration of the different spatial structures increased. The most perceptible difference, in contrast, was the increasing number of 'foreign' divinities who were accorded spaces within Greek sanctuaries, although, as the Delos example shows, many of these were specifically so located as to minimise their visual impact on the wider space (cf. Figure 2.4).

The overall similarity of Classical and Hellenistic approaches to sacred space thus chimes in with the findings of other recent scholarship, which has equally stressed the lack of change in conceptions of the divine image

164   *Conclusion: space and society in the Greek and Roman worlds*

between the Classical and Hellenistic worlds (cf. Mylonopoulos 2010), instead putting an emphasis on the new ways in which space, architecture and image worked together to create impact and mould interpretation (e.g. Schultz 2007). Thus while in many other aspects (and particularly kinds of space and sculpture) of the Hellenistic world much more dramatic changes may well have taken place, sacred space and sacred sculpture seem to have struck a note of continuity. As a result, different kinds of spaces (in this book we have examined the difference between Hellenistic approaches to civic spaces, such as the agora at Cyrene, and to sacred space, such as at Delos) would have offered different perceptions on what the transition between the Classical and Hellenistic worlds meant, and offered different venues for those keen to stress either difference or similarity.

With the advent of Roman influence, as might be expected, approaches to space changed more radically. Current scholarship has emphasised the importance of the centre-and-periphery model, as well as the much more tightly interconnected and wider network of the Mediterranean world, as key factors in defining Roman approaches to space (cf. Foxhall et al. 2007: 108; Purcell 2007: 189; Talbert 2010: 256). Yet I would argue that in many ways the case-studies deployed here complicate that picture. The study of tomb communities at Ostia, Pompeii and Rome underlines how Rome was sometimes not the first to begin a tradition, but in fact the slowest to take it up (particularly in terms of Late Republican tomb elaboration). In such cases, the periphery was not following the centre, but the reverse. Equally, the differences between cities on display in tomb community dynamics had the potential, I argued in Chapter 3, to undercut the centre-and-periphery model by creating a powerful sense of alienation between such communities and thus underlining difference rather than integration and the slavish following of the centre (cf. Figure 3.10).

The *Geography* of Strabo, as seen in Chapter 5, also offers a complication of the centre-and-periphery model by placing Greece as an equally key part of both the historic Greek and the present Roman world. In addition, the Roman world itself appears keen to reconnect parts of the Greek world much more strongly than is often acknowledged. It was, after all, in the Roman period that the strongest relationships between Syracuse and Corinth were enunciated in the Romano-Greek literary sources, when, in terms of power politics, those two places could not have been more remote.

At the same time, Roman approaches to and conceptualisation of the wider world stage also changed significantly from those of the Romans' Classical and Hellenistic predecessors. Scholarship on Classical approaches to the geographical extent of the wider world has stressed a move from

Herodotus' focus on knowing the world as a matter of knowing the extent of the sea (e.g. Hdt. 1.47), to Plato's Greek cities seen as frogs around the Mediterranean pond (Plato *Phaedo* 109b), to the centre-and-periphery models put forward by Plato, Aristotle and Isocrates, with Greece placed at the centre (cf. Cole 2010; Romm 2010). Hellenistic models continued to play with these options of a centre-and-periphery model as well as models in which the world was defined by water and land mass (cf. Geus 2003). The Roman conceptualisation, as we have seen, favoured the centre-and-periphery model, but one resolutely focused on land rather than open sea, and traversed, as well as understood, through set linear itineraries, within a culture that privileged the social importance of walking and its connection to learning (cf. O'Sullivan 2011). This shift in the conceptualisation of the wider world is dramatically apparent in Strabo's *Geography*. Strabo, as a Greek writer from Asia Minor within the Roman world, is stuck in the gulf between the Greek/Hellenistic and Roman attitudes, taking on elements of each. He describes, for example, the earth as being given form by the sea, echoing Hellenistic approaches (*Geography* 2.5.17), but he tours that world resolutely in an ordered itinerary by land/coastal sea voyage that equally betrays his Roman mindset (cf. Salway 2004: 96).

What the example of Strabo's split Greek/Roman approach to conceptualising and investigating the world highlights is the complexity of the ways in which these two worlds meshed, as Rome's power came to expand and include that of Greece and the Hellenistic kingdoms. Much has been written about how Rome perceived and interacted with Greece and its legacy from historical, philosophical, literary and archaeological viewpoints. I would argue that the study of attitudes to space can contribute actively to improving our understanding of the texture and depth of this relationship by revealing not only how Rome came to occupy the physical spaces of the Greek world (cf. Alcock 1993), but also how that occupation impacted upon the perception and construction of Greek space and spatial relationships as witnessed through the material as well as literary, epigraphic and historical sources.

In terms of the perception and construction of Greek space and spatial relationships, we have seen not only how Strabo's account was split between Greek and Roman ways of understanding and investigating the world, but also how he actively incorporated Greece as a physical feature of the Roman world's landscape thanks to its historical and present importance. We have seen, further, how Roman influence had drastically changed the nature and meaning of parts of the Greek landscape (e.g. converting the narrow pass of Thermopylae from Greece's 'shackles' into an open and convenient through-point). In a similar vein, the output of different writers who rebranded the relationship between Syracuse and Corinth, bringing them closer together at a time when socio-politically they were far apart, underlines the way in which the Roman world could actively rearticulate and reframe the space of Greece. Both sides had the potential to recharacterise not only the physical and perceptual spaces they occupied, but also, as a result, the relationship between them and their respective histories.

Yet what the picture offered by Roman engagement with the physical spaces of Greece underlines particularly is how sensitive and subtle that process often was. At Cyrene, for example, the early Roman presence in the agora was, if anything, tentative and respectful. Moreover, the Roman powers appear to have actively sought to avoid 'memory politics'. For example, it was not an important religious or civic structure that they turned into the early temple for the worship of Augustus in the agora at Cyrene, but instead a recently constructed, still functioning, fountain house (cf. Figure 1.7). Equally, on Delos, early Roman presence is perceptible through the subtle insertion of the deity Roma into pre-existing civic and religious structures. In later periods of the Roman Empire, of course, the Roman presence was much less tentative and the changes it wrought on the physical space of Greece more insistent and dominating. Yet even at this time it is noticeable how much more respectful Roman rulers remained towards cult buildings in contrast to civic ones (the last building to remain functional in Cyrene's agora was one of its earliest cult structures). Moreover, it was through the sacred spaces of the Greek world that later emperors such as especially Hadrian created notions of panhellenic Greece: the sanctuary of Apollo at Cyrene, for example, was the space in which Hadrian enunciated Cyrene's part in the *Panhellenion* he created, rather than its agora (cf. Walker 1985).

Therefore just as sacred space provided the strongest note of continuity between the Classical and Hellenistic worlds, so too it appears to have been not only the most respected genre of space for the Romans (as one might expect, given their similar religious systems), but also in many ways the most useful kind of space for the continued enunciation of Roman reconceptualisations of the Greek world. Yet that relationship continued to be a two-way process. It has been argued, for example, that it was particularly through Greek sacred spaces that Rome received many of the varied cult practices from the eastern half of its Empire (e.g. Egyptian cults first came to Italy through Delos (Malaise 1972)). In the process of integration between the world of Greece and Rome, therefore, sacred space played a key role in what was a strong dialectical relationship.

Consideration of approaches to, and conceptualisations of, space further highlights not only the complexity of the relationship between Greece and Rome, nor only the way in which both sides had the power to reframe that relationship, but also, on the ground, how the process of engagement by Rome with the Greek world was often subtle and sensitive, and impacted as much on Rome as it did on Greece. I would argue that the importance of sacred space in facilitating and defining that process has been traditionally undervalued. Not only was it in regard to sacred spaces that Classical, Hellenistic and Roman approaches to space were most akin, but, more importantly, and in part as a result, it was they that provided the most effective spaces for engagement, interaction and rearticulation between those different cultures over the course of the Greek and Roman worlds.

SPACE AND SOCIETY, SPACE AND HISTORY

How does thinking about space thus improve our historical understanding of the ancient world? Most importantly, it highlights how dynamically the ancient world was perceived, negotiated and constructed. It places the emphasis not only on the multiple factors affecting the development of a particular space or spatial relationship at a particular point in time, but also on the multiple ways in which that space could be experienced at any one time and over time. It makes the physical landscape not just a setting for historical action, but rather a fundamental participant in that action, as reflector and articulator of social values, phenomena and identities. In turn, because space exists at so many levels of resolution from the micro- to the macro-level, as well as being both a physical and a conceptual entity, a spatial approach allows for, and encourages, comparative historical analysis between a very wide range of different kinds of spaces. That analysis could be conducted, for example, between different kinds of physical space (mountains, plains), or social space (civic, sacred, funerary, military), between different resolutions of space (private house to entire *oikoumene*), different genres of space (countryside, city), and different perceptual spaces (as in the relationships of proximity and distance between poleis), as well as between a mixture of all of these.

Yet a spatial approach also has the advantage of being applicable across a very wide time frame of historical inquiry. For the earliest historical periods a spatial approach can offer another tool for exploration and analysis of the material evidence (e.g. the Archaic development of Delos, which is often left unstudied by scholars who focus on Delian inscriptions and thus typically only on the Hellenistic and later periods). Yet in later periods, in which there is adequate literary, epigraphic and material evidence, a spatial approach can also focus on the different constructions of a particular space as between literary, epigraphic and material sources, emphasising the often radical difference in characterisations of particular phenomena between different kinds of evidence. Moreover, because space, as physical and conceptual entity, does exist as a construct within all the types of evidence, a spatial approach, as a result, allows for a uniquely joined-up interdisciplinary understanding of the dynamic, polyvalent ways in which the ancient world constructed, perceived and negotiated its ideas and values (cf. Sauer 2004: 11). In turn, by thinking about how spaces were constructed, used and perceived in different periods and parts of the ancient world through different sources, a spatial approach offers us, as we have seen here, another way in which to conceptualise what, if anything, distinguished one particular period or area of the ancient world from another, and how they subsequently engaged each other.

What next for spatial scholarship? As the wealth of material evidence for different kinds of spaces at different times and places in the ancient world increases (thanks both to traditional and to new forms of excavation and survey technique), so too will our ability to investigate and understand a much wider range of spaces and spatial relationships across the ancient world. In particular, I would argue that spatial approaches need, where possible, to become more sensitive to factors affecting the perception and experience of space, which are notoriously difficult to observe in the archaeological record, factors such as smell and touch (cf. Hamilakis et al. 2002; Betts 2011: 118), as well as the ways in which users negotiated spaces through different patterns of movement (cf. Laurence and Newsome 2011). As a result, our understanding of how different kinds of space, places and periods related to one another, and the ways in which the ancients perceived those connections, will continue to become more sophisticated. In the Greek world, that will allow us in particular to push further our understanding of the balance in similarity and difference between its many constituent groups and entities. Equally, in the Roman world, such advances will allow us to move to a more subtle understanding of the balance between centre and periphery. Yet it is also crucial that spatial approaches continue to widen their remit so as to be as interdisciplinary as possible. In particular, that means more joined-up thinking among those interested in space as constructed within different types of evidence. Similarly, we need to continue to study the interplay between physical and conceptual constructions of particular spaces and spatial relationships within and between different kinds of evidence, in order to think about how the two overlap, influence and/or contradict one another. If we can do that, then a spatial approach will have truly earned its place as a fundamental part of historical enquiry.

Bibliographic essay

INTRODUCTION

From the 1970s the concept of space began to morph from that of a mathematical, geographical, bounded, static entity to that of a more fluid social construct (cf. Gregory and Urry 1985). At the same time, archaeological and anthropological theorists, particularly Bourdieu and Lefebvre, developed complex understandings of social behaviour and the way in which space affected that (Bourdieu 1977; Lefebvre 1991 (1974)). These theories developed in tandem with the debate between structuralism and functionalism, and the eventual middle position of structuration as advocated by Giddens (1984), in which space was firmly represented as both product and producer of social action, as well as observed norms (in particular Bourdieu's concept of 'habitus'). This in turn was complemented by an increasing appreciation of the complex ways in which physical and mental perceptions of spaces overlapped and interacted with one another (cf. Lefebvre 1991 (1974); Soja 1996).

Methods of studying physical spaces have varied from a syntactical approach to the reading of space as a fixed cross-cultural language, on the one hand, (e.g. Hillier and Hanson 1984; for criticism of the space syntax approach: Pearson and Richards 1994), to, on the other, the foregrounding of the particularity of different types of space depending on their debated meaning and use (cf. the debate on the relationships of 'space' and 'place': Broadbent et al. 1980; Hirsch and O'Hanlon 1995; Casey 1996; Feld and Basso 1996). More recently, there has been increasing interest in capturing the variety of ways in which ancient viewers constructed their 'experience' of spaces and places and in the implications of the latter for our understanding of place/space (Tilley 1994; Hamilakis et al. 2002; Tilley and Bennett 2004; Fitzjohn 2007; Lane 2007).

All these types of spatial approach have normally been conducted at either the micro or the macro level of spatial resolution (cf. Clarke 1977). At the micro level, important cross-cultural work on individual structures has been carried out by, for example, Rapoport (1980; 1982; 1990). At the macro level, the multiplicity of meanings in the landscape across many different cultures has been the subject of much investigation (Hodder and Orton 1976; Barrett 1984; Certeau 1984; Bender 1993; Snead and Preucel 1999; Bradley 2000). In contrast, the 'middle' level – that of the built site – has failed to attract sufficient recent spatially orientated attention (cf. Scott 2010: 21–3).

In 2002, space was the focus for that year's issue of the *Journal of Social Archaeology*, and has since been highlighted in a number of volumes as a key feature of classical archaeological scholarship in the early twenty-first century (Meskell and Preucel 2004; Penz et al. 2004; Alcock and Osborne 2007). It has also been identified as one of the most promising topics for the successful engagement within literary, epigraphic and archaeological material combined (cf. Sauer 2004). The focus now is on how, on the one hand, to understand space's dynamic, fractured, and polyvalent development, interaction and meaning without, on the other hand, allowing interpretation of it to become diluted, endless and ineffective (cf. Blake 2004; Gardner 2004a; 2004b; Morris 2004; Bentley 2006).

CHAPTER 1: INHERITING AND ARTICULATING A COMMUNITY: THE AGORA AT CYRENE

A variety of ancient sources treat of Cyrene, the myths of its foundation and subsequent turbulent political history (amongst others: Pindar, Herodotus, Callimachus, Diodorus, Pausanias and Synesius). Historical scholarship on the city has been heavily focused on three aspects: first, on how Cyrene's foundation and changing political structure work as a motif within the corpus of a particular ancient author (e.g. Calame 1990; Lloyd 1990a; Vanicelli 1993; Osborne 2010: 8–17; Calame 2003); second, on how to extract a 'historical' timeline for the city's development from the varying myths, stories and viewpoints on offer (cf. Chamoux 1953: 33–212; Applebaum 1979: 8–68; Giannini 1990: 51–95; Calame 2003); third, on how to use ancient texts to visualise the key physical elements of the city (e.g. Goodchild 1971: 17–56; Bacchielli 1990).

Scholarship has been surprisingly slow to consider public spaces such as agoras (as opposed to private domestic space) as a candidate for spatial analysis (cf. Lofland 1989); perhaps this is reaction to such a strong previous focus on public space. There has been no major assessment of Greek agoras since Martin (1951), although see Dickenson's recent completion of a thesis on Greek public space in Hellenistic and Roman periods (Dickenson 2012). Lefebvre, in his pioneering work on social space, considered the Greek agora to be principally an empty space, in contrast to the Roman forum, which was filled with objects and things (Lefebvre 1991 (1974): 237). Runciman argued that the Hellenic polis (and its central agora) was an evolutionary dead end (Runciman 1990). Recent analyses (Morgan and Coulton 1997; Millett 1998; Vlassopoulos 2007) have, however, sought to breathe fresh life into agora studies.

There has been a wide range of publications as a result of the continuing excavations at Cyrene. The Italian excavations have been published in a series of volumes (*Monografie di Archeologia Libica* (*MAL*)) covering different parts of the site (e.g. *necropoleis*, agora); and the excavations of the extramural sanctuary of Demeter and Persephone have been published by an American team (e.g. White 1990). As already indicated, however, this has led to the excavations of different parts of the agora being split up and published in different volumes (Stucchi 1965; Bacchielli 1981; Ermeti 1981; Stucchi and Bacchielli 1983; Purcaro 2001). Reports on the southern side of the agora are still to be made fully available, but an overview of its development, as well as a first attempt to bring the different sides of the agora together, can be found as part of a more general guide to the archaeological site (Bonacasa and Ensoli 2000). Several edited volumes on the archaeology of Cyrene have also been published (e.g. Barker et al. 1985; Stucchi 1990; Fabbricotti and Menozzi 2006), as well as major volumes on the city's architecture (Stucchi 1975), and more recently on the site as a whole as part of the Italian excavation series (Luni 2006). A guide to the vast body of Cyrenean inscriptions is also available (Marengo 1991). Historical syntheses of Cyrene (as well as neighbouring settlements within Cyrenaica) have also been written (Freeman 1950: 181–202; Waisglas 1955; Goodchild 1971; Applebaum 1979; Barker et al. 1985; Laronde 1987; Catani and Marengo 1998; Gentili 1990; Reynolds 1994; Polidori et al. 1999; Gasperini and Marengo 2007). Work has also been conducted on the religious landscape of the city (Callot 1999).

CHAPTER 2: NETWORKS OF POLYTHEISM: SPACES FOR THE GODS AT DELOS

The main literary sources for the mythology and development of religious cult at Delos are the *Homeric Hymn to Delian Apollo* and Callimachus' *Hymn to Delos*. For Delos' involvement in the political affairs of the wider Greek world, particularly in the fifth century BC, the main sources are Herodotus and Thucydides, and there are briefer mentions in a wider variety of sources (e.g. Strabo). The abundant epigraphy found on Delos is published both in *Inscriptiones Graecae* (*IG*) volume XI (2 and 4), as well as in seven volumes in the *Inscriptions de Délos* (*ID*) series (published by de Boccard, Paris). A *Choix d'inscriptions de Délos avec traduction et commentaire* was also brought out in 1921 (Durrbach 1921), and has been recently updated in *Nouveau Choix d'inscriptions de Délos: lois, comptes et inventaires* (Prêtre 2002). In addition, an index of Delian inscriptions is available, although only volume I has appeared in print (Tréheux 1992). M-C. Hellmann has also made extensive use of the Delian inscriptions in her publications on the vocabulary of Greek architecture (Hellmann 1992), and a recent synthesis on the Delian inventories has been written by Hamilton (2000).

The archaeological material has been extensively published in the *Exploration archéologique de Délos* (*EAD*) series. Volume I is a general description and presentation of the cartography of the island, volume III is a history of cartography of the island, but other volumes are focused on a different physical structure (currently 41 volumes have been published from 1909 to 2003). In addition, volume XXVIII is actually focused on the graffiti inscriptions found in gymnastic buildings around the island, and volume XXX on funerary inscriptions. The list of volumes and their contents can be found in Bruneau and Ducat 2005:19–20. The French Archaeological School in Athens publishes a guide to the Delos excavations (*Guide de Délos*), now in its fourth edition, that is very worthwhile both for detailed study and for using on site: Bruneau and Ducat 2005. *BCH* has also dedicated several supplements to a collection of articles on Delos (*BCH* Supplements 1, 10, 41 and 47). In addition, there are various works of synthesis on different aspects of the political and religious life of the island, as well as its topography and architecture (e.g. Roussel 1915–16; 1916; Vallois 1944–78; Gallet de Santerre 1958; Bruneau 1970; Vial 1984; Bruneau et al. 1996; Étienne 1996; Chankowski 2008). In English there are very few comprehensive works: e.g. Laidlaw (1933) and Rauh (1993). A longer list of useful articles can be found in Bruneau and Ducat 2005:23. There has been a similar, but by no means as extensive, focus on Delos' art and mosaic collection (e.g. Marcadé 1969; Stewart 1979: 65–100), as well as on its urban development and housing (Deonna 1948; Papageorgiou-Venetas 1981). The relationship between Delos and Italy has been of understandable interest to Italian scholars (Coarelli et al. 1983).

CHAPTER 3: SPACES OF ALIENATION: STREET-LINING ROMAN CEMETERIES

Factors affecting tomb design and placement include patterns of burial, regulations surrounding burial and acculturated practices across the Empire. In terms of patterns of burial, scholars have long ago established the chronological shifts in preferences for inhumation and cremation in the Roman world (Davies 1977 for Italy; Carroll 2006 for western Europe; Hope 2009: 81). Those preferences can be broadly understood as: inhumation for the early/middle Republic; cremation from the end of the first century BC for Rome and everywhere by the first century AD; and a return to inhumation by the early second century AD in Rome and everywhere by the third century AD.

The evidence for regulation of burial is patchier, yet seems to indicate both certain basic rules and a large degree of variation from city to city. The best-known stipulation is that of extra-mural burial. Rome's Law of the Twelve Tables, dating perhaps as far back as 450 BC, specifies that burial (and cremation) must take place outside the city (Cic. *Leg.* 2.23.58). Similar, even more detailed, laws (e.g. the *Lex Ursonensis* from Ursa in Spain (*CIL* 1.594)) are attested for cities around the Roman Empire (cf. Robinson 1992: 126; Hope 2007: 130). The problem of maintaining this rule – or rather its not-infrequent violation through the practice of 'body-dumping', particularly in Rome – is marked in several inscriptional and literary sources (cf. Kaser 1978; Robinson 1992: 124–6; Hope 2009: 89, 154). Yet official exceptions were also made at Rome, not only for emperors and war heroes but also for families who wished to continue using older tombs the original construction of which had been outside the pomerium but, thanks to subsequent city expansion, were now inside (Coates-Stephens 2004: 61; Hope 2007: 135–6). Tombs, once constructed, however, were in no way 'safe' from further change. The evidence, ranging from epitaph-inscribed threats of fines or 'other-world' punishments for those who disturb tombs (e.g. *CIL* 14.1153), to encouragements to return to the grave regularly to honour the deceased (Hope 2009: 73–8, 85), to obvious neglect of tombs as witnessed by graffiti or rubbish dumping (e.g. Cooley and Cooley 2004: 139), to their occupation by an entirely different family, and even to their disturbance by grave-diggers digging a fresh plot (Sidonius Apollinaris 12; Reece 1977), shows how tombs could be disturbed and their configuration changed. In addition to unintended changes, tombs could also deliberately be sub-divided and sold off (e.g. Meiggs 1973: 462), as well as be made subject to authorised changes by the state (Robinson 1992: 124–6). Tombs were thus understood, for a whole number of reasons, to be not necessarily 'static structures' (Hope 1997: 86).

As regards burial practice and tomb architecture across the Empire, scholars have pointed both to general similarity in tomb types across the Roman world and to geographical variation in styles of tomb commemoration (as well as in the spatial arrangement of cemeteries) motivated by the particular acculturation of Roman and local practice: tower-tombs, for example, are mostly found in the eastern provinces (Toynbee 1971: 79, 164; MacDonald 1986: 166; Dyson 1992: 145, 150; von Hesberg 1994: 64; Hope 1998; 2000b; 2001; 2007: 145; 2009: 165–6).

More work still needs to be done on tombs from the Roman world. In part, this is due to the incomplete nature of tomb preservation and excavation. While certain stretches of tombs along major roads out of Rome have survived, many have not. At Ostia, for example, tombs are thought to have continued along the Via Ostiensis for perhaps as much as seven miles outside the city on the route to Rome. Equally, the real size of the burial area at Isola Sacra is only now becoming clear through current investigation and publication (Meiggs 1973: 455; Baldassarre 1987; 2001; Heinzelmann 2001: 373). Other cemeteries are inaccessible and can be glimpsed only in small pockets (e.g. the Vatican Necropoleis: Liverani and Spinola 2010). A similar picture can be drawn for other major cities (e.g. Pompeii, Aquileia in Italy). But equally crucial has been the way the material has been studied. Monumental tombs have occupied excavators' attention, until recently, when there has been more of an effort to understand the full spectrum of burial practices. A large proportion of scholarly activity has also been focused on the sculptured sarcophagi, exterior reliefs and interior decoration of tombs (e.g. Kleiner 1987), or alternatively on the vast number of surviving epitaphs (cf. Hope 2009: 171). Much of this work has been conducted in terms of typologies or in disregard of spatial context. Equally, despite recent work on urban society, much of it has neglected to include tombs within its analysis (e.g. Cornell and Lomas 1995).

CHAPTER 4: A SPATIAL APPROACH TO RELATIONSHIPS BETWEEN COLONY AND METROPOLIS: SYRACUSE AND CORINTH

Recent work on colonisation has been developing on several fronts. First, scholarship has become more aware of the importance of distancing itself from the implicit modern connotations of the term 'colonisation' (cf. Snodgrass 2002; Shepherd 2005b). Second, thanks to new excavations in areas such as around the Black Sea, scholarly understanding of the different kinds of processes of settlement foundation practised at different places in the Mediterranean and Black Sea region is increasing (cf. Tsetskhladze and de Angelis 1994; Tsetskhladze 1998; 2002). Third, thanks to the constantly improving archaeological understanding of areas around later colonies, scholarship has been able to reinterpret early contacts between Greeks and these areas (Finley 1976; Graham 1990; Ridgway 1990; Osborne 1998; 2010; van Dommelen

1998; Blake 2004: 243–8; Hall 2004; Owen 2005; Hodos 2006; Descoeudres 2008). In particular, this has led to a portrayal of colonial foundations not as 'bolt out of the blue' events, but rather as processes which formed part of a much longer continuum of contact within a much more fluid Mediterranean world.

Fourth, there have been strong advances in understanding the literary sources not as unimpeachable fact, but as narrative retellings structured for the worlds and particular time periods in which they were created. As a result, scholarship has begun to think through how these later, varying portrayals of colonisation (often emphasising the arrival of an individual 'oikist', internal civic stasis leading to the search for a colony, and the role of Delphi) served particular purposes (cf. Dougherty 1993a; Yntema 2000; Calame 2003; Wilson 2006: 27, 51; Hall 2008). Scholars have focused on how tightly such stories were 'woven into the larger fabric of Greek cultural memory' (Dougherty 1993b: 4). Scholarship has also demonstrated the role of colonial foundation stories as justifications for later actions (Wilson 2006; Dominguez-Monedro 2010: 51); these include attempts to create retrospectively a concept of 'oikist' cult for current political gain (Malkin 1987: 201; Antonaccio 1999). Also noted is the correlation between the intensity of mythical stories surrounding certain colonies and the severity of the challenge currently faced by their founding city (cf. Malkin 1994b).

Scholarship on colonies in Sicily has a long history (cf. Freeman 1891; Dunbabin 1948; Finley 1979; Boardman 1999). Colonial foundations in Sicily, for example, have traditionally been thought of as 'unprecedentedly planned' (Snodgrass 1994: 1). Yet this broad brush approach has recently been finessed so as to compare individual settlements; thus Syracuse is now portrayed as a more haphazard settlement in comparison with Megara Hyblaia, which was laid out almost immediately on a planned 'Greek' city grid (cf. Malkin 2002). Foundations in Sicily have also been recast as settlements growing out of long-term trading connections rather than as the result of particular events on the mainland, and a whole spectrum of relationships has been posited between Sicilian colonies and their Greek founding cities, as well as between subsequent colonies set up by those original foundations (cf. Malkin 1994a: 1). Scholarship particularly on Syracuse and Corinth, and the relationship between them (Dunbabin 1948; Freeman 1950: 81–126; Graham 1983; Finley 1979; Salmon 1984), has a long history as well, although the archaeological evidence from these settlements is difficult to interpret, both because of the existence of modern Syracuse lying over much of the ancient city and because of the destruction of much of the Archaic and Classical city of Corinth by the Romans in 146 BC (the American School of Classical Studies at Athens excavation reports on Corinth, de Waele 1961; for the excavation publications at Syracuse and Corinth, see Gabba and Vallet 1980; Pugliese-Carratelli 1985–88; 1996; Williams and Bookidis 2003).

CHAPTER 5: THE PLACE OF GREECE IN THE *OIKOUMENE* OF STRABO'S *GEOGRAPHY*

The latest commentary on the text of Strabo's *Geography* is Radt (2002). Past scholarship has focused on Strabo's biographical origins and on the debated question of the date of his surviving works (Lasserre 1982; Clarke 1999a: 228–39; Dueck 2000: 1–30; Engels 2010); on the cultural world in which he was writing (Clarke 1999a: 334–5; Dueck 2000: 85–106; Braund 2005; Maas 2007; Pretzler 2007); and on the differentiation between his two major works, the *Geography* and the *Historica Hypomnemata* (most of which is now lost: Engels 2008; 2010: 72). Scholarship on his surviving work, the *Geography*, has examined the influences on him of poets, historians and geographers (e.g. Dueck 2000: 31–84; 2010), with whom Strabo actively engages in the first two books of his work (e.g. 1.1.2–11 (his respect for Homer); 1.3.1–21 (criticism of the works of Eratosthenes, Hipparchus, Posidonius and Polybius)), and on Strabo's actual first-hand knowledge of places he describes (Weller 1906; Wallace 1979: 168–72; Engels 1999: 28–32; Dueck 2000: 15–30). There have been two recent monographs focusing on Strabo's work, one from the point of view of his mix of geography and history (Clarke 1999a), the other more focused on his biographical details and literary style (Dueck 2000), along with a very useful edited volume that approaches the *Geography* from a variety of thematic, literary and geographical standpoints (Dueck et al. 2005).

His work has also been examined in a series of thematic and systematic studies in Italian scholarship. A major source of this scholarship has been the University of Perugia, under the auspices of which there has been published not just a bibliographical résumé of everything published on Strabo from the fifteenth century until 1980, organised by year and subject area (Biraschi et al. 1981), but also edited volumes on thematic aspects of the *Geography* (Prontera 1984; Maddoli 1986), besides further continuing thematic discussions (particularly on Strabo's use of Homer (Biraschi 1984; 1986; 1994b) and systematic regional surveys of Strabo's presentation of Asia Minor, Italy, Greece and Magna Graecia (Biffi 1988; Maddoli 1988; Biraschi 1994a; Musti 1994; Biraschi and Salmeri 2000). Strabo will also be a focus of the Key Themes in Ancient History volume on *Geography in the Ancient World* (Dueck and Brodersen 2012).

Bibliography

Adams, C. and Roy, J. eds. (2007) *Travel, Geography and Culture in Ancient Greece, Egypt and the Near East.* Oxford.
Alcock, S. (1993) *Graecia Capta: The Landscapes of Roman Greece.* Cambridge.
  (2002) *Archaeologies of the Greek Past: landscapes, monuments and memories.* Cambridge.
Alcock, S. and Osborne, R. eds. (1994) *Placing the Gods: sanctuaries and sacred space in Ancient Greece.* Oxford.
  eds. (2007) *Classical Archaeology.* Oxford.
Alcock, S., Cherry, J. F. and Elsner, J., eds. (2001) *Pausanias: travel and memory in Roman Greece.* Oxford.
Algra, K. (1995) *Concepts of Space in Greek Thought.* Leiden.
Allison, P. (2004) *Pompeian Households: an analysis of the material culture.* Los Angeles.
Almagor, E. (2005) 'Who is a barbarian? The barbarians in the ethnological and cultural taxonomies of Strabo', in Dueck, Lindsay and Pothecary 2005: 42–55.
Alonso-Núñez, J. M. (1987) 'Augustan world history and Pompeius Trogus', *G&R* 34: 56–72.
Amiotti, G. (1994) 'Fenomeni naturali della Calcidia', in Biraschi 1994a: 201–9.
Antonaccio, C. M. (1999) 'Colonization and the origins of hero cult', in Hägg, R., ed. *Ancient Greek Hero Cult,* 109–21. Athens.
  (2001) 'Ethnicity and colonisation', in Malkin 2001: 113–58.
Applebaum, S. (1979) *Jews and Greeks in Ancient Cyrene.* Leiden.
Arena, R. ed. (1998) *Iscrizioni Greche Arcaiche di Sicilia e Magna Grecia.* Alessandria.
Ashmore, W. and Knapp, A. B. eds. (1999) *Archaeologies of Landscape: Contemporary Perspectives.* Oxford.
Audiat, J. (1970) *Le Gymnase (EAD 28).* Paris.
Aujac, G. (1994) 'L'Eubée: l'île des merveilles', in Biraschi 1994a: 213–36.
Bacchielli, L. (1981) *L'Agorà di Cirene 2,1: l'area settentrionale del lato ouest della platea inferiore (MAL 15).* Rome.
  (1985) 'Modelli politici e modelli architettonici a Cirene durante il regime Democratico', in Barker, Lloyd and Reynolds 1985: 357–62.
  (1990) 'I "luoghi" della celebrazione politica e religiosa a Cirene nella poesia di Pindaro e Callimaco', in Gentili 1990: 5–33.
Baladié, R. (1980) *Le Péloponnèse de Strabon: étude de géographie historique.* Paris.

Baldassarre, I. (1987) 'La necropolis dell'Isola Sacra (Porto)', in von Hesberg and Zanker 1987: 125–38.
Baldassarre, I. (2001) 'La nécropole de l'Isola Sacra', in Descoeudres 2001: 385–90.
Barker, G. (1996) *A Mediterranean Valley: landscape archaeology and annales history in the Biferno Valley*. London.
Barker, G., Lloyd, J. and Reynolds, J. eds. (1985) *Cyrenaica in Antiquity*. Oxford.
Barletta, B. A. (1983) *Ionic Influence in Archaic Sicily: the monumental art*. Gothenburg.
Barrett, S. R. (1984) *The Rebirth of Anthropological Theory*. Toronto.
Baslez, M.-F. (1982) *Les Étrangers à Délos: formes et évolution de la vie de relation dans un sanctuaire panhéllenique (Doctoral Thesis)*. Université de Paris I.
Benchimol, E. and Sagnier, B. (2008) 'Un trésorarchaïque du sanctuaire à Délos (Trésor 5): étude architecturale', *BCH* 132: 1–113.
Bender, B. (1993) *Landscape: politics and perspectives*. Oxford.
Benevolo, L. (1980) *The History of the City*. London.
Bentley, R. A. (2006) 'Academic copying, archaeology and the English language', *Antiquity* 80: 196–201.
Bérard, J. (1957) *La colonisation grecque de l'Italie méridionale et de la Sicile dans l'antiquité: histoire et légende*, 2nd edn. Paris.
Berger, S. (1992) *Revolution and Society in Greek Sicily and Southern Italy*. Stuttgart.
Bergmann, B. (2007) 'Housing and households (Roman world)', in Alcock and Osborne 2007: 224–43.
Berve, H. and Gruben, G. (1963) *Greek Temples, Theatres and Shrines*. London.
Betts, E. (2011) 'Towards a multisensory experience of movement in the city of Rome' in Laurence and Newsome 2011: 118–32.
Biffi, N. (1988) *L'Italia di Strabone: testo, traduzione e commento dei libri V e VI della Geografia*. Genova.
Bintliff, J. (2006) 'City-country relationships in the "normal polis"', in Rosen and Sluiter 2006: 13–32.
Biraschi, A.-M. (1984) 'Strabone e la difesa di Omero nei prolegomena', in Pronter 1984: 129–58.
  (1986) 'Strabone e gli onomata omerici. A proposito di Strabo VIII.3.2', in Maddoli 1986: 67–77.
  ed. (1994a) *Strabone e la Grecia*. Napoli.
  (1994b) 'Strabone e Omero. Aspetti della tradizione omerica nella descrizione del Peloponneso', in Biraschi 1994a: 22–57.
Biraschi, A.-M., and Salmeri, G. eds. (2000) *Strabone e l'Asia Minore*. Naples.
Biraschi, A.-M., Maribelli, P., Massaro, G. D. and Pagnotta, M. A. eds. (1981) *Strabone: saggio di Bibliografia 1469–1978*. Perugia.
Bjur, H. and Santillo-Frizell, B. eds. (2009) *Via Tiburtina: space, movement and artefacts in the urban landscape* Rome.
Blake, E. (2004) 'Space, spatiality and archaeology', in Meskell, L. and Preucel, R., eds., *A Companion to Social Archaeology*, 230–54. Oxford.
Boardman, J. (1999) *The Greeks Overseas*, 4th edn. London.
Bodel, J. (1997) 'Monumental villas and villa monuments', *JRA* 10: 5–35.

(2008) 'From columbaria to catacombs: collective burial in pagan and Christian Rome', in Brink, L. and Green, D., eds., *Commemorating the Dead: texts and artifacts in context*, 177–242. Berlin.
Bon, S. E., and Jones, R. (1997) *Sequence and Space in Pompeii*. Oxford.
Bonacasa, N. and Ensoli, S. eds. (2000) *Cirene*. Milan.
Bookidis, N. (1995) 'Archaic Corinthian sculpture: a summary', in Pugliese-Carratelli 1995: 231–56.
Bourdieu, P. (1977) *Outline of a Theory of Practice*. Cambridge.
Bousquet, J. (1938) 'Nouvelles inscriptions de Delphes III: Compte du IVième siècle', *BCH* 62: 348–57.
Bowersock, G. W. (1961) 'Eurycles of Sparta', *JRS* 51: 112–18.
Bradley, R. (2000) *Archaeology of Natural Places*. London.
Brand, S. (1994) *How Buildings Learn What Happens After They Are Built*. London.
Braund, D. (1985) 'The social and economic context of the Roman annexation of Cyrenaica', in Barker, Lloyd and Reynolds 1985: 319–26.
  (2005) 'Greek geography and Roman Empire: the transformation of tradition in Strabo's Euxine', in Dueck, Lindsay and Pothecary 2005: 216–34.
Bregman, J. (1982) *Synesius of Cyrene: philosopher-bishop*. Berkeley.
Broadbent, G., Bunt, R. and Llorens, T. (1980) *Meaning and Behaviour in the Built Environment*. Chichester.
Brodersen, K. (1995) *Terra cognita: Studien zur römischen Raumerfassung*. Hildesheim.
Broodbank, C. (1999) 'Kythera survey: preliminary report on the 1998 season', *ABSA* 94: 191–214.
Bruhn, J., Croxford, B. and Grigoropoulos, D., eds. (2005) *TRAC 2004*. Oxford.
Bruneau, Ph. (1968) 'Contributions à l'histoire urbaine de Délos à l'époque hellénistique et à l'époque impériale', *BCH* 92: 633–709.
  (1970) *Recherches sur les cultes de Délos à l'Époque Hellénistique et à l'Époque Impériale*. Paris.
  (2006a) 'Isis Pélagia à Délos', in Moretti 2006: 1–12.
  (2006b) 'Isis Pélagia à Délos (compléments)', in Moretti 2006: 13–20.
  (2006c) 'L'autel des cornes à Délos', in Moretti 2006: 943–56.
  (2006d) 'L'hymne Délos de Callimaque et les cultes Déliens', in Moretti 2006: 786–90.
  (2006e) 'Le dromos et le temple C du Sarapieion de Délos', in Moretti 2006: 499–526.
  (2006f) 'Les cultes de l'établissement des Poseidoniastes de Bérytos à Délos', in Moretti 2006: 438–72.
Bruneau, Ph., and Ducat, J. (2005) *Guide de Délos*. Athens.
Bruneau, Ph., and Fraisse, P. (2002) *Le monument à abside et la question d'Autel des cornes (EAD 40)*. Paris.
Bruneau, Ph., Brunet, M., Farnoux, A. and Moretti, J-C. (1996) *Délos: Île sacrée et ville cosmopolite*. Paris.
Bulard, M. (1926) *La religion domestique dans la colonie Italienne de Délos, d'après les peintures murales et les autels historiés (BEFAR 131)*. Paris.

Burrell, B. (2009) 'Reading, hearing and looking at Ephesos', in Johnson, W. and Parker, H., eds., *Ancient Literacies: the culture of reading in Greece and Rome*, 69–95. Oxford.
Buxton, R. (1992) 'Imaginary Greek mountains', *JHS* 112: 1–15.
Cahill, N. (2002) *Household and City Organisation at Olynthus*. New Haven.
Calame, C. (1990) 'Narrating the foundation of a city: the symbolic birth of Cyrene', in Edmunds, L., ed. *Approaches to Greek Myth*, 275–341. Baltimore.
  (2003) *Myth and History in Ancient Greece: the symbolic creation of a colony*. Trans. D. Bermann. Princeton.
  (2009) *Poetic and Performance Memory in Ancient Greece: heroic reference and ritual gestures in time and space*. Trans. H. Patton. Harvard.
Callot, J. (1999) *Recherches sur les cultes en Cyrénaïque durant le haut-empire romain*. Paris.
Carroll, M. (2006) *Spirits of the Dead: Roman funerary commemoration in Western Europe*. Oxford.
Carruseco, J. ed. (2010) *Topos-Chora: l'espai a Grècia I: perspectives interdisciplinàries*. Tarragon.
Casey, E. (1996) 'How to get from space to place in a fairly short stretch of time. Phenomenological prolegomena', in Basso, K. H. and Field, S., eds., *Sense of Place*, 13–52. Washington.
Catalano, P. (2008) 'Les ensembles funéraires de l'époque impériale à Rome', *Les Dossiers d'Archéologie* 330: 10–13.
Catani, E. and Marengo, S. M. eds. (1998) *La Cirenaica in età antica*. Rome.
Cerchiai, L., Janelli, L. and Longo, F. (2004) *Greek Cities of Magna Graecia and Sicily*. Verona.
Certeau, M. de (1984) *The Practice of Everyday Life*. Trans. S. Rendall. Berkeley.
Chamoux, F. (1953) *Cyrène sous la monarchie des Battiades*. Paris.
Chankowski, V. (2008) *Athènes et Délos à l'époque classique: recherches sur l'administration du sanctuaire d'Apollon délien (BEFAR 331)*. Paris.
Chapouthier, F. (1935) *Le sanctuaire des dieux de Samothrace (EAD 16)*. Paris.
Chevallier, R. (1974) *Littérature Gréco-Romaine et Géographie Historique*. Paris.
Clarke, D. (1977) *Spatial Archaeology*. London.
Clarke, K. (1999a) *Between Geography and History: Hellenistic Constructions of the Roman World*. Oxford.
  (1999b) 'Universal perspectives in historiography', in Kraus, C. S., ed. *The Limits of Historiography: genre and narrative in ancient historical texts*: 249–79. Leiden.
Coarelli, F. (1983) 'L'agora des Italiens a Delo: il mercato degli schiavi?', in Coarelli, F., Musti, D. and Solin, H., eds., *Delo e l'Italia*, 119–46. Rome.
  (2002) *Pompeii*. New York.
Coarelli, F., Musti, D. and Solin, H. eds. (1983) *Delo e l'Italia*. Rome.
Coates-Stephens, R. (2004) *Porta Maggiore: monument and landscape: archaeology and topography of the southern Esquiline from the Late Republican Period to the present*. Rome.

Cole, S. G. (2004) *Landscapes, Gender and Ritual Space: the Ancient Greek experience*. Berkeley.
 (2010) 'Geography and difference in the early Greek world', in Raaflaub and Talbert 2010: 197–214.
Constantakopoulou, C. (2007) *The Dance of the Islands: insularity, networks, the Athenian Empire, and the Aegean world*. Oxford.
Cooley, A. E. and Cooley, M. G. (2004) *Pompeii: a sourcebook*. London.
Cornell, T. and Lomas, K. eds. (1995) *Urban Society in Roman Italy*. London.
Coulton, J. J. (1974) 'Towards understanding Doric design: the stylobate and intercolumniations', *ABSA* 69: 61–86.
Courbin, J. (1980) *L'oikos des Naxiens (EAD 33)*. Paris.
Courbin, P. (1987) 'Le temple archaïque de Délos', *BCH* 111: 63–78.
Courby, M. F. (1912) *La portique d'Antigone ou du Nord-Est et les constructions voisines (EAD 5)*. Paris.
 (1931) *Les temples d'Apollon (EAD 12)*. Paris.
Curtius, E. (1851–2) *Peloponnesos. Eine historisch-geographische Beschreibung der Halbinsel*. Gotha.
Curty, O. (1995) *Les parentés légendaires entre cités grecques*. Geneva.
Davies, G. (1977) 'Burial in Italy up to Augustus', in Reece, R., ed. *Burial in the Roman World*, 13–19. London.
Day, H. W. (2011) *The Aurelian Wall and the Refashioning of Imperial Rome AD 271–855*. Cambridge.
De Caro, S. (1979) 'Scavi nell'area fuori Porta Nola a Pompei', *Cronache pompeiane* 5: 61–101.
 (1983) *Un impegno per Pompeii: Fotopiano e documentazione della necropoli di Porta Nocera*. Milan.
Dearden, C. W. (1990) 'Fourth century drama in Sicily: Athenian or Sicilian', in Descoeudres 1990: 231–42.
Delorme, J. (1961) *Les palestres (EAD 25)*. Paris.
Dench, E. (2007) 'Ethnography and history', in Marincola 2007b: 493–503.
Deonna, W. (1948) *La vie privée des Déliens*. Paris.
Descoeudres, J. P., ed. (1990) *Greek Colonists and Native Populations*. Oxford.
 ed. (2001) *Ostia: port et portique de la Rome antique*. Geneva.
 ed. (2008) 'Central Greece on the eve of the colonisation movement', in Tsetskhladze 2008: 289–382.
Di Donato, R. (2001) *Geografia e storia della letteratura greca arcaica: contributi a una antropologia storica del mondo antico*. Milan.
Di Vita, A. (1990) 'Town planning in the Greek colonies of Sicily from the time of their foundation to the Punic wars', in Descoeudres 1990: 343–64.
Dickenson, C. (2012) *On the Agora: power and public space in Hellenistic and Roman Greece* (Proefschrift). Groningen.
Dinsmoor, W. B. (1927) *The Architecture of Ancient Greece*. London.
Dixon, S. (2011) '*Portrait statue monuments on the dromos at Delos*', Unpublished conference paper, APA/AIA San Antonio, Texas.
Dobres, M. A., and Robb, J. E. eds. (2000) *Agency in Archaeology*. London.

Dominguez-Monedro, A. J. (2010) 'La organización simbólica del espacio en el mundo griego: el caso locrio', in Carruseco 2010: 75–84.
Dougherty, C. (1993a) 'It's murder to found a colony', in Dougherty, C. and Kurke, L., eds., *Cultural Poetics in Archaic Greece: cult, performance, politics*, 178–200. Cambridge.
  (1993b) *The Poetics of Colonisation: from city to text in Archaic Greece*. Oxford.
Doxiadis, C. A. (1972) *Architectural Space in Ancient Greece*. Cambridge, Mass.
Dubois, L. (1989) *Inscriptions grecques dialectales de Sicile*. Vol. 1. Paris.
Dueck, D. (2000) *Strabo of Amasia: a Greek man of letters in Augustan Rome*. London.
  (2005) 'Strabo's use of poetry', in Dueck, Lindsay and Pothecary 2005: 86–107.
  (2010) 'The geographical narrative of Strabo of Amasia', in Raaflaub and Talbert 2010: 236–51.
Dueck, D. and Brodersen, K. (2012) *Geography in Classical Antiquity*. Cambridge.
Dueck, D., Lindsay, H. and Pothecary, S. eds. (2005) *Strabo's Cultural Geography: the making of a kolossourgia*. Cambridge.
Dunbabin, T. J. (1948) *The Western Greeks: the history of Sicily and South Italy from the foundations of the Greek colonies to 480 BC*. Oxford.
Duncan-Jones, R. (1982) *The Economy of the Roman Empire: quantitative studies*, 2nd edn. Cambridge.
Durrbach, F. (1921) *Choix d'inscriptions de Délos*. Paris.
Dürrwächter, C. (2009) *Time, Space and Innovation: an archaeological case-study on the Romanisation of the north-western provinces*. Oxford.
Durry, M. (1938) *Les Cohortes Prétoriennes*. Paris.
Dyson, S. (1992) *Community and Society in Roman Italy*. Baltimore.
  (2003) *The Roman Countryside*. London.
Eck, W. (1998) 'Grabmonumente und sozialer Status in Rom und Umgebung', in Fasold, P., Fischer, T., von Hesberg, H. and Witteyer, M., eds., *Bestattungssitte und kulturelle Identität. Grabanlagen und Grabbeigaben der frühen römischen Kaiserzeit in Italien und den Nord-West-Provinzen*, 9–40. Cologne.
Edlund-Berry, I. (2006) 'Ritual space and boundaries in Etruscan religion', in Grummond, N. T. de, and Simon, E., eds., *The Religion of the Etruscans*, 116–31. Austin.
Elsner, J. (2001) 'Structuring "Greece": Pausanias' periegesis as a literary construct', in Alcock, Cherry and Elsner 2001: 3–20.
Emmerson, A. L. C. (2011) 'Evidence for Junian Latins in the tombs of Pompeii', in *JRA* 24: 161–90.
Emmerson, A. L. C. (forthcoming) 'Reconstructing the funerary landscape of Pompeii's Porta Stabia', in *RStPomp* 21.
Engelmann, H. (1975) *The Delian Aretalogy of Serapis*. Leiden.
Engels, D., Geis, L. and Kleu, M. eds. (2010) *Zwischen Ideal und Wirklichkeit: Herrschaft auf Sizilien von der Antike bis zum Spätmittelalter* Stuttgart.
Engels, J. (1999) *Augusteische Oikumenegeographie und Universalhistorie im Werk Strabons von Amaseia*. Stuttgart.
  (2005) 'Andres eudoxoi or "men of high reputation" in Strabo's *Geography*', in Dueck, Lindsay and Pothecary 2005: 129–43.

(2007) 'Geography and history', in Marincola 2007b: 541–52.
(2008) 'Universal history and cultural geography of the *oikoumene* in Herodotus' Historiai and Strabo's Geographika', in Pigon 2008: 144–61.
(2010) 'Strabo and the development of ancient Greek universal historiography', in Liddel and Fear 2010: 71–86.
Ermeti, A. L. (1981) *L'Agorà di Cirene 3,1: Il monumento navale (MAL 16)*. Rome.
(2002) 'Gli altari marmorei dell' Agorà di Cirene: la ricostruzione', *QuadALibia* 16: 87–97.
Erskine, A. ed. (2009) *A Companion to Ancient History*. Chichester.
Étienne, R. ed. (1996) *L'Espace Grec: 150 ans de fouilles de l'EFA*. Paris.
Fabbricotti, E. and Menozzi, O. eds. (2006) *Cirenaica: studi, scavi e scoperte*. Oxford.
Feld, S. and Basso, K. eds. (1996) *Senses of Place*. Santa Fe, NM.
Figueira, T. (2008) 'Colonisation in the Classical period', in Tsetskhladze 2008: 427–524.
Finley, M. I. (1976) 'Colonies – an attempt at a typology', *Transactions of the Royal Historical Society* 26: 167–88.
(1979) *A History of Ancient Sicily to the Arab Conquest*, 2nd edn. London.
Fischer-Hansen T., ed. (1995) *Ancient Sicily*. Copenhagen.
Fitter, C. (1995) *Poetry, Space, Landscape: towards a new theory*. Cambridge.
Fitzjohn, M. (2007) 'Viewing places: GIS applications for examining the perception of space in the mountains of Sicily', *World Archaeology* 39.1: 36–50.
Flohr, M. (2007) 'Nec quicquam ingenium habere potest officina? Spatial contexts of urban production at Pompeii', *BABesch* 82: 129–48.
Foxhall, L., Jones, M. and Forbes, H. (2007) 'Human ecology and classical landscape', in Alcock and Osborne 2007: 91–117.
Freeman, E. (1891) *History of Sicily*. Oxford.
Freeman, K. (1950) *Greek City-States*. London.
Gabba, E. and Vallet, G. eds. (1980) *La Sicilia Antica*. Vols. I–II. Naples.
Gallet de Santerre, H. (1958) *Délos primitive et archaïque*. Paris.
(1959) *La terrasse des lions, le Létoön, le monument de granit (EAD 24)*. Paris.
Gardner, A. (2004a) 'Introduction: social agency, power and being human', in Gardner 2004b: 1–18.
ed. (2004b) *Agency Uncovered: archaeological perspectives on social agency, power and being human*. London.
Gasperini, L. (1990) 'Le laminette plumbee iscritte dal ripostiglio dell'agorà di Cirene', in Stucchi 1990: 17–34.
Gasperini, L. and Marengo, S. M. eds. (2007) *Cirene e la Cirenaica nell' antichità*. Tivoli.
Gates, C. (2011) *Ancient Cities: the archaeology of urban life in the ancient Near East and Egypt, Greece and Rome*. London.
Gell, A. (1998) *Art and Agency: an anthropological theory*. Oxford.
Gentili, B. ed. (1990) *Cirene: storio, mito, letteratura*. Urbino.
Georgiades, T. (1993) *Archaia Makedonia kata ton Strabona*. Athens.
Geus, K. (2003) 'Space and Geography', in Erskine, A., ed. *Companion to the Hellenistic World*, 232–46. Oxford.

Giannini, P. (1990) 'Cirene nella poesia greca: tra mito e storia', in Gentili 1990: 51–95.
Giddens, A. (1984) *The Constitution of Society*. Cambridge.
Goodchild, R. (1971) *Kyrene und Apollonia*. Zurich.
  (1976) *Libyan Studies: select papers of the late R. G. Goodchild*, ed. J. Reynolds. London.
Gowland, R. and Garnsey, P. (2010) 'Skeletal evidence for health, nutritional status and malaria in Rome and the Empire', in Eckardt, H., ed., *Roman Diasporas: archaeological approaches to mobility and diversity in the Roman Empire*, 131–56. Portsmouth, Rhode Island.
Graham, A. J. (1983) *Colony and Mother City in Ancient Greece*, 2nd edn. Manchester.
  (1990) 'Pre-colonial contacts: questions and problems', in Descoeudres 1990: 45–60.
Graham, E. (2005) 'The quick and the dead in the extra-urban landscape: the Roman cemetry at Ostia', in Bruhn, Croxford and Grigoropoulos 2005: 133–43.
Grahame, M. (2000) *Reading Space: social interaction and identity in the houses of Roman Pompeii. A syntactical approach to the analysis and interpretation of built space*. Oxford.
Gray, C. L. (2006) 'The bearded rustic of Roman Attica', in Rosen and Sluiter 2006: 349–68.
Gregory, D. and Urry, J. eds. (1985) *Social Relations and Spatial Structures*. Basingstoke.
Grey, E. (2005) 'Beyond the temple: blurring the boundaries of "sacred space"', in Bruhn, Croxford and Grigoropoulos 2005: 109–18.
Groskurd, C. G. (1831–34) *Strabons Erdbeschreibung in siebenzehn Büchern nach berichtigtem griechischen Texte unter Begleitung kritischer erklärender Anmerkungen verdeutscht*. Berlin.
Habsburg, M. von (1985) 'Egyptian influence in Cyrenaica during the Ptolemaic period', in Barker, Lloyd and Reynolds 1985: 357–62.
Hackens, T., Holloway N. D., and Holloway R. R., eds. (1983) *Crossroads of the Mediterranean*. Louvain-La-Neuve.
Hadzis, C. (1995) 'Fêtes et cultes à Corcyre et à Corinthe, calendrier d'Épire, calendriers des cités coloniales de l'Ouest et calendrier de Corinthe', in Pugliese-Carratelli 1995: 445–61.
Hales, S. (2003) *The Roman House and Social Identity*. Cambridge.
Hall, J. M. (1997) *Ethnic Identity in Greek Antiquity*. Cambridge.
  (2002) *Hellenicity: Between Ethnicity and Culture*. Chicago.
  (2004) 'How "Greek" were the early Western Greeks?', in Lomas, K., ed., *Studies in Honor of Brian Shefton*, 35–54. Leiden.
  (2008) 'Foundation stories', in Tsetskhladze 2008: 383–426.
Hamilakis, Y., Pluciennik, M. and Tarlow, S. eds. (2002) *Thinking Through the Body: archaeologies of corporeality*. London.
Hamilton, R. (2000) *Treasure Map: A Guide to the Delian inventories*. Michigan.
Hansen, M. H., and Nielsen, T. H. (2004) *An Inventory of Archaic and Classical Poleis: an investigation conducted by the Copenhagen Polis Centre for the Danish National Research Foundation*. Oxford.

Harding, P. (2007) 'Local history and atthidography', in Marincola 2007b: 180–8.
Harley, J. and Woodward, D. eds. (1987) *The History of Cartography*. Chicago.
Harrison, T. (2007) 'The place of geography in Herodotus' Histories', in Adams and Roy 2007: 44–65.
Heinzelmann, M. (2000) *Die Nekropolen von Ostia: Unterschungen zu den Gräberstrassen vor der Porta Romana und an der Via Laurentina*. Munich.
(2001) 'Les nécropoles d'Ostie: topographie, développement, architecture, structure sociale', in Descoeudres 2001: 373–84.
Hellmann, M.-C. (1992) *Recherches sur le vocabulaire de l'architecture grecque, d'après les inscriptions de Délos*. Paris.
Hellmann, M.-C., and Fraisse, P. (1979) *Le monument aux héxagones et le portique des Naxiens (EAD 32)*. Paris.
Hermansen, G. (1981) *Ostia: Aspects of Roman City Life*. Alberta.
Herzog, R. and Klaffenbach, G. (1952) *Asylieurkunden aus Kos*. Berlin.
Hesberg, H. von (1994) *Monumenta: I sepolcri Romani e la loro Architettura*. Milan.
Hesberg, H. von and Panciera, S. (1994) *Das Mausoleum des Augustus*. Munich.
Hesberg, H. von and Zanker, P., eds. (1987) *Römische Gräberstrassen: Selbstdarstellung – Status – Standard*. Munich.
Higbie, C. (2003) *The Lindian Chronicle and the Greeks' Creation of Their Past*. Oxford.
Hillier, B. and Hanson, J. eds. (1984) *The Social Logic of Space*. Cambridge.
Hirsch, E. and O'Hanlon, M. eds. (1995) *The Anthropology of Landscape: Perspectives on Place and Space*. Oxford.
Hodder, I. and Orton, C. (1976) *Spatial Analysis in Archaeology*. Cambridge.
Hodos, T. (2006) *Local Responses to Colonisation in the Iron Age Mediterranean*. London.
Holleran, C. (2011) 'The street life of ancient Rome' in Laurence and Newsome 2011: 246–61.
Holloway, R. R. (1983) 'Recent research in prehistoric Sicily and recent research in Greek and Punic Sicily', in Hackens, Holloway and Holloway 1983: 261–76.
(1991) *The Archaeology of Ancient Sicily*. London.
Hope, V. M. (1997) 'A roof over the dead: communal tombs and family structure', in Laurence, R. and Wallace-Hadrill, A., eds., *Domestic Space in the Roman World: Pompeii and Beyond*, 69–88. Portsmouth.
(1998) 'Negotiating identity and status: the gladiators of Roman Nimes', in Laurence and Berry 1998: 179–95.
(2000a) 'Fighting for identity: the funerary commemoration of Italian gladiators', in Cooley, A. E., ed., *The Epigraphic Landscape of Roman Italy*, 93–114. London.
Hope, V. M. (2000b) 'Inscription and sculpture: the construction of identity in the military tombstones of Roman Mainz', in Oliver, G., ed., *The Epigraphy of Death: studies in the history and society of Greece and Rome*, 155–86. Liverpool.
(2000c) 'The city of Rome: capital and symbol', in Huskinson, J., ed. *Experiencing Rome: culture, identity and power in the Roman Empire*, 63–93. London.

(2001) *Constructing Identity: the Roman funerary monuments of Aquileia, Mainz and Nimes*. Oxford.
(2007) *Death in the Ancient World: a sourcebook*. London.
(2009) *Roman Death: the dying and the dead in ancient Rome*. London.
Hope, V. M., and Huskinson, J. eds. (2011) *Memory and Mourning: studies on Roman death*. Oxford.
Horden, P. and Purcell, N. (2000) *The Corrupting Sea: a study of Mediterranean history*. Oxford.
Hüttl, W. (1929) *Verfassungsgeschichte von Syrakus*. Prague.
Hutton, W. (2005) 'The construction of religious space in Pausanias', in Elsner, J. and Rutherford, I., eds., *Pilgrimage in Graeco-Roman and Early Christian Antiquity*, 291–317. Oxford.
Jackson, J. B. (1984) *Discovering the Vernacular Landscape*. New Haven.
Jacob, C. (1991) *Géographie et ethnographie en Grèce ancienne*. Paris.
Jacquemin, A. (1985) 'Trois bases à relief de Délos', *BCH* 109: 569–83.
(1991) 'Offrandes monumentales Italiotes et Siciliotes à Delphes', in Pugliese-Carratelli, G., ed., *La Magna Grecia e I grandi santuari della madrepatria*, 193–204. Taranto.
Jaeger, M. (1997) *Livy's Written Rome*. Ann Arbor.
Jashemski, W. (1979) *The Gardens Of Pompeii, Herculaneum and the Villas Destroyed by Vesuvius*. New Rochelle.
Jeffery, L. H. (1973–4) 'Demiourgoi in the Archaic Period', *Archeologia Classica* 25–6: 319–30.
Jones, F. (2011) *Virgil's Garden: the nature of bucolic space*. Bristol.
Jones, H. L. (trans. 1927–31) *The Geography of Strabo (8 volumes)*. Cambridge, Mass.
Jones, N. (2004) *Rural Athens Under the Democracy*. Philadelphia.
Jones, S. (1997) *The Archaeology of Ethnicity: constructing identities in the past and present*. London.
Jong, I. de ed. (2012) *Space in Ancient Greek Literature: studies in ancient Greek narrative*. Vol. III. Leiden.
Kaiser, A. (2000) *Urban Dialogue: an analysis of the use of space in the Roman city of Empuries, Spain*. Oxford.
Karageorghis, V. ed. (2002) *The Greeks Beyond the Aegean: from Marseilles to Bactria*. New York.
Karlsson, L. (1995) 'The symbols of freedom and democracy on the bronze coinage of Timoleon', in Fischer-Hansen 1995: 149–69.
Kaser, M. (1978) 'Zum römischen Grabrecht', *ZSS* 95: 15–92.
Keay, S., Millett, M., Paroli, L. and Strutt, K. (2005) *Portus: an archaeological survey of the port of Imperial Rome*. London.
Kent, J. H. (1952) 'The victory monument of Timoleon at Corinth', *Hesperia* 21: 9–18.
Kent, S. ed. (1990) *Domestic Architecture and the Use of Space: an interdisciplinary cross-cultural study*. Cambridge.
Kilian-Dirlmeier, I. (1985) 'Fremde Weihungen in griechischen Heiligtümern vom 8. bis zum Beginn des 7. Jahrhunderts v. Chr.', *JRGZ* 32: 215–54.

Kleiner, D. (1987) *Roman Imperial Funerary Altars with Portraits.* Rome.
Kockel, V. (1983) *Die Grabbauten vor dem Herkulaner Tor in Pompeji.* Mainz am Rhein.
Konstan, D. (2002) 'Narrative Spaces', in Paschalis, M. and Frangoulidis, S., eds., *Space in the Ancient Novel,* 1–11. Groningen.
Koortbojian, M. (1996) 'In commemorationem mortuorum: text and image along the "street of tombs"', in Elsner, J., ed., *Art and Text in Roman Culture,* 210–34. Cambridge.
Kramer, G. (1844) *Strabonis Geographica recensuit, commentario critico instruxit.* Berlin.
La Bédoyère, G. de (2010) *Cities of Roman Italy: Pompeii, Herculaneum, Ostia.* London. La Bianca, O. and Scham, S. eds. (2006) *Connectivity in Antiquity: globalisation as a long term historical process.* London.
Laidlaw, W. (1933) *A History of Delos.* Oxford.
Lamari, A. (2010) *Narrative, Intertext and Space in Euripides' Phoenissae.* Berlin.
Lane, M. (2007) 'Viewing space', *World Archaeology* 39.1: 1–3.
Langton, J. (1988) 'The two traditions of Geography: historical geography and the study of landscapes', *Geografiska Annaler* 70B: 17–25.
Lapalus, E. (1939) *L'agora des Italiens (EAD 19).* Paris.
Larmour, D. and Spencer, D. eds. (2007) *The Sites of Rome: time, space, memory.* Oxford.
Laronde, A. ed. (1987) *Cyrène et la Libye hellénistique: Libykai Historiai: de l'époque républicaine au principat d'Auguste.* Paris.
  ed. (1990) 'Cyrène sous les derniers Battiades', in Gentili 1990: 35–50.
Lasserre, F. (1982) 'Strabon devant l'Empire romain', *Aufstieg und Niedergang der Römischen Welt II* 30.1: 867–96.
Launaro, A. (2011) *Peasants and Slaves: The Rural Population of Roman Italy (200 BC to AD 100).* Cambridge.
Laurence, R. (1994) *Roman Pompeii: space and society.* London.
  (1995) 'The organisation of space in Pompeii', in Cornell, T. and Lomas, K., eds., *Urban Society in Roman Italy,* 63–78. London.
  (1999) *The Roads of Roman Italy: mobility and cultural change.* London.
Laurence, R. and Berry, J. eds. (1998) *Cultural Identity in the Roman Empire.* London.
Laurence, R. and Newsome, D. eds. (2011) *Rome, Ostia, Pompeii: movement and space.* Oxford.
Laurence, R. and Wallace-Hadrill, A. eds. (1997) *Domestic Space in the Roman World: Pompeii and beyond.* Portsmouth.
Laurence, R., Esmonde-Cleary, S. and Sears, G. (2011) *The City in the Roman West c.250 BC–AD 250.* Cambridge.
Leach, E. (1988) *The Rhetoric of Space: literary and artistic representations of landscape in Republican and Augustan Rome.* Princeton.
Lefebvre, H. (1991 (1974)) *The Production of Space.* Oxford.
Lehmler, C. (2005) *Syrakus unter Agathokles und Hieron II: Die Verbindung von Kultur und Macht in einer hellenistischen Metropole.* Frankfurt.

Leighton, R. (1999) *Sicily Before History: an archaeological survey from the Palaeolithic to the Iron Age*. London.
Leontis, A. (1995) *Topographies of Hellenism: mapping the homeland*. Ithaca.
Leroux, G. (1909) *La salle hypostyle (EAD 2)*. Paris.
Liddel, P. and Fear, A. eds. (2010) *Historiae Mundi: studies in universal historiography*. London.
Lindsay, H. (2005) 'Amaysa and Strabo's patria in Pontus', in Dueck, Lindsay and Pothecary 2005: 180–99.
Liverani, P. and Spinola, G. (2010) *The Vatican Necropoles: Rome's city of the dead*. Vatican City.
Lloyd, A. B. (1990a) 'Herodotus on Egyptians and Libyans', in Reverdin, O. and Grange, B., eds., *Hérodote et les peuples non-Grecs*, 215–44. Geneva.
  (1990b) 'The cities of Cyrenaica in the 3rd century AD', in Stucchi 1990: 41–53.
Lofland, L. (1989) 'Social life in the public realm – a review', *Journal of Contemporary Ethnography* 17(4): 886–92.
Loicq-Berger, M.-P. (1967) *Syracuse: histoire culturelle d'une cité grecque*. Brussels.
Lomas, K. (1998) 'Roman imperialism and the city in Italy', in Laurence and Berry 1998: 64–78.
  ed. (2004) *Greek Identity in the Western Mediterranean*. Leiden.
Londey, P. (1990) 'Greek colonists and Delphi', in Descoeudres 1990: 117–27.
Low, S. M. (2000) *On the Plaza: the politics of public space and culture*. Austin.
Luni, M. (1990) 'Il Ginnasio-Caesareum nel contesto del rinnovamento urbanistico della media età ellenistica e della prima età imperiale', in Stucchi 1990: 87–120.
  (2006) *Cirene 'Atene d'Africa', MAL 28*. Rome.
Luni, M. and Mei, O. (2006) 'L'area sacra a Sud del Ginnasio ellenistico – Forum di Cirene', in Fabbricotti, E. and Menozzi, O., eds., *Cirenaica: studi, scavi e scoperte*, 3–16. Oxford.
Ma, J. (2009) 'The city as memory', in Boys-Stone, G., Graziosi, B. and Vasunia, P., eds., *The Oxford Handbook of Hellenic Studies*, 248–259. Oxford.
Maas, M. (2007) 'Strabo and Procopius: classical geography for a Christian Empire', in Amirav, H. and Romeny, B. H., eds., *From Rome to Constantine: studies in honour of Averil Cameron*, 67–84. Leuven.
MacDonald, W. L. (1986) *The Architecture of the Roman Empire Volume II: an urban reappraisal*. New Haven.
MacKendrick, P. (1980) *The North African Stones Speak*. London.
Maddoli, G. ed. (1986) *Strabone: contributi allo studio della personalità e dell'opera (volume II)*. Perugia.
  ed. (1988) *Strabone e l'Italia antica*. Naples.
Malaise, M. (1972) *Les conditions de pénétration et de diffusion des cultes égyptiens en Italie*. Leyde.
Malkin, I. (1984) 'The origins of the colonists of Syracuse: Apollo of Delos', *Kokalos* 30–31: 53–5.
  (1987) *Religion and Colonisation in Ancient Greece*. Leiden.

(1994a) 'Inside and outside: colonisation and the formulation of the mother-city', in D'Agostino, B. and Buchner, G., eds., *Apoikia: I più antichi insediamenti greci in occidente: funzioni e modi dell'organizzazione politica e sociale*, 1–10. Naples.
  (1994b) *Myth and Territory in the Spartan Mediterranean*. Cambridge.
  ed. (2001) *Ancient Perceptions of Greek Identity*. Cambridge, Mass.
  (2002) 'Exploring the validity of the concept of "foundation"', in Gorman, V. B. and Robinson, E. W., eds., *Oikistes: studies in constitutions, colonies and military power in the ancient world (Fest. A. J. Graham)*, 195–225. Leiden.
Malkin, I., Constantakopoulou, C. and Panagopoulou, K. eds. (2009) *Greek and Roman Networks in the Mediterranean*. London.
Malmberg, S. and Bjur, H. (2011) 'Movement and urban development at two city gates in Rome: the Porta Esquilina and Porta Tiburtina' in Laurence and Newsome 2011: 361–85.
Marcadé, J. (1950) 'Notes sur trois sculptures archaïques récemment reconstituées à Délos', *BCH* 74: 181–215.
Marcadé, J. (1969) *Au musée de Délos*. Paris.
March, C. (2009) *Spatial and Religious Transformations in the Late Antique Polis: a multi-disciplinary analysis with a case-study of the city of Gerasa*. Oxford.
Marengo, S. M. (1991) *Lessico delle iscrizioni greche della Cirenaica*. Rome.
Mari, M. (2010) 'Funerali illustri e spazio pubblico nella Grecia antica', in Carruseco 2010: 85–102.
Marincola, J. (2007a) 'Universal history from Ephorus to Diodorus', in Marincola 2007b: 171–9.
  ed. (2007b) *A Companion to Greek and Roman Historiography (Volumes 1 and 2)*. Oxford.
Martin, R. (1951) *Recherches sur l'agora grecque: études d'histoire et d'architecture*. Paris.
Massaro, G. D. (1986) 'I moduli della narrazione storica nei libri di Strabone sull'Italia meridionale', in Maddoli 1986: 81–120.
Meiggs, R. (1973) *Roman Ostia*, 2nd edn. Oxford.
Meiggs, R. and Lewis, D. (1988) *A Selection of Greek Historical Inscriptions to the End of the Fifth Century* BC (rev. edn). Oxford.
Mertens, D. (1990) 'Some principal features of west Greek colonial architecture', in Descoeudres 1990: 374–83.
  (1996) 'Greek architecture in the West', in Pugliese-Carratelli 1996: 315–36.
  (2010) 'La formación del espacio en las ciudades coloniales', in Carruseco 2010: 67–74.
Meskell, L. and Preucel, R. W. eds. (2004) *A Companion to Social Archaeology*. Oxford.
Miller, M. (1970) *The Sicilian Colony Dates: studies in chronography*. Albany.
Millett, P. (1998) 'Encounters in the agora', in Cartledge, P., Millett, P. and Von Reden, S., eds., *Kosmos: essays in order, conflict and community in Classical Athens*, 203–28. Cambridge.
Molinier, S. (1914) *Les 'maisons sacrées' de Délos au temps de l'indépendance de l'île*. Paris.

Momigliano, A. (1982) 'The origins of universal history', *Annali della Scuola Normale Superiore di Pisa* 12: 533–60.
Morcillo, M. G. (2010) 'The glory of Italy and Rome's universal destiny in Strabo's Geographika', in Liddel and Fear 2010: 87–101.
Morel, J-P. (1983) 'Greek colonisation in Italy and the West (problems of evidence and interpretation)', in Hackens, Holloway and Holloway 1983: 123–62.
Moretti, J.-C., ed. (2006) *Études d'archéologie délienne par Ph. Bruneau (BCH Supp. 47)*. Paris.
Moretti, J.-C. and Fincker, M. 2008 'Un autel de Dionyos à Délos', *BCH* 132: 116–52.
Morgan, C. (1988) 'Corinth, the Corinthian gulf and western Greece during the 8th century BC', *ABSA* 83: 313–38.
  (1990) *Athletes and Oracles: the transformation of Olympia and Delphi in the eighth century BC*. Cambridge.
Morgan, C. and Coulton, J. J. (1997) 'The polis as a physical entity', in Hansen, M. H., ed. *The Polis as an Urban Centre and as a Political Community*, 87–143. Copenhagen.
Morgan, C. and Hall, J. M. (1996) 'Achaian poleis and Achaian colonisation', in Hansen, M. H., ed., *Introduction to the Inventory of Poleis*, 164–232. Copenhagen.
Morris, J. (2004) 'Agency theory applied: a study of later prehistoric lithic assemblages from north-west Pakistan', in Gardner 2004b: 51–64.
Mossé, C. (1970) *La colonisation dans l'antiquité*. Paris.
Mouritsen, H. (1997) 'Mobility and social change in Italian towns during the Principate', in Parkins, H., ed., *Roman Urbanism: beyond the consumer city*, 59–82. London.
Moyer, I. (2011) *Egypt and the Limits of Hellenism*. Cambridge.
Muir, E. and Weissman, F. (1989) 'Social and symbolic places in Renaissance Venice and Florence', in Agnew, J. A. and Duncan, J. S., eds., *The Power of Place: bringing together geographical and sociological imaginations*, 81–103. London.
Müller, C. and Hasenohr, C. eds. (2002) *Les Italiens dans le monde grec: IIe siècle av. JC. – Ier siècle ap. JC. Circulation, Activités, Intégration (BCH Supp. 41)*. Paris.
Murray, O. and Price, S. R. F. eds. (1990) *The Greek City: from Homer to Alexander*. Oxford.
Musti, D. (1994) *Strabone e la Magna Grecia: città e popoli dell' Italia antica*. Esedra.
Mylonopoulos, I. (2010) 'The myth of artistic innovation: hellenistic divine images and the power of transition', Unpublished conference paper, *Rethinking the Gods: post-Classical approaches to sacred space (Conference Oxford 2010)*.
Nevett, L. C. (1999) *House and Society in the Ancient Greek World*. Cambridge.
  (2010) *Domestic Space in Classical Antiquity*. Cambridge.
Nicolet, C. (1980) *Insula sacra: la loi Gabinia Calpurnia de Délos (58 av. J.C.)*. Paris.
O'Sullivan, T. (2011) *Walking in Roman Culture*. Cambridge.
Osborne, R. (1987) *Classical Landscape with Figures: the Ancient Greek city and its countryside*. London.
  (1998) 'Early Greek colonisation: the nature of Greek settlements in the West', in Fisher, N. and Van Wees, H., eds., *Archaic Greece: new approaches and new evidence*, 251–70. London.

(2010) *Greece in the Making c.1200–479* BC, 2nd edn. London.
Osborne, R. and Tanner, J. eds. (2007) *Art's Agency and Art History*. Oxford.
Osterhammel, J. (1998) 'Die Wiederkehr des Raumes. Geopolitik, Geohistorie und historische Geographie', *Neue politische Literatur* 43: 374–97.
Owen, S. (2005) 'Analogy, Archaeology and archaic Greek colonisation', in Owen and Hurst 2005: 5–22.
Owen, S. and Hurst, H. eds. (2005) *Ancient Colonisations: analogy, similarity and difference*. London.
Owen, S. and Preston, L. eds. (2009) *Inside the City in the Greek World: studies of urbanism from the Bronze Age to the Hellenistic period*. Oxford.
Panichi, S. (2005) 'Cappadocia through Strabo's eyes', in Dueck, Lindsay and Pothecary 2005: 200–15.
Papageorgiou-Venetas, A. (1981) *Recherches urbaines sur une ville antique: Délos*. Munich.
Paschalis, M. and Frangoulidis, S. eds. (2002) *Space in the Ancient Novel*. Groningen.
Patterson, J. (2000) 'On the margins of the city of Rome', in Hope, V. M. and Marshall, E., eds., *Death and Disease in the Ancient City*, 85–103. London.
Patterson, L. (2010) *Kinship Myth in Ancient Greece*. Austin.
Pearson, M. and Richards, C. eds. (1994) *Architecture and Order: approaches to social space*. London.
Pelling, C. (2007) 'The Greek historians of Rome', in Marincola 2007b: 244–58.
Penz, F., Radick, G. and Howell, R. eds. (2004) *Space in Science, Art and Society*. Cambridge.
Picard, C. (1921) *L'Établissement des Poseidoniastes de Bérytos (EAD 6)*. Paris.
Pigon, J. ed. (2008) *The Children of Herodotus: Greek and Roman historiography and related genres*. Newcastle upon Tyne.
Plassart, A. (1928) *Les sanctuaires et les cultes de Mont Cynthe (EAD 11)*. Paris.
Polacco, L., Anti, C. and Trojani, M. (1981) *Il teatro antico di Siracusa*. Rimini.
Polidori, R., Di Vita, A., Di Vita-Evrard, G. and Bacchielli, L. eds. (1999) *Libya: lost cities of the Roman Empire*. Cologne.
Polignac, F. de (1995) *Cults, Territory and the Origins of the Greek City-State*, 2nd edn. Trans. J. Lloyd. Chicago.
Pomtow, H. (1895) 'Ein sicilisches Anathem in Delphi', *Ath. Mitt.* 20: 483–94.
Pothecary, S. (2005a) 'Kolossourgia: "a colossal statue of a work"', in Dueck, Lindsay and Pothecary 2005: 5–26.
  (2005b) 'The European provinces: Strabo as evidence', in Dueck, Lindsay and Pothecary 2005: 161–79.
Prandi, L. (1994) 'La "successione delle penisole" e la Grecia di Strabone', in Biraschi 1994a: 11–21.
Prêtre, C. (2002) *Nouveau choix d'inscriptions de Délos: lois, comptes et inventaires*. Paris
Pretzler, M. (2005) 'Comparing Strabo with Pausanias: Greece in context vs. Greece in depth', in Dueck, Lindsay and Pothecary 2005: 144–60.
  (2007) 'Greek intellectuals on the move: travel and paideia in the Roman Empire', in Adams and Roy 2007: 123–38.

Prontera, F. ed. (1984) *Strabone: contributi allo studio della personalità e dell'opera.* Vol. I. Perugia.
Pugliese-Carratelli, G. ed. (1985–88) *Magna Graecia: il mediterraneo, le metropoleis e la fondazione delle colonie.* Milan.
  ed. (1995) *Corinto e l'Occidente.* Taranto.
  ed. (1996) *The Western Greeks: classical civilisation in the western Mediterranean.* London.
Purcaro, V. (2001) *L'Agorà di Cirene 2, 3: L'area meridionale del lato ouest dell'agorà (MAL 24).* Rome.
Purcell, N. (1987) 'Tomb and suburb', in Hesberg and Zanker 1987: 25–42.
  (2005) 'The boundless sea of unlikeness? On defining the Mediterranean', in Malkin, I., ed. *Mediterranean Paradigms and Classical Antiquity,* 9–29. London.
  (2007) 'Urban spaces and central places (Roman world)', in Alcock and Osborne 2007: 182–202.
Raaflaub, K. and Talbert, R. eds. (2010) *Geography and Ethnography – Perceptions of the World in Pre-Modern Societies.* Chichester.
Radt, S. (2002) *Strabons Geographika.* Vols. I–VIII. Göttingen.
Rapoport, A. (1969) *House Form and Culture.* New Jersey.
  (1980) 'Vernacular architecture and the cultural determinants of form', in King, A., ed., *Buildings and Society,* 283–305. London.
  (1982) *The Meaning of the Built Environment: a nonverbal communication approach.* Beverley Hills.
  (1990) 'Systems of activities and systems of settings', in Kent, S., ed., *Domestic Architecture and the Use of Space,* 9–20. Cambridge.
Rauh, N. K. (1993) *The Sacred Bonds of Commerce: religion, economy and trade: society at hellenistic and Roman Delos.* Amsterdam.
Reece, R. ed. (1977) *Burial in the Roman World.* London.
Rehm, R. (2002) *The Play of Space: spatial transformation in Greek tragedy.* Princeton.
Reichert-Südbeck, P. (2000) *Kulte von Korinth und Syrakus: Vergleich zwischen einer Metropolis und ihrer Apoikia.* Dettelbach.
Reynolds, J. (1977) 'The cities of Cyrenaica in decline', in Duval, P. M. and Frézouls, E., eds., *Thèmes de recherches sur les villes antiques d'Occident,* 53–8. Paris.
  ed. (1994) *Cyrenaican Archaeology.* London.
Rhodes, P. J., and Osborne, R. (2003) *Greek Historical Inscriptions 404–323 BC.* Oxford.
Richardson, L. (1988) *Pompeii: an architectural history.* Baltimore.
Richmond, A. (1930) *The City Wall of Imperial Rome: an account of its architectural development from Aurelian to Narses.* Oxford.
Ridgway, D. (1990) 'The first Western Greeks and their neighbours 1935–1985', in Descoeudres 1990: 61–72.
Ridley, R. T. (1996) 'The Praetor and the pyramid: the tomb of Gaius Cestius in history, archaeology and literature', *Bollettino di Archeologia* 13–15: 1–30.
Robert, F. (1952) *Trois sanctuaires sur le rivage occidental (EAD 20).* Paris.

Robertson, N. (2010) *Religion and Reconciliation in Greek Cities: the sacred laws of Selinus and Cyrene.* Oxford.
Robinson, O. F. (1992) *Ancient Rome: city planning and administration.* London.
Romm, J. S. (1992) *The Edges of the Earth in Ancient Thought.* Princeton.
  (2010) 'Continents, climates and cultures: Greek theories of global structure', in Raaflaub and Talbert 2010: 15–35.
Rosen, R. and Sluiter, I. eds. (2006) *City, Countryside and the Spatial Organisation of Value in Classical Antiquity.* Leiden.
Roussel, P. (1915–16) *Les cultes égyptiens à Délos du IIIe au Ier siècle av. J.-C.* Paris.
  (1916) *Délos colonie Athénienne.* Paris.
Roux, G. (1973) 'Salles de banquets à Délos', *BCH* Supp. 1 (Fest. G. Daux): 525–54.
Runciman, W. G. (1990) 'Doomed to extinction: the polis as an evolutionary dead end', in Murray and Price 1990: 347–67.
Sakellariou, M. B. (1996) 'The metropolises of the western Greek colonies', in Pugliese-Carratelli 1996: 177–88.
Salmeri, G. (2000) 'Nota Conclusiva', in Biraschi and Salmeri 2000: 567–85. Naples.
Salmon, J. B. (1984) *Wealthy Corinth: a history of the city to 338 BC.* Oxford.
Salway, B. (2004) 'Sea and river travel in Roman itinerary literature', in Talbert and Brodersen 2004: 43–96.
  (2007) 'The perception and description of space in Roman itineraries', in Rathmann, M., ed., *Wahrnehmung und Erfassung geographischer Räume in der Antike* 181–209. Mainz.
Santucci, A. (1998) 'Il santuario dell'Anax nell' Agorà di Cirene', in Catani and Marengo 1998: 523–36.
Sauer, E. ed. (2004) *Archaeology and Ancient History: breaking down the boundaries.* London.
Schlögel, K. (2007) *Im Raume lesen wir die Zeit. Über Zivilisationsgeschichte und Geopolitik.* Frankfurt.
Schroer, M. (2006) *Räume, Orte, Grenzen. Auf dem Weg zu einer Soziologie des Raumes.* Frankfurt.
Schultz, P. (2007) 'Leochares' Argead Portraits in the Philippeion', in Schultz, P. and von den Hoff, R., eds., *Early Hellenistic Portraiture: image, style, context,* 205–36. Cambridge.
Scott, M. C. (2007) 'Putting architectural sculpture into its archaeological context: the case of the Siphnian treasury at Delphi', *BABesch* 82.2: 321–31.
Scott, M. C. (2010) *Delphi and Olympia: the spatial politics of Panhellenism in the Archaic and Classical periods.* Cambridge.
  (2011) 'Displaying lists of what is (not) on display: the uses of inventories in Greek sanctuaries', in Haysom, M. and Wallensten, J., eds., *Current Approaches to Religion in Ancient Greece,* 239–52. Stockholm.
  (forthcoming) 'The spatial indeterminacy and social life of athletic facilities', in Christesen, P. and Kyle, D., eds., *A Companion to Sport and Spectacle in the Ancient World.* Oxford.
Scully, V. (1969) *The Earth, the Temple and the Gods: Greek sacred architecture.* New York.

Seaford, R. (2012) *Cosmology and the Polis: the social construction of space and time in the tragedies of Aeschylus*. Cambridge.
Shepherd, G. (1993) *Death and Religion in Archaic Greek Sicily: a study in colonial relationships*. Cambridge.
  (1995) 'The pride of most colonials: burial and religion in the Sicilian colonies', in Fischer-Hansen 1995: 51–82.
  (1999) 'Fibulae and females: intermarriage in the Western Greek colonies and evidence from the cemeteries', in Tsetskhladze, G. R., ed. *Ancient Greeks East and West*, 267–300. Leiden.
  (2000) 'Greeks bearing gifts: religious relationships between Sicily and Greece in the Archaic Period', in Smith, C. and Serrati, J., eds., *Sicily from Aeneas to Augustus: new approaches in archaeology and history*, 55–72. Edinburgh.
  (2005a) 'Dead men tell no tales: ethnic diversity in Sicilian colonies and the evidence of the cemeteries', *Oxford Journal of Archaeology* 24: 115–36.
  (2005b) 'The advance of the Greek: Greece, Great Britain and archaeological Empires', in Owen and Hurst 2005: 23–44.
Sjöqvist, E. (1973) *Sicily and the Greeks: studies in the interrelationships between the indigenous populations and the Greek colonists*. Michigan.
Smagacz, M. (2008) *The Revitalisation of Urban Space*. Pisa.
Smith, A. (2001) *Differential Use of Constructed Sacred Space in Southern Britain, From the Late Iron Age to the Fourth Century AD*. Oxford.
Smith, M. ed. (2003) *The Social Construction of Ancient Cities*. Washington.
Snead, J. E., and Preucel, R. W. (1999) 'The ideology of settlement: ancestral Keres landscapes in the Northern Rio Grande', in Ashmore and Knapp 1999: 169–200.
Snodgrass, A. M. (1991) 'Archaeology and the study of the Greek city', in Rich, J. W. and Wallace-Hadrill, A., eds., *City and Country in the Ancient World*, 1–24. London.
  (1994) 'The nature and standing of early Western colonies', in Tsetskhladze and de Angelis 1994: 1–10.
Snodgrass, A. M. (2001) 'Pausanias and the chest of Kypselos', in Alcock, Cherry and Elsner 2001: 127–41.
  (2002) 'The history of false archaeology', *AWE* 1: 19–23.
Soja, E. (1996) *Thirdspace: journey to Los Angeles and other real and imagined places*. Oxford.
Sokolowski, F. (1969) *Lois sacrées des cités grecques*. Paris.
Sorabji, R. (1988) 'Theophrastus on Place', in Fortenbaugh, W. and Sharples, R., eds., *Theophrastean Studies: on natural science, physics and metaphysics, ethics, religion, and rhetoric*, 139–66. New Brunswick.
Souvatzi, S. (2008) *A Social Archaeology of Households in Neolithic Greece*. Cambridge.
Spawforth, A. and Walker, S. (1985) 'The world of the Panhellenion I: Athens and Eleusis', *JRS* 75: 78–104.
  (1986) 'The world of the Panhellenion II: three Dorian cities', *JRS* 76: 88–105.
Spencer, D. (2006) 'Horace's garden thoughts: rural retreats and the urban imagination', in Rosen and Sluiter 2006: 239–74.

(2010) *Roman Landscape: culture and identity*. Cambridge.
Spieser, J.-M. (2001) *Urban and Religious Spaces in Late Antiquity and Early Byzantium* Aldershot.
Sprawski, S. (2008) 'Writing local history: Archemachus and his Euboika', in PIGON 2008: 102–18.
Squarciapino, M. (1955) *Scavi di Ostia: le necropoli (parte 1): le tombe di età repubblicana e augustea*. Rome.
Stackelberg, K. von (2009) *The Roman Garden: space, sense and society*. London.
Steinsapir, A. (2005) *Rural Sanctuaries in Roman Syria: creation of a sacred landscape*. Oxford.
Stevens, K. (forthcoming) 'Mapping intellectual change: Hellenistic geography in Aristotle and Theophrastus', in Barker, E., Bouzarovski, S. and Isaksen, L., eds., *New Worlds Out of Old Texts: developing techniques for the spatial analysis of ancient narratives*.
Stewart, A. (1979) *Attika: studies in Athenian sculpture of the Hellenistic Age*. London.
Stucchi, S. (1965) *L'Agorà di Cirene 1: Il lati nord ed est della platea inferiore (MAL 7)*. Rome.
(1975) *Architettura Cirenaica (MAL 9)*. Rome.
ed. (1990) *Giornata Lincea di Archeologia Cirenaica*. Rome.
Stucchi, S. and Bacchielli, L. (1983) *L'Agorà di Cirene 2,4: Il lato sud della platea inferiore e il lato nord della terrazzo superiore (MAL 17)*. Rome.
Syme, R. (1995) *Anatolica: Studies in Strabo (ed. by A. Birley)*. Oxford.
Talbert, R. (1974) *Timoleon and the Revival of Greek Sicily*. Cambridge.
(2004) 'Cartography and taste in Peutinger's Roman map', in Talbert and Brodersen 2004: 113–41.
(2010) 'The Roman world view: beyond recovery?', in Raaflauband Talbert 2010: 252–72.
Talbert, R. and Brodersen, K. eds. (2004) *Space in the Roman World: its perception and presentation*. Munster.
Tanner, J. (2006) *The Invention of Art History in Ancient Greece*. Cambridge.
Terrenato, N. (2007) 'The essential countryside', in Alcock and Osborne 2007: 139–61.
Thomas, J. (2001) 'Archaeologies of place and landscape', in Hodder, I., ed. *Archaeological Theory Today*, 165–86. Cambridge.
Thompson, H. A., and Wycherley, R. E. (1972) *The Agora of Athens: the history, shape and use of an ancient city centre*. Princeton.
Thylander, H. (1952) *Inscriptions du port d'Ostie (vols. I and II)*. Lund.
Tilley, C. (1994) *A Phenomenology of Landscape: places, paths and monuments*. Oxford.
Tilley, C. and Bennett, W. (2004) *The Materiality of Stone: explorations in landscape phenomenology*. Oxford.
Todd, M. (1978) *The Walls of Rome*. London.
Toynbee, J. M. C. (1971) *Death and Burial in the Roman World*. London.
Tréheux, J. (1992) *Index des inscriptions de Délos: 1. Les étrangers à l'exclusion des Athéniens de la cléruchie et des Romains*. Paris.

Trexler, R. (1980) *Public life in Renaissance Florence*. London.
Trotta, F. (2005) 'The foundation of Greek colonies and their main feature in Strabo: a portrayal lacking homogeneity?', in Dueck, Lindsay and Pothecary 2005: 118–28.
Tsetskhladze, G. R. (1998) *The Greek Colonisation of the Black Sea Area*. Stuttgart.
  (2002) 'Greeks beyond the Bosphorus', in Karageorghis 2002: 129–66.
  ed. (2008) *Greek Colonisation: an account of Greek colonies and other settlements overseas*. Vol. II. Leiden.
Tsetskhladze, G. R. and Angelis, F. de, eds. (1994) *The Archaeology of Greek Colonisation: essays dedicated to Sir John Boardman*. Oxford.
Vallois, R. (1923) *La portique de Philippe (EAD 7.1)*. Paris.
Vallois, R. (1944–78) *L'architecture hellénique et héllénistique à Délos jusqu'à l'éviction des Déliens (166 av. J.-C.), BEFAR 157*. Paris.
Vallois, R. and Poulsen, G. (1914) *La salle hypostyle, EAD 2bis*. Paris
van der Vliet, C. L. (1984) 'L'ethnographie de Strabon: idéologie ou tradition', in Prontera 1984: 27–86.
van Dommelen, P. (1998) *On Colonial Grounds: a comparative study of colonialism and rural settlement in first millennium BC West Central Sardinia*. Leiden.
  (2005) 'Urban foundations? Colonial settlement and urbanization in the Western Mediterranean', in Osborne, R. and Cunliffe, B., eds., *Mediterranean Urbanisation 800–600 BC*, 143–67. Oxford.
van Dyke, R. M. and Alcock, S. E. eds. (2003) *Archaeologies of Memory*. Oxford.
van Haverbeke, H., Poblome, J., Vermeulen, F., Waelkens, M. and Brulet, R. eds. (2008) *Thinking About Space: the potential of surface survey and contextual analysis in the definition of space in Roman times*. Turnhout.
Vanicelli, P. (1993) *Erodoto e la storia dell'alto e medio arcaismo (Sparta–Tessaglia–Cirene)*. Rome.
Várhelyi, Z. (2010) *The Religion of Senators in the Roman Empire: power and the beyond*. New York.
Vatin, C. (1965) 'Délos prémycénienne', *BCH* 89: 185–315.
Veronese, F. (2006) *Lo spazio e la dimensione del sacro: santuari Greci e territorio nella Sicilia arcaica*. Padova.
Vial, C. (1984) *Délos Indépendante 314–167: Étude d'une communauté civique et de ses institutions (BCH Supp. 10)*. Paris.
Vidal-Naquet, P. (1986) *The Black Hunter: forms of thought and forms of society in the Greek world*. Trans. A. Szegedy-Maszak. Baltimore.
Visscher, F. de (1965) *Les édits d'Auguste découverts à Cyrène*. Osnabrück.
Vlassopoulos, K. (2007) 'Free spaces: identity, experience and democracy in classical Athens', *Classical Quarterly* 57: 33–52.
Vout, C. (2007) 'Sizing up Rome, or theorizing the overview', in Larmour and Spencer 2007: 295–322.
  (forthcoming) 'Roman funerary art and the rhetoric of unreachability', in Elsner, J. and Meyer, M., eds., *Art and Rhetoric*. Cambridge.
Waele, F.-J. de (1961) *Corinthe*. Paris.

Waisglas, A. (1955) *A Historical Study of Cyrene from the Fall of the Battiad Monarchy to the Close of the Fourth Century* BC. Columbia.
Walker, S. (1985) 'The architecture of Cyrene and the Panhellenion', in Barker, Lloyd and Reynolds 1985: 97–104.
Wallace, P. W. (1979) *Strabo's Description of Boeotia: a commentary*. Heidelberg.
Wallace-Hadrill, A. (1988) 'The social structure of the Roman house', *PBSR* 56: 43–97.
  (1994) *Houses and Society in Pompeii and Herculaneum*. Princeton.
Ward-Perkins, J. B. (1974) *Cities of Ancient Greece and Italy: planning in classical antiquity*. New York.
Weller, C. H. (1906) 'The extent of Strabo's travel in Greece', *Classical Philology* 1: 339–56.
White, D. ed. (1990) *The Extramural Sanctuary of Demeter and Persephone at Cyrene, Libya: Final Report*. Vol. IV. Philadelphia.
Will, Edouard (1955a) *Korinthiaka: Recherches sur l'histoire et la civilisation de Corinthe des origines aux guerres médiques*. Paris.
Will, Ernest (1955b) *Le Dôdékathéon, EAD 22*. Paris.
Will, Ernest and Schmidt, M. (1985) *Le sanctuaire de la déesse syrienne, EAD 35*. Paris.
Williams, C. K. and Bookidis, N. eds. (2003) *Corinth: the centenary 1896–1996*. Athens.
Wilson, J. P. (2006) 'Ideologies of Greek colonisation', in Bradley, G. and Wilson, J., eds., *Greek and Roman Colonisation*, 25–58. Swansea.
Wilson, R. J. A. (1990) *Sicily Under the Roman Empire: the archaeology of a Roman province 36* BC *–* AD *535*. Warminster.
Witcher, R. (2009) 'The countryside', in Erskine 2009: 462–74.
Woodard, R. D. (2006) *Indo-European Sacred Space: Vedic and Roman cult*. Chicago.
Woodhead, A. G. (1962) *The Greeks in the West*. London.
Woolf, G. (2011) *Tales of the Barbarian: ethnography and empire in the Roman West*. Oxford.
Yntema, D. (2000) 'Mental landscapes of colonisation: the ancient written sources and the archaeology of early colonial Greek south-eastern Italy', *BABesch* 75: 1–49.
Zambon, E. (2008) *Tradition and Innovation: Sicily between Hellenism and Rome*. Stuttgart.
Zanker, P. (1975) 'Grabreliefs römischer Freigelassener', *JDAI* 90: 267–315.
Zimmerman, S. and Weissman, R. eds. (1989) *Urban Life in the Renaissance*. London.

Index

Achilles 7
Actaeon 133
Actium 142, 154, 157
Adonis 66, 74
Aeschylus 121, 123
Aetnaeae (Aeschylus) 121, 123
Agamemnon 42
agency 9
agoras
  'agora-type' spaces 11
  in Corinth 128
  in Cyrene *see under* Cyrene
  in Delos 60, 62, 72–4
    'agora of the Gods' 53, 57–8, 62, 65
  importance in Greek culture 10
  of the Ionian Confederation 52
  of the Italians 73, 74
  open for the gathering of citizens 161
  as public space 10, 15
  purposes, flexibility of 10–11
  spatial analysis 171–2
  in Syracuse 132
  of Theophrastus 73
Alcibiades 125, 135
Alcibiades (Plutarch) 135
Alcock, S. 5, 8, 165, 171
Alexander the Great 25, 26, 28, 139
  in Strabo's *Geography* 142, 143, 147, 148
Algra, K. 3
Allison, P. 4
Almagor, E. 140
Alonso-Núñez, J. M. 139
Amazons 147
Amiotti, G. 141
Anaximander of Miletus 7
Angelis, F. de 174
Anios 53, 58, 67, 74
Anoubis 64, 71
Antigonous I 54
Antigonus Gonatas 61, 62
Antiochus III 61

Antonaccio, C. M. 111, 120, 125, 129, 175
Antony 147
Aphrodite
  at Corinth 117
  at Delos 59–60, 65, 76
  in Syracuse's colonies 117
Apollo 45
  at Corinth 115, 116
  at Cyrene 15, 17, 21, 23, 26, 28–9, 33, 37–9, 40–1, 44, 166
  at Delos *see under* networks of polytheism: spaces for the gods at Delos
  at Delphi 128
  at Ortygia/Syracuse 115
  at Tenea 134
Apollodorus 149
Apollonius 63–4
Appian 109
Applebaum, S. 17, 19, 21–4, 34, 37, 39, 171, 172
Arcesilaus III 19
Arcesilaus IV 22
archaeology and site excavation
  American School of Classical Studies at Athens 175
  colonisation knowledge from excavations 174
  Cyrene *see under* Cyrene
  French Archaeological School 172
  Geographical Information Systems 6, 9
  historical focus on public architecture 10
  Ortygia 112
  sanctuary excavation reports 6
  surface-survey/field survey 6, 9
    in Greece 6–7
    in Italy 7
  tomb excavation incomplete 174
Archias 125–6, 133–4
Archilochus 149
architecture in Corinth and Syracuse 115–17
Arena, R. 120, 122
Aristaeus (Anax) 23, 25, 30, 38, 43, 44, 161
Aristotle 7, 144, 162, 165

Index

art in Corinth and Syracuse 115–17
Artemis 45
  Artemis Hekate 74
  Artemis Leucophryene 130
  Artemis Lochia 56
  at Delos *see under* networks of polytheism:
    spaces for the gods at Delos
  at Syracuse 117
Ascalon 70, 71
Asclepius
  at Cyrene 24, 26, 32, 39
  at Delos 65
Ashmore, W. 6
Asia Minor 130, 131, 135, 165
  in Strabo's *Geography* 140–1, 146, 147–8, 156, 176
asylia ('asylum') 130
Athena 127
  Athena Cynthia 56, 65, 70
  Athena Lindia 132
  Athena Paeon 57
  Athena Polias 53, 67
  Athena Soteria 67
  at Delos 49, 53, 56, 57, 65, 66, 67, 70
  at Syracuse 112
    at Ortygia 115, 122
Athens 9, 10, 24
  agora, stoa of Zeus Eleutherius in 24, 28, 43
  boule 127
  Cephalus 121
  and Cyrene 22
  dedications 122
  at Delos *see under* networks of polytheism:
    spaces for the gods at Delos
  Demeter 122
  democracy 24
  government system 26
  Ionians supporting 125
  mixed community 162
  Piraeus 66
  poets 121
  Sicilian expedition 121, 122, 124–5, 126
  stoas 24, 25, 26, 28
  in Strabo's *Geography* 152, 153, 154, 155
  and Syracuse 121, 122, 126–8, 129
  theatre/Athenian tragedy 121, 127
  Tisias 121
Attalus I 62
Attica 122
Audiat, J. 74
Augustus
  burial 102
  and Cyrene 34, 36
  in Strabo's *Geography* 147, 148, 154, 157
Aujac, G. 143
Aulus Hirtius 99

Bacchielli, L. 20, 23–6, 30, 32–3, 36–9, 41, 171
Bacchus 39
Bacchylides 121
Baladié, R. 140–1, 154
Baldassarre, I. 174
Barker, G. 7, 172
Barletta, B. A. 115, 116
Barrett, S. R. 170
Baslez, M.-F. 66, 69
Basso, K. 170
Battus 17, 18–19, 20, 22–6, 28, 30–1, 38, 41, 43, 44
Benchimol, E. 52
Bender, B. 6, 170
Bendis 66, 74
Bennett, W. 6, 170
Bentley, R. A. 171
Bérard, J. 110
Berger, S. 124
Bergmann, B. 4
Berve, H 115
Betts, E. 109, 168
Biffi, N. 145, 176
Bintliff, J. 8
Biraschi, A.-M. 140, 141, 150, 156, 176
Bjur, H. 5, 97, 98, 100
Black Hunter, The (Vidal-Naquet) 3
Blake, E. 5, 171, 175
Boardman, J. 17, 175
Bodel, J. 77, 102
Boeotia 140, 144, 151, 153–4
Bon, S. E. 5
Bonacasa, N. 17, 19, 23–4, 27–8, 30, 32, 34, 37–9, 41–2, 172
Bookidis, N. 116, 175
boundaries
  between city and countryside 3
  marked boundaries of the agora 10–11, 14
  in Cyrene 17, 19, 20, 25, 32
Bourdieu, P. 170
Bousquet, J. 128
Bowersock, G. W. 152
Bradley, R. 170
Braund, D. 34, 176
Bregman, J. 42
Broadbent, G. 170
Brodersen, K. 7, 139, 176
Broodbank, C. 6
Bruneau, Ph. 45, 51, 53, 55, 57–62, 64–73, 75, 172, 173
buildings, domestic *see* houses and domestic space
Bulard, M. 69
burials and tombs *see under* Corinth; Ostia; Pompeii; Rome; Syracuse
Burrell, B. 5, 8

Index

Buxton, R. 3
Byzantium 144, 149

Cahill, N. 4
Calame, C. 3, 15, 171, 175
Callimachus 45, 59, 60, 171, 172
Callot, J. 37, 39, 40, 172
Camarina 130
Cambyses 19
Carroll, M. 173
Carruseco, J. 6
Carthage/Carthaginians 121, 128–9, 131, 155
cartography 139–40, 157, 172
Casey, E. 170
Catalano, P. 96, 105
Catani, E. 172
cemeteries *see* street-lining Roman cemeteries
Cephalus 121
Cerchiai, L. 115, 121, 133
Certeau, M. de 170
Chalcidice 141
Chamoux, F. 21, 33, 171
Chankowski, V. 53, 173
Chapouthier, F. 63
Chevallier, R. 139
Choix d'inscriptions de Délos avec traduction et commentaire (Durrbach) 172
Cicero 74, 97, 98, 104, 108, 131, 173
cities 4–5
  and countryside 3, 5, 8
  see also individual cities
Clarke, D. 170
Clarke, K. 139, 140, 142, 145, 147–8, 176
Claudius 36, 78, 83, 104
Claudius Gothicus 41
Coarelli, F. 73, 88, 89, 94, 173
Coates-Stephens, R. 78, 99, 104, 173
Coelius Antipater 145
Cole, S. G. 5, 7, 139, 165
colonies/colonisation *see* relationships between colony and metropolis: Syracuse and Corinth
columbaria (communal tomb forms) 77, 82, 84, 103, 104
Commodus 37
Companion to Ancient History (Erskine) 14
Constantakopoulou, C. 6, 50, 52
Constantine I 79
Cooley, A. E./Cooley, M. G. 87, 95, 173
Copenhagen Polis Centre 5
Corcyra 120, 123, 124, 128
Core
  at Corinth 122
  at Cyrene *see under* Cyrene
  at Syracuse 122

Corinth 17, 174–5
  active at Delphi and Olympia 118
  alphabet 120
  architecture, art and trade 115–17
  calendar 120
  coinage 129, 130
  colonies 124
  destruction 69, 113, 155, 175
  literary sources 122–6
  material and epigraphic sources 120–2
  religious practice and burial 117–20
    Aphrodite sanctuary 117
    Apollo temple 115, 116
    burial practices 118–19, 120
    Core 122
    Hera's sanctuary 113, 117
    Poseidon worship 117, 128
  rulers 118
  in Strabo's *Geography* 152, 154, 155, 157
  Syracuse, relationship with *see under* Syracuse
  urban expansion 113
Corinthian order 39
Cornell, T. 174
Cos 130
Coulton, J. J. 115, 162, 171
countryside 3, 5, 8
Courbin, J. 51
Courbin, P. 51
Courby, M. F. 50, 52, 55, 59, 62
Crete
  and Cyrenaica 34, 41
  in Strabo's *Geography* 153
Cumae 121, 122, 146
Curtius, E. 156
Curty, O. 130
Cypselus 118
Cyrenaica 14, 15, 22, 33, 152, 172
  and Crete 34, 41
Cyrene 10–11
  acropolis 15, 17
  agora at Cyrene 14–44, 159, 161, 163–4, 166, 171–2
  agro-pastoral citizenry 23, 30, 43
  from Augustus to Hadrian 34–49
  Battus/tomb 17, 18–19, 20, 22–6, 28, 30–1, 38, 41, 43, 44
  boule/'council' 26
  bouleuterion/civic council building 24, 25, 26, 29–30
  boundaries 17, 19, 20, 25, 32
  Capitolium 39, 41, 42, 43–4
  changes in second half of fourth century 26–8
  civic and religious memory 36, 37, 44, 166
  conclusion 43–4

Index

delineation, integration and enlargement (550–500 BC) 19–22
Demiurgi/financial officers and/or magistrates 24, 25
Demiurgi stelae 24, 25, 29, 34
democracy 22–5, 28, 44
destruction in Jewish revolt and reconstruction 37–8, 39, 40, 41
development as civic centre 21–2, 27–8, 37, 44
development as religious centre 20–1, 22, 33
earliest structures/oikos within the future agora 17, 18
edicts of Augustus 34
end of Cyrene's agora 40–2
gerousia/'senate' 26, 29–30, 34, 38
hestiatorion/public dining room 22, 23, 26
importance 39
location and initial developments (650–550 BC) 15–19
magistrates' building and 'sala dei sedili' 32, 39, 42
monument alpha 32, 39, 43
monumental altars 27, 28, 32
nomophylakeion/'law archive' 27, 32, 33, 37, 39, 42
prosperity and uncertainty (401–300 BC) 25–9
prytaneion/'city-hall' 20, 21, 23, 25, 26, 27, 39, 41, 42
Ptolemaic period (301–96 BC) 29–34
reflecting/formulating changing realities 11
ritual structures 17, 18, 19–20, 21, 22
ship monument 30–1, 32, 43
skyrota/processional route 17, 20, 22, 23, 26, 40
statues/honorific monuments 30–2, 33, 36, 37, 38, 39, 43
stoa 19–20, 22, 24–9, 32–3, 37, 38, 41, 43–4
wellhouse 28, 33, 36, 40, 43, 166
archaeology and excavations 18, 28, 171–2
earliest habitation 17
pottery origins 17
reports 14, 19, 171–2
Berenice 29, 30, 32
married Ptolemy III 29, 30
ship monument 30–1, 32
Claudiopolis, renamed as 41
coinage 21, 22
decline after loss of status 41–2
defensive construction 41, 42
Delphi 17, 19, 22, 118, 123
treasury 29
earthquakes 41, 42
and Egypt/Persia 19, 20, 22, 29
enlargement near Caesarium 40, 44

failure to link political history with spatial development of public spaces 15
foundations and legends 14, 15–17, 18, 20, 23, 24–5, 30
gymnasium/Ptolemaium 34
as Roman forum/Caesarium 37, 39, 40, 44
political history/rulers 14, 17, 18–19, 20, 21–2
Arcesilaus III 19
Arcesilaus IV 22
Battus 17, 18–19, 20, 22–6, 28, 30–1, 38, 41, 43, 44
civil war 23
control passed to Rome 29, 34
democracy 22–5, 28, 44
Demonax of Mantinea 19, 24, 43
Diagramma stele 26, 29
Hadrian 37, 38, 39, 40
instability in second half of fourth century 25–6, 28
Jewish revolt 37
Magas 26, 28, 29
Marcus Aurelius 37, 40
Ptolemaic period 29, 32, 33, 39, 43
Septimius Severus 40
timocratic constitution 23, 26, 29
prosperity 22
and uncertainty (401–300 BC) 25–9
religion and gods
Apollo/oikos 17, 19, 20, 21, 23, 24
Apollo sanctuary 15, 17, 21, 23, 26, 28–9, 33, 37–9, 40–1, 44, 166
Aristaeus/sanctuary 23, 25, 30, 38, 43, 44, 161
Artemis sanctuary 28
Asclepius 24, 26, 32, 39
Augustus sanctuary/temple 36, 37, 38, 40, 41, 42, 43, 166
Bacchus 39
Damoteleis divinities 27
Demeter statue 36
Demeter and Core sanctuary 15, 21, 23–4, 37, 38, 171
Demeter and Core temenos/temple 19–20, 21, 22, 23, 30, 33, 43
Dioscuri 23, 25, 26
Hestia 23
Opheles/oikos 17, 18, 19, 20, 21, 24, 26, 32, 39, 44
Persephone 171
Roma/temple 37, 39, 41, 44
Zeus 23, 37
Zeus sanctuary/temple 15, 21, 32, 33, 37, 38, 39, 42, 43–4

Davies, G. 86, 97, 98, 102, 173
Day, H. W. 105

Index

De Caro, S. 88
Dearden, C. W. 121, 127
Deinomenes 132
Delorme, J. 61, 66
Delos
  agoras 60, 72–3
  Apollonia festival 60
  Archaic development 45, 167–8
  Athenian influence/control 52–3, 66–8
  athletics facilities 60–1
  civic and religious financial funds 61
  Delia festival 54, 56, 66
  Delian League 45, 54, 55
  epigraphy 172
  foundation 53, 61
  gymnasium 66, 73–4, 75
  habitation 48
  historical importance 45
    and Ionian Confederation 51, 52
  independence 54, 58, 66, 67
  'League of Islanders' 54
  Mt Cynthus *see under* networks of polytheism: spaces for the gods at Delos
  Naxians 51–2
  networks of polytheism *see* networks of polytheism: spaces for the gods at Delos
  pantheon 59, 60
  purification 50, 51, 54, 60
Delphi 50, 144
  Apollo's temple 128
  and colonisation 134, 175
  and Cyrene *see under* Cyrene
  Delphic Oracle 17, 19, 54, 110, 133
  sanctuary 121, 122, 150
  and Syracuse/Corinth 123, 128, 129, 134
Delphian peace conference 127
Demeter
  at Athens 122
  at Cyrene *see under* Cyrene
  at Syracuse 117, 122
Demetrius Poliorcetes 61
democracy
  Athens 24
  Cyrene 22–5, 28, 44
Demonax of Mantinea *see under* Cyrene
Demos 67
Dench, E. 140
Deonna, W. 69, 173
Descoeudres, J.-P. 175
Di Donato, R. 139
Di Vita, A. 113
Dinsmoor, W. B. 115
Diocletian 41
Diodorus Siculus 23, 98, 124, 127, 128, 129, 131–3, 171

Diogenes Laertius 127
Dion 128, 132, 133
Dionysus 59, 65, 74, 75
Dionysius of Halicarnasus 101, 108, 148, 158
Dionysus I 126–7, 129, 132
Dionysus II 128, 132
Dioscuri
  at Cyrene 23, 25, 26
  at Delos 60, 65, 67, 70
Dixon, S. 62
Dobres, M. A. 9
Dominguez-Monedro, A. J. 175
Dorians 125, 134
Doric style 39, 41
Dougherty, C. 133, 134, 175
Doxiadis, C. A. 5
Dubois, L. 122
Ducat, J. 45, 53, 59–61, 64, 66, 68–71, 172, 173
Ducetius 123
Dueck, D. 7, 140, 141, 142, 145, 147, 149, 155, 176
Dunbabin, T. J. 110, 116, 175
Duncan-Jones, R. 101
Durrbach, F. 172
Dürrwächter, C. 6
Durry, M. 103
Dyson, S. 7, 78, 87, 102, 174

Eck, W. 102
Edlund-Berry, I. 6
Egypt 147
  and Cyrene 19, 25, 29, 33
  deities installed on Delos 63–5, 71–2, 74, 166
  Probus as prefect 41
Eileithyia 48, 56
Elsner, J. 3
Emmerson, A. L. C. 87, 94
Engels, D. 131, 139, 140, 141, 148, 176
Ensoli, S. 17, 19, 23–4, 27–8, 30, 32, 34, 37–9, 41–2, 172
Ephorus 144, 150
Epidamnus 124
epigraphic sources 120–2, 172
Eratosthenes 153, 176
Ermeti, A. L. 32, 171
Erskine, A. 14
Étienne, R. 69, 173
Etruscan culture 6
Euboea 143
excavation *see* archaeology and site excavation
Exploration archéologique de Délos (EAD) 172

Fabbricotti, E. 172
Fear, A. 139
Feld, S. 170
festivals 129, 132

Index

Apollonia 60
Delia 54, 56, 66
Lenaia 127
Figueira, T. 125
Fincker, M. 59
Finley, M. I. 111, 116–17, 122, 131, 174, 175
Fitter, C. 3
Fitzjohn, M. 6, 170
Flohr, M. 5
Foxhall, L. 7, 164
Fraisse, P. 52, 55
Frangoulidis, S. 3
Freeman, K. 172, 175

Gabba, E. 175
Gallet de Santerre, H. 51–2, 53, 68, 173
gardens 4, 104
Gardner, A. 9, 171
Garnsey, P. 96, 105
Gasperini, L. 24, 172
Gates, C. 4
Gaul 145
Gela 116–17, 121, 123, 130
Gell, A. 9
Gelon 121–2, 123, 132, 133
Gentili, B. 172
geography 139–40
  Greek geographical literary tradition 141, 142
  Greek interest in 10
  Homer as 'founder of the science of Geography' 141
  Geography (Strabo) 131
  see also place of Greece in the *oikoumene* of Strabo's *Geography*
Geography in the Ancient World (Dueck/Brodersen) 176
Georgiades, T. 140
Geus, K. 139, 144, 153, 165
Giannini, P. 171
Giddens, A. 170
gods *see* sacred space and religion
Goodchild, R. 34, 41, 171, 172
Gowland, R. 96, 105
Graham, E. 111, 116, 135, 174, 175
Grahame, M. 4, 78
Gray, C. L. 78
Great Mother of the Gods 130
Greece
  ancients' perception of/interconnectedness of their world 7
  interest in geography 10
  cities *see* cities
  colossus statues 157
  countryside *see under* countryside
  domestic buildings/houses 4

literature *see under* literature
landscape as a rhetorical discourse 3
myths 146–7
in Strabo's *Geography see* place of Greece in the *oikoumene* of Strabo's *Geography*
religion *see under* sacred space and religion
Greeks beyond the Aegean (Karageorghis) 14
Gregory, D. 170
Grey, E. 6
Groskurd, C. G. 156
Gruben, G. 115
Guide de Délos, (French Archaeological School) 172

'habitus' 170
Hadrian
  and Cyrene 37, 38, 39, 40
  Mausoleum 104
  Panhellenion 37, 135, 166
Hadzis, C. 120
Hagesias of Syracuse 123
Hales, S. 4
Hall, J. M. 8, 116, 125, 175
Hamilakis, Y., 168, 170
Hamilton, R. 172
Hansen, M. H., 5
Hanson, J. 170
Hapsburg, M. von 33
Harding, P. 139
Harley, J. 139
Harrison, T. 139
Hasenohr, C. 73
Heinzelmann, M. 79, 80, 81–3, 99, 174
Hellenes 125, 149
Hellmann, M.-C. 52, 172
Hera
  at Corinth 113, 117
  at Delos *see under* networks of polytheism: spaces for the gods at Delos
Heracles 123, 145
  at Delos 65, 70–1, 74
Heraclists of Tyre 70
Herculaneum gate at Pompeii 91–4, 95, 107
Hercules 143
Hermansen, G. 78
Hermes 65, 66, 74
Herodotus 7, 17, 123, 124, 125, 126, 139, 149, 165, 171, 172
Herzog, R. 130
Hesberg, H. von 96, 101, 174
Hesiod 139, 149
Hestia 23, 67
HESTIA research project 1, 3
Hieron 121, 122, 132
Hieron II 130–1, 132
Higbie, C. 132

Hillier, B. 170
Himera 121, 122
Hipparchus 176
Hippocrates 132
Hirsch, E. 170
Historica Hypomnemata (Strabo) 176
Histories (Herodotus) 17
Hodder, I. 170
Hodos, T. 120, 175
Holloway, R. R. 112, 115, 130
Homer
  Catalogue of Ships 150, 151
  as 'founder of the science of Geography' 141, 145, 150
  in Strabo's *Geography* 141, 145, 147, 148, 149, 156, 176
  Greece as space of Homer 150–2
Homeric Hymn to Delian Apollo 45, 50, 172
Hope, V. M. 77, 78, 96, 98, 100, 102, 173, 174
Horace 104
Horden, P. 6
houses and domestic space 9
  Greek houses and domestic space 4
  prevalence of recent spatial analysis of private space 10
  Roman houses and domestic space 4, 7
  as important extension of the self 4
  villa landscape 7
Huskinson, J. 77
Hüttl, W. 110
Hutton, W. 3
Hymn to Delos (Callimachus) 59, 172
Hyperborean virgins 54, 61

Iberia 142, 144–5
Iliad (Homer) 7, 150
Inscriptiones Graecae (IG) 172
Inscriptions de Délos (ID) 172
Ionians 125
  Ionian Confederation 51, 52
Isis 30
  at Delos 64, 71
Isocrates 165
Isola Sacra 80, 174
Italy 5–7, 12, 87, 97–8, 130, 134, 135
  and Delos 173
  in Strabo's *Geography* 131–2, 137, 142, 143, 145–6, 147, 152–4, 176

Jackson, J. B. 77
Jacob, C. 139
Jacquemin, A. 59, 122
Jaeger, M. 77
Jashemski, W. 4
Jason, Medea and the Golden Fleece 147

Jeffrey, L. H. 24
Jones, F. 3, 4
Jones, N. 3, 8
Jones, R. 5
Jones, S. 8
Jong, I. 3
Journal of Social Archaeology 171
Jupiter Optimus Maximus 131
Justinian 7, 158

Kaiser, A. 5
Kant, Immanuel 3
Karageorghis, V. 14
Karlsson, L. 129
Kaser, M. 173
Keay, S. 78
Kent, S. 4, 128, 131
Key Themes in Ancient History (Nevett) 4
Key Themes in Ancient History (Zuiderhoek) 4
Kilian-Dirlmeier, I. 117–18
Klaffenbach, G. 130
Kleiner, D. 174
Knapp, A. B. 6
Kockel, V. 94
kolossourgia 140
Koortbojian, M. 77
Kramer, G. 156

La Bédoyère, G. de 78, 79, 83, 86, 89
La Bianca, O. 7
Laidlaw, W. 66–8, 71–2, 173
Lamari, A. 3
landscapes 6, 7, 134
  maps 7
  multiple ways of understanding same physical landscape 3, 170
  as a rhetorical discourse 3
  Roman impact on 7, 105
  and sacred space 5, 6
Lane, M. 170
Langton, J. 139
Lapalus, E. 73
Lares Compitales 73
Larmour, D. 5, 77, 97
Laronde, A. 21, 22, 28, 29, 33, 36, 172
Lassere, F. 176
Launaro, A. 7
Laurence, R. 4, 5, 77, 78, 94, 98, 168
Leach, E. 3
Lefebvre, H. 137, 161, 170, 171
Lehmler, C. 130, 131
Leighton, R. 112
Lenaia festival 127
Leontis, A. 3
Leroux, G. 59

Leto 45, 53, 54, 56, 57, 62, 66, 68, 73, 74
Lewis, D. 25, 120, 122
Libitina 97
Liddel, P. 139
Lindsay, H. 140
literature 3
    Greek literature 3
    historical focus on public architecture 10
    Latin literature 3, 4
    literary sources relating to Corinth and Syracuse 122–6
Liverani, P. 96, 103, 104, 174
Livy 98, 104, 131
Lloyd, A. B. 41, 171
Lofland, L. 171
Loicq-Berger, M.-P. 121
Lomas, K. 8, 78, 174
Londey, P. 134
Low, S. M. 11
Luni, M. 34, 37, 39, 40, 172

Ma, J. 5
Maas, M. 141, 176
MacDonald, W. L. 174
Maddoli, G. 176
Magas 26, 28, 29
Magnesia 130
Maia 73
Malaise, M. 166
Malkin, I. 6, 8, 111–13, 117, 123, 133, 134, 175
Malmberg, S. 97, 98, 101
maps 7, 14, 153
    orbis terrarum 7
    Periegesis as a 'cognitive map' 3
Marathon 122
Marcadé, J. 53, 173
Marcellus 131
March, C. 5
Marcus Agrippa 7
Marcus Aurelius 37, 40
Marengo, S. M. 172
Mari, M. 132
Marincola 139
Mark Anthony 99
Martial 97, 108
Martin, R. 52, 174
Massaro, G. D. 145
Megara Hyblaia 113, 120, 134, 175
Mei, O. 40
Meiggs, R. 25, 81–3, 85, 120, 122, 174
memory
    civic, cultural and religious 36, 37, 44, 106, 124, 166, 175
    and identity in space/spatial study 8
Menozzi, O. 172

Mercury 73
Mertens, D. 112, 113, 115, 116, 121
Meskell, L 8, 171
metropolis and colony *see* relationships between colony and metropolis: Syracuse and Corinth
Miller, M. 111
Millett, P. 10, 171
Mithridates 142
Mithridates VI 73, 154
Molinier, S. 64, 69
Momigliano, A. 139
Monografie di Archeologia Libica (MAL) 171
Morcillo, M. G. 140, 145
Morel, J.-P. 111
Moretti, J.-C 59
Morgan, C. 113, 116, 162, 171
Morris, J. 171
Mossé, C. 110
mountainous spaces 3, 51
    Mt Cynthus *see under* networks of polytheism: spaces for the gods at Delos
Mouritsen, H. 101
Moyer, I. 64
Müller, C. 73
Murray, O. 5
Musti, D. 145, 176
Mylonopoulos, I. 164
myths 146–7, 172

Natural History (Pliny) 101
Naxos 52, 118
Nemesis 39
Nero 83, 103, 104
networks and network theory 6, 7
networks of polytheism: spaces for the gods at Delos 11, 45–76, 159–60, 162–4, 166, 172–3
    Anios 53, 57, 67, 74
    Anoubis 64, 71
    Aphrodite 59–60, 65, 76
    Apollo and Artemis sanctuary 48–54, 74, 75, 162, 163
    agoras, ringed by 72–4
    Artemision 48, 51, 57, 58, 61, 68
    balance between the deities 51 53
    boundaries 52
    diversification of Artemis worship 68
    Grand Temple 55, 58–9
    and Hellenistic rulers 61–2
    increasing separation of sanctuary 54, 57, 66
    Neorion 61
    new structures and temples to Apollo 52–3, 54–5, 57, 66–8
    preservation of Apollo temples/destruction of Artemis' 55, 57

Index

networks of polytheism (cont.)
  private worship 51, 59–60, 64, 68, 69–70, 71, 76
  reassertion of Artemis 65, 76
  ritual tombs of figures/divinities involved with the deities 50, 54, 61
  as space used for agora of Ionian Confederation 52
  structures for social functions 54
archaeological material, publication of 172–3
Archegesion 52, 53, 56, 67
Ascalon, 70, 71
Asclepius 65
Athena 49, 53, 56, 57, 65, 66, 67, 70
Cynthion 65
Demos 67
developing the network: 700–500 BC 48–54
  Athenian influence 52–3, 57
  creation of specific spatial relationships between deities 51
  female divinities, preference for 50, 51
  habitation reframed as area of religious worship 49–50, 52
  Lions terrace processional way 51–2, 53, 54, 62
  Naxian investments 51–2
  new cult of Leto and Anios 53
  oikos of the Naxians 51
Dionysus 59, 65, 74, 75
Dioscuri/*dioscurion* 60, 65, 67, 70
Egyptian deities/sanctuaries 63–5, 71–2, 74
Eileithyia 48, 56
festivals 54, 56, 66
foreign deities 62–5, 70–2, 166
Hera 48–9, 56–7, 65, 71
  estranged spatial position reflecting hostility to Apollo and Artemis 50–1
  sanctuary renovated 54
  worshipped usually in own sanctuary 51, 53, 54
Heracles 65, 70–1, 74
Hermes 65, 66, 74
Hestia 67
Hyperborean virgins 54, 61
Isis 64, 71
Lares Compitales 73
Leto/sanctuary 45, 53, 54, 57, 62, 68, 74
  cult in decay 66, 73, 74
  temonos 56, 66, 73
Maia 73
making way for a wider world: 314–166 BC 58–66
  a changing network of polytheism 65–6
  Delian predominance over the religious landscape 58–61
  Hellenistic rulers and the Apollo and Artemis sanctuary 61–2
  spaces for foreign deities in the religious landscape 62–5
Mercury 73
Mt Cynthus
  cults 48–9, 50–1, 56–8, 62–5, 69–71, 74, 75
  only accessible on foot 51
  renewed interest in cults on Mt Cynthus 56–7
mythology and development of religious cult, literary sources for 172
networks of polytheism in a changing world: 166–69 BC 66–75
  Athenian efforts to change the network 66–8
  the impact of cosmopolitanism 68–75
Nike 67
Pan 75
Poseidon 59, 65, 71, 73
reconfiguring the network: 500–314 BC 54–8
  associating Apollo with Athena 57
  Athenian investment in Apollo 54–6, 57
  Delia festival 54, 56, 66
  increased worship of Apollo/marginalisation of Artemis 55–6, 57
  internationalisation of Delos 56, 57–8
  new Apollo cults 57
  renewed interest in cults on Mt Cynthus 56–7
Roma 67, 73
Samothraceion sanctuary 62–3, 70
Sarapis and Sarapeions 63–5, 70, 71–2, 74, 75
Stesileos' private cult 59–60, 65, 75
syncretised forms of worship 70, 71, 74
Syrian cults/sanctuaries 71, 72, 74, 75
Zeus 53, 56, 57, 65, 67, 70, 75
  cults and foreign deities 70, 71
  spatial location 50
Nevett, L. C. 3
Newsome, D. 5, 77, 168
Nicolet, C. 75
Nielsen, T. H. 5
Nike 30, 67
Nikopolis 154
Nolan gate at Pompeii 87–8
Nouveau Choix d'inscriptions de Délos: lois, comptes et inventaires (Prêtre) 172
Nucerian gate at Pompeii 89–91

O'Hanlon, M. 170
oikoumene see place of Greece in the *oikoumene* of Strabo's *Geography*
Olympia 22, 30, 50, 118, 131
  Iamidai prophetic family 123
  Olympic contests 118

sanctuary 121–2
Zeus 123
Olympian 6 (Pindar) 123
Orpheles 17, 18, 19, 20, 21, 24, 26, 32, 39, 44
Orton, C. 170
Ortygia *see under* Syracuse
Osborne, R. 5, 8, 9, 17, 29, 66, 110, 126–7, 171, 174
Osterhammel, J. 4
Ostia 4, 131
  C. Cartilius Poplicola 80
  history and geography 78–9
  material survival 5
  as port of Rome 78
  tombs and burial 78–86, 174
    approaching Ostia through its tombs 85
    elaboration of tombs 81, 83, 106
    freedmen 85
    future generations, tombs for 86
    group burial 81
    Isola Sacra 80, 174
    Porta Laurentina 79, 80, 81–2
    Porta Marina 79, 80
    Porta Romana 79–80, 83–4
    social mixing 106
O'Sullivan, T. 5, 8, 77, 109, 158, 165
Ovid 101, 108
Owen, S. 5, 175

Paionios 30
Pan 75
Panciera, S. 102
Panhellenion (Hadrian) 37, 135
Panichi, S. 140
Papageorgiou-Venetas, A. 51, 56, 59, 173
Parthia/Parthians 142, 147
Paschalis, M. 3
Patras 154
Patterson, J. 78
Patterson, L. 125
Pausanias 3, 134, 140, 141, 158, 171
Pearson, M. 170
PELAGIOS research project 1
Pelling, C. 139, 148
Peloponnese
  Peloponnesian War 125
  Return of the Heraclidae to the Peloponnese 142
  in Strabo's *Geography* 149, 156
Penz, F. 171
Perachora 117, 118
Periander 118
Periegesis (Pausanias) 3
Persae (Aeschylus) 121
Persephone 171
Persia/Persians 121

and Cyrene 19, 20, 22
Perugia school 140, 176
Petronius 108
Peutinger map 7
Phaedo (Plato) 165
Philetaerus 61, 62
Philostratus 70
Philip V of Macedon 62
Picard, C. 73
Pigon, J. 139
Pillars of Hercules 143
Pindar 18, 22, 23, 121, 122, 123, 125, 126, 133, 171
Pithecusae 143
place of Greece in the *oikoumene* of Strabo's *Geography* 12–13, 137–58, 160–1, 164–5, 175–6
  approaching space and Strabo 139–41
    aims and methods of Strabo in conceptualising *Geography* 139–40
    the inhabited world/ *oikoumene* 139, 140–1
    Strabo's terminology for *Geography* 140
    texts offering 'focused universality' 139
  Boeotia 140, 144, 151, 153–4
  conclusions 155–8
  Greece and the framework of Strabo's project 141–4
    Euboea 143
    Greek conception of world/denunciating Roman contribution 141–2, 143
    Homer as starting point 141
    key temporal moments in *Geography* 142–3
    position of Greece at end of Europe 143–4
  Greece as a space within the *Geography* 148–55
    Greece as a microcosm of the *oikoumene* 148–50
    Greece as a space in Strabo's present-day world 152–5
  place of Greece in other spaces of the *oikoumene* 144–8
    Asia Minor 147–8
    Greek myths 146–7
    Iberia 142, 144–5
    Italy and Sicily 145–6, 147, 148, 156, 176
Plassart, A. 56, 65, 70
Plataea 121
Plato 7, 127, 128, 144, 165
Pliny 101, 105, 152
Plutarch 128, 129, 130, 132, 133–5
poetry/poets 121, 140, 176
Polacco, L. 121
poleis 110, 117, 146, 152, 156, 162, 163
Polidori, R. 20, 24, 37, 172
Polignac, F. De 5, 33
Politics (Aristotle) 162
Polybius 132, 158, 176

Pompeii 4
  amphitheatre 94
  destruction 86, 94
  history 85–6, 89–90
    conversion to Roman colony 89
    immigration 90
    material survival 5
    society 95
  tombs and burial 85–95, 174
    M. Alleius Minius 87
    approaching Pompeii through its tombs 94–5
    burial of women 88, 96
    Gn. Clovatius 87
    elaboration of tombs 90, 94, 107
    Epidii family 87
    Eumachia 90, 95
    freedman 87, 90, 93, 94, 95, 96
    future generations, tombs for 90, 94–5, 107
    Herculaneum gate 91–4, 95, 107
    Marcus Tullius 87
    Nolan gate 87–8
    Nucerian gate 89–91
    M. Porcius 94
    seat-tombs/bench tombs 87–8, 90, 94
    social mixing 106
    Stabian gate 86–7
    Vesuvian gate 88
  women 88, 95, 99
Pompey 147
Pomtow, H. 128
Porta Laurentina at Ostia 79, 80, 81–2
Porta Marina at Ostia 79, 80
Porta Romana at Ostia 79–80, 83–4
Portus 78–9, 80
Poseidon 59, 67
  at Corinth 117, 128
  at Delos 59, 65, 71, 73
Poseidoniasts of Beirut 72–3
Posidonius 176
Pothecary, S. 140, 157
Potidaea 124
pottery 17
  Corinthian 116–17
  Sicel 120
Poulsen, G. 59
Prandi, L. 144, 149
Preston, L. 5
Prêtre, C. 172
Pretzler, M. 140, 141, 142, 143, 151, 152, 176
Preucel, R. W. 8, 170, 171
Price, S. R. F. 5
Probus 41
Procopius 158
Production of Space (Lefebvre) 137

Prontera, F. 176
Ptolemais 41, 42
Ptolemy I 25–6, 28, 29
  Diagramma stele 26, 29
Ptolemy III 29, 30, 32
Ptolemy VIII 29
Pugliese-Carratelli, G. 175
public space *see* agoras
Punic Wars 131
Purcaro, V. 20, 38, 171
Purcell, N. 5, 6, 78, 98, 101, 110, 164
Pyrrhus of Epirus 130–1, 132
Pythian I (Pindar) 12–23

Raaflaub, K. 139
Radt, S. 175
Ranchman, W. G. 163, 171
Ransom of Hector (Dionysius I) 127
Rapoport, A. 4, 170
Rauh, N. K. 69, 72, 73, 173
Reece, R. 173
Rehm, R. 3
Reichert-Südbeck, P. 117
relationships between colony and metropolis:
  Syracuse and Corinth 12, 110–36, 160, 162, 166, 174–5
  colonisation studies 110–11, 160, 174–5
    purposes served by portrayals of colonisation 175
  conclusion 135–6
  Syracuse and Corinth in the Archaic Period 111–20
    architecture, art and trade 115–17
    relationship between Syracuse and Corinth in context 119–21
    religious practice and burial 117–19, 119–20
    urban layout 111–15
  Syracuse and Corinth in the fifth century BC 120–6
    Syracuse and Corinth in the literary sources 122–6
    Syracuse and Corinth in the material and epigraphic sources 120–2, 130
  Syracuse and Corinth in the fourth century BC 126–30
  Syracuse and Corinth from the third century onwards 130–5
  see also Syracuse
religion *see* sacred space and religion
Return of the Heraclidae to the Peloponnese 142
Reynolds, J. 37, 172
Rhodes 132
Rhodes, P. J. 29, 66, 126–7
Richards, C. 170
Richardson, L. 88, 94

Index

Richmond, A. 105
Ridgway, D. 174
Ridley, R. T. 102
Robb, J. E. 9
Robert, F. 60, 67
Robertson, N. 21, 23
Robinson, O. F. 97, 104, 173, 174
Roma
  at Cyrene 37, 39, 41, 44
  at Delos 67, 73
Roman Empire/Roman world
  cities *see* cities
  countryside 3, 5, 8
  and Cyrene *see under* Cyrene
  burials and tombs *see under* Rome
  domestic buildings/houses *see under* houses and domestic space
  'hodological'/itinerary-led understanding of wider world 7, 10
  literature 3, 4
  religion *see* sacred space and religion
  Romans' perception of their world 7
  roads 7, 97–8
Rome 9
  centrality of Rome as model for urban space in Roman world 5, 9–10
  corn supply from Delos 74–5
  foundation 145
  material survival of Rome 5
  regional landscape studies counteracting focus on 7
  roads 7, 97–8
  society 99–100
  and Syracuse 131–2
  tombs and burial
    after Augustus 101–4
    approaching Rome through its tombs 105–6
    'body-dumping' 173
    Caius Cestius' pyramid 102, 105
    Claudii Marcelli 104
    collegia 99
    elaboration of tombs 98, 101–2, 105, 106
    elites' burial 102
    Esquiline 97–8, 104
    Eurysaces (baker) 99, 104
    first century BC 90–101
    up to first century BC 97–8
    freedmen 99, 103, 106
    imperial household 104–5
    Law of the Twelve Tables 173
    'lunatic fringe' burials 102, 105
    Metelli 104
    monuments underlining foreign trading and military might 103
    plebs urbana 96, 105

Scipios 98, 104
second century AD onwards 104–5
slaves 99, 103, 104, 106
Sepulcrum Scipionis 102
Servilii 104
working-class Romans 103
Romm, J. S. 7, 139, 144, 165
Romulus and Remus 145
Rosen, R. 3, 5, 78
Roussel, P. 64, 66–72, 173

sacred space and religion 5–6, 162–7
  asylia ('asylum') 130
  Corinth *see under* Corinth
  crucial role of sacred space in transmission of culture 6
  Cyrene *see* Cyrene
  excavation reports, approach of 6
  gods *see individual gods*
  in landscape 5, 6
  networks of polytheism *see* networks of polytheism: spaces for the gods at Delos
  Syracuse *see under* Syracuse
Sakellariou, M. B. 117
Salamis 121
Salmeri, G. 147, 148, 176
Salmon, J. B. 111, 113, 129, 130, 133, 175
Salway, B. 7, 144, 145, 165
Samos 118
Samothrace 62–3
Santillo-Frizell, B. 5
Santucci, A. 23
Sarapis 63–5, 70, 71–2, 74, 75
Sauer, E. 8, 168, 171
Scham, S. 7
Schlögel, K. 4
Schmidt, M. 72
Scholia Vetera 123
Schroer, M. 4
Schultz, P. 164
Scipio Africanus 102
Scott, M. C. 5, 9, 29, 118, 121–2, 132, 161–2, 170
Scully, V. 5, 50
Seaford, R. 3
Segesta 121, 125
Selinous 125
Seneca (the younger) 104
Septimius Severus 40
Servius Sulpicius Rufus 97
Shepherd, G. 116–17, 118–19, 120, 121, 132, 174
Sicel/Sicels 120, 123, 126, 129
Sicily
  foundations 175
  and relationships between Syracuse and Corinth 116, 120, 122, 125–33, 135

Sicily (cont.)
　in Strabo's *Geography* 143, 145–6, 148, 152, 156
　Sicilians as *Hellenes* 125
Sidonius Apollinaris 173
Signer, B. 52
Simonides 121
Sjöqvist, E. 120, 123, 128
Sluiter, I. 3, 5, 78
Smith, A. 6
Smith, M. 4
Snead, J. E. 170
Snodgrass, A. M. 111, 116, 118, 174, 175
Soja, E. 170
Sophron 127
Sorabji, R. 3
Sosicrates 61
Souvatzi, S. 4
spaces and society in the Greek and Roman worlds 1–2
　alienation, spaces of *see* street-lining Roman cemeteries
　as basis of all intuitions 3
　changing conceptualisations in literary works 3
　concept of space 170
　conclusions 159–69
　　classical, Hellenistic and Roman approaches to space 161–7
　　space and society, space and history 167–9
　earliest discussions 2–7
　identity and space/spatial study 8
　methods of studying physical spaces 170–1
　　micro and macro level of spatial resolution 170
　multiple interpretations and attitudes towards 8
　as part of the study of history 8–10
　　advantages of spatial study 9–10
　　integrated approach to ancient world 9
　relationships *see* relationships between colony and metropolis: Syracuse and Corinth
　sacred space and religion *see* sacred space and religion
Space in Literature project 3
Spain 173
Sparta/Spartans 124–5, 127
　and Cyrene 23
　government system 26
　in Strabo's *Geography* 152, 154, 155
Spawforth, A. 135
Spawski, S. 139
Spencer, D. 3, 5, 77, 78, 97
Spes Vetus 99
Spieser, J.-M. 5
Spinola, G. 96, 103, 104, 174
Squarciapino, M. 83

Stabian gate at Pompeii 86–7
Stackelberg, K. von 4
Steinsapir, A. 6
Stevens, K. 3
Stewart, A. 173
Strabo 131–2, 134, 172
　Geography see place of Greece in the *oikoumene* of Strabo's *Geography*
　influences 140, 176
street-lining Roman cemeteries 11–12, 77–109, 160, 164, 173–4
　changing preferences for inhumation and cremation 77, 173
　columbaria 77, 82, 84, 103, 104
　conclusion 107–9
　fines for tomb desecration 80
　importance of roads along which tombs lay 77–8
　Ostia 78–85, 174
　　approaching Ostia through its tombs 85–6
　　Porta Laurentina 79, 80, 81–2
　　Porta Marina 79, 80
　　Porta Romana 79–80, 83
　　see also under Ostia
　Pompeii 85–95, 174
　　approaching Pompeii through its tombs 95–6
　　freedman burials 87, 90, 91, 92, 95, 96
　　Herculaneum gate 91–94, 95, 106
　　Nolan gate 87–8
　　Nucerian gate 89–91
　　seat-tombs/bench tombs 87–8, 90, 94
　　Stabian gate 86–7
　　Vesuvian gate 88
　　see also under Pompeii
　regulation of burial 173–4
　Rome 96–109
　　after Augustus 101–4
　　approaching Rome through its tombs 105–6
　　first century BC 98–101
　　second century AD onwards 104–5
　　up to the first century BC 97–8
　　see also under Rome
　tomb types and acculturation of Roman and local practice 174
　tombs not 'static structures' 173–4
　visitors' perceptions 78, 94–6, 100–1, 102, 103, 105, 106–9
　women 89, 95, 99
structuration 170
Stucchi, S. 18, 20, 22, 24–6, 28, 32, 36–9, 41, 171–2
Sulla 99
Syme, R. 140
Symposium (Xenophon) 127
Synesius, Bishop 42, 171

Syracuse 174–5
  alphabet 120
  architecture, art and trade 115–17
  calendar 120
  Cephalus 121
  coinage 129
  colonies 130
  and Corinth in the fifth century BC 120–6
    Athens 121, 122
    Gelon's takeover 121–2
    Hagesias of Syracuse 123, 133
    Hieron 121, 122
    increasingly dominant role within Sicily 122–3
    political affairs in fifth century 123–4
    Tisias 121
  and Corinth in the fourth century BC 126–30
    Athens 126–8
    Dion 128, 132, 133
    Dionysus I 126–7, 129, 132
    Dionysus II 128, 132
    Timoleon 128–9, 130, 131, 132, 133
  and Corinth from third century onwards 130–5
    Asia Minor 130
    Dion/Dionysius I's appeals to Corinth for help 132
    Greece relationship declining 130, 132
    'Greekness' of Syracuse 131–2
    Hieron II 130–1, 132
  foundation 111–12, 123, 130, 133–4
    by Archias 125–6, 133
    refounded by Gelon 133
  layout as a settlement 175
  literary sources 122–6
  material and epigraphic sources 120–2, 130
  Ortygia 112, 115, 122
  and other cities and sanctuaries in Greece 122
  poets visiting 121
  religious practice and burial 117–20
    Aphrodite worship in Syracuse's colonies 117
    Apollo temple 115
    Artemis and acculturation 117
    Athena/Athenaion and temples 115, 122
    burial practices 118, 120
    Core 122
    Demeter 117, 122
    Great Mother of the Gods 130
  reputation for luxury 128, 132
  and Rome 131–2
  theatre 121, 127
  unexcavated beneath the modern city 113
  urban space/layout 113–15
  Zeus temple 115
Syria 61
  Syrian cults/sanctuaries on Delos 71, 72, 74, 75

Talbert, R. 7, 128, 135, 139, 164
Tenea 134
Tanner, J. 9
Terrenato, N. 7
theatre 121, 127
  amphitheatre at Pompeii 94
  Theatrum Minus 94
Themis 39
Theophrastus 73
Thera 25
Thermopylae 154–5, 165–6
Thomas, J. 6
Thompson, H. A. 10
Thucydides 45, 50, 54, 111, 124–6, 130, 133, 149, 172
Thylander, H. 80
Tiberius 36, 81
Tilley, C. 6, 170
Timaeus 128
Timoleon 128–9, 130, 131, 132, 133
  heroön established for 132–3
Tisias 121
Todd, M. 105
tombs *see* street-lining Roman cemeteries
TOPOI research project 1
Toynbee, J. M. C. 86, 98, 99, 102, 104, 174
trade in Corinth and Syracuse 115–17
Trajan 78, 84, 104
Tréheux, J. 172
Trojan War 142, 147
Trotta, F. 140
Tsetskhladze, G. R. 174.
Tyche 39, 71
Tyndaris 121

universal history 137, 139
Urry, J. 170

Vallet, G. 175
Vallois, R. 48, 51, 53, 59, 62, 173
van Dommelen, P. 113, 116, 174
van Dyke, R. M. 8
van Haverbeke, H., 6
Vanicelli, P. 171
Várhelyi, Z. 102
Varro 109
Vatin, C. 48
Veronese, F. 6
Vesuvian gate at Pompeii 89
Vesuvius 94,
Vial, C. 173
Vibius Pansa, C. 99
Vidal-Naquet, P. 3
Visscher, F. de 34
Vlassopoulos, K. 5, 10, 162, 171
Vout, C. 98, 109

Waele, F.-J. De 175
Waisglas, A. 172
Walker, S. 37
Wallace, P. W. 140, 151, 152, 176
Wallace-Hadrill, A. 4
Walker, S. 135
Ward-Perkins, J. B. 5
water 7, 134, 165
  supply 62–3, 65, 99, 154
Weller, C. H. 152, 176
White, D. 23, 171
Will, Ernest 62, 72, 117
Williams, C. K. 175
Wilson, J. P. 125, 135, 175
Witcher, R. 7
women
  gendered division of particular spaces 4
  in Pompeii 88, 95, 99
Woodard, R. D. 6
Woodhead, A. G. 110
Woodward, D. 139
Woolf, G. 140, 145
Wycherley, R. E. 10

Xenophon 127

Xerxes 123

Yntema, D. 175

Zambon, E. 131
Zanker, P. 100
Zeus 150
  at Athens 24, 28
  at Cyrene *see under* Cyrene
  at Delos *see under* networks of polytheism: spaces for the gods at Delos
  Olympia temple 123
  at Syracuse 115
  Zeus Cynthius 65, 71
  Zeus Du[sares] 71
  Zeus Eleutherius 24, 28, 43, 129
  Zeus Hadad 71
  Zeus Hypsistus (Ba'al) 70, 71
  Zeus Ktesios 71
  Zeus Olympius 115
  Zeus Ourios 71
  Zeus Polieus 53, 67
  Zeus Sabazios 71, 75
  Zeus Soter 37, 67
Zuiderhoek, A. 4

Printed in Great Britain
by Amazon